CHARLES OLSON & ROBERT CREELEY:

THE COMPLETE CORRESPONDENCE

VOLUME 8

EDITED BY

GEORGE F. BUTTERICK

BLACK SPARROW PRESS

SANTA ROSA   1987

ACKNOWLEDGEMENTS

The originals of these letters are in the collections of the University of Connecticut Library, Storrs, and Washington University Libraries, St. Louis, and are printed here with those libraries' kind cooperation. Grateful acknowledgement must continue to be made to Donald Allen, who provided typescripts of many of Charles Olson's letters; to Timothy Murray of Washington University Libraries, who provided copies of letters as well as photographs from among Robert Creeley's papers; to Cid Corman, for his permission to publish a photograph of his November 1951 letter to Robert Creeley; to Seamus Cooney and Eric Purchase, who meticulously helped to read proofs; to Julie Voss, able coordinator at Black Sparrow; and to John Martin for his continued faith in monumental projects.

This project was supported by a matching grant from the National Endowment of the Arts.

Cover photograph by Gerard Malanga.

LIBRARY OF CONGRESS CATALOGING-IN-PUBLICATION DATA
(Revised for volume 8)

Olson, Charles, 1910–1970.
  Charles Olson & Robert Creeley : the complete correspondence.
  Limited ed. of 250 copies.
  Includes bibliographical references and indexes.
  1. Olson, Charles, 1910–1970 — Correspondence.
2. Creeley, Robert, 1926 —   — Correspondence.
3. Poets, American — 20th century — Correspondence.
I. Creeley, Robert, 1926–   . II. Butterick, George F.
III. Title.
PS3529.L655Z544   811'.54 [B]   80-12222
ISBN 0-87685-400-5 (v. 1)
ISBN 0-87685-401-3 (deluxe : v. 1)
ISBN 0-87685-399-8 (pbk. : v. 1)
ISBN 0-87685-705-5 (v. 8)
ISBN 0-87685-706-3 (deluxe : v. 8)
ISBN 0-87685-704-7 (pbk. : v. 8)

318164

TABLE OF CONTENTS

Editor's Introduction

Olson becomes a family man for the first time at age 40. Creeley has to shift his typewriter upstairs or down every time he wants to use it, or after every four pages or so, because of the painfully cramped house in France. The letters go on, despite these realities and because of them.

Creeley is embattled at Fontrousse, unable to speak the language, indeed unwilling to learn ("No interest, finally; hate the tightness of it"). Little gets written, and frustration rules. He takes it out on the landscape, accusing it of being "placid," a "hell of a waste of space, from any angle I can see" — although he's kept those angles decidedly narrow. He writes, October 4th, of sitting in the house all day; "see no one, and when someone goes by, feel very shy, & sometimes duck back on the stairs, so as not to be seen."

Greater aplomb, however, can be found in his writing and in his thinking. His October 8th letter discusses "sequence" and how "the most basic thing I have ever felt about any continuity, of reality, is that it could not be anticipated." Any attempt to force or anticipate creation flattens the result: "One sees that reality somehow manages a continuity that is exact in every particular. One hardly says it, but even so, what is remarkable about reality is that, nothing *else* could really have happened . . ." The goal is to have an art of the same character. The letter contains some of Creeley's most succinct and applicable thinking on key theoretical issues that he and Olson have been discussing the past several months — the "single intelligence," the extension of form from content, the "conjectural method," as well as the value Creeley has found in Stendhal.

The correspondence continues to be highly, almost exclusively, personal. Little seeps into the exchange from the larger world — the Korean War, McCarthy's intimidation campaign, Europe still struggling to its feet. Indeed, it is a bleak Europe Creeley looks out of his doorway and sees after four months (November 19th): "The whole place . . . is *dead*, there is the war coming, so surely you can *smell* it; death everywhere I have been."

Whereas Creeley is very concentrated in his thinking, Olson is grandiose, sweeping, surging, perilous, as usual. His October 9th letter proposes nothing less than "The Etymology of All Things." It is a characteristic gesture, ambitious on a scale that distinguishes him from other poets to this day. There is, for example, the excitement with which he passes on to Creeley what he accepts to be the first alphabetic writing: "READ IT, LAD: it is the 1st sentence writ in yr language." It is exactly such gestures that make him so attractive. It is his belief, his underlying optimism, as much as the details — that it is possible to *know*, and that it is possible to know *everything*. No wonder we are so ready to accept Maximus. The enthusiasm over the earliest phonetic writing also reflects his sense of the "archaic." If he is willing to start with such basics, literally A, B, C ("A is a BULL / B, is a HOUSE / C, is a T-SQUARE . . ."), then so are we.

Creeley's conceptualizing takes a different but no less engaging metaphor: "Poultry still seems to be the more or less 'perfect' attention to go along with writing" (October 10th). He offers as his exemplary artist his old friend Ira Grant, the poultry breeder, and arrives at this beautiful truth: "Of course, poultry-breeding so taken may seem a gratuitous art, i.e., a man like Ira breeds for a 'perfection' that cannot be proven, i.e., it is only proven by one man's conception of it. Even so, what else is a perfection, but just so, one man's idea of it?"

Olson continues to resent the comparisons made of his work with Pound's, which are superficial and dismissive more often than not. It is partly the sensitivity of an emerging artist, but more importantly he recognizes that such comparisons are frequently made by those critics who simply prefer, without stating it, the work of Eliot — academic formalists, strict traditionalists. "In fact it is not those who know Pound that say this easy business of, like him, you, are like him, but, those who still pipe for TSE, always, it is they — and the intent is, to beat me with that stick." He quite properly cries, having been publishing poems only since 1946, "for christ sake, just give me my air." And he is true to add, "whatever it is," because he is in the very act of discovering it.

Olson's relation to Pound is tested again in a more immediately personal way with a visit from John Kasper, one of the publishers of the Square Dollar series masterminded by Pound. (In some accounts, Kasper was sent as a mole or double-agent by Pound into the Black Mountain encampment. The same Kasper would eventually swing further out than even Pound's St. Elizabeths' orbit and gain nationwide notoriety as a racist incendiary for the White Citizens Council.) Olson is at least pleased that Kasper doesn't judge his work by Pound's, but "wants to publish me for myself." One beneficial by-product of the visit is that Olson realizes that he has a "conspiracy" of his own to offer, a program or curriculum (as he would later offer "A Plan for a Curriculum of the Soul") for an alternative culture morphology.

Meanwhile, Olson is fully engaged in teaching at Black Mountain. His writing students at the time include Fielding Dawson and Joel Oppenheimer. As a member of the faculty, he also shares responsibility for the government of that "polis." There is no doubt he strongly believes in the place and in such a concept of education. At the same time, he writes Creeley (October 12th) that what keeps him there is basically the need to meet the requirements of foundations, those that offer the grants that would free him to follow his own work, for institutional "affiliation." One even wonders if Connie's words upon emerging from the web of anesthesia after giving birth to their daughter — "We *can* move, move, MOVE" — don't mean that now they can move from Black Mountain to some more attractive and independent alternative, as discussed in previous letters. As Olson writes November 7th, "The drainage of this place is beyond belief, the wear of it."

The aspect of Black Mountain that initially attracted him, as he indicates again on November 18th, is what he calls the "Chinese," learned from Robert Payne ("the scholar lives in the imperial city, does his work, and, once a month, tells the children what he had found out" — I, 28). Ideally, he would like a Black Mountain relocated "about half way between Washington & NY — thus enabling such as [dancer Katherine] Litz and myself to visit, and have an income, at the same time live in the imperial cities!" What keeps his hopes up, meanwhile, is the possibility of establishing printing opportunities at Black Mountain, though these fail to get very far.

In his October 18th letter, Olson again calls for the exploration of language to its roots, specifically the "hieroglyphic" nature of language and, through that, to language as gesture. He also returns to his concept of "objectism," related to his revisionist humanism of "Human Universe" as well as to his activism, whereby man is viewed as instrument, as "a force of work not as source of wonder." Olson's letter a few days later, from October 20th or thereabouts, is an even more significant one, a major sweep. It directly supplements "Human Universe," which he had rewritten in September. He outlines again the limits of logic and classification, part of his overall objection to the partitioning of reality. He also presents the "SINGLE FACT" from which all "laws" must follow, and which can be taken as a summarization of Olsonism: "reality is this instant & me." (The egotism, too, seems unavoidable.) In consequence, art is only the ability "to state or to make an equivalent of, this fact." Olson offers an alternative metaphysic, opposing "the act of rhythm" to "the act of logic." Somehow — the clearest thing here is his insistence — there is a "law of rhythm" that results in "form." Without such form, "content degenerates to no more than *agitated material*, which is chaos, and immoral. Form, then, is the only measure of the moral, and rhythm is the only mechanic of the moral." Actually, as written (VIII, 70), this last statement remains a question, as once again Olson's thoughts are more exploratory than fixed — like the "'Projective Verse" essay itself — despite the assertive, dogmatic tone.

He continues to explore related matters in this, one of the liveliest theoretical letters in the series. To the "either-or" he prefers the "multiple" — "which is the real biz of reality, that it is multiple, and does not STOP." The "instant" is the "immensity," and only art does not divide reality. Mythology, he insists, is being "reconstituted from the ground"; the "archaic" is once again our condition; while we ourselves are what he calls here, too, "post-modern man."

The environment in which Creeley receives such immense propositions is only three rooms large, shared by his wife, two sons, and, for three weeks, his friends the Berlins. The autumn chill is driven away only by a wood fire, the fuel for which Creeley must gather daily. His wife Ann must use a washing stone for the family's laundry, which would include diapers for young Thomas.

Creeley's November 29th letter reveals more of his miserable state. A week might go by when the only time he spends out of the house or even his room is to go to the toilet. "I never say anything more than hello, to anyone, because I don't speak the language, like they say, and even if I did, I don't think I would to most of those that go by us here." Even Ashley Bryan, about whom he writes so fondly, he has only seen some half dozen times in six months. He reports spending an entire afternoon in a morose torpor just looking out the window, and feeling "dirty, even sick" with the loss of motive. Given these details, the letters loom more consequentially for his survival than might otherwise have been imagined.

Nevertheless, Creeley manages "Jardou," with its lovely final sentence, and Olson gives the story a close reading. His comments have been inserted here as they appear on Creeley's typescript, to allow the reader to judge for himself his critical acuity, even though that interrupts the narrative flow. Creeley's poem "The Dead" (part of his November 19th letter), not otherwise published and sent to Olson without any enthusiasm, actually anticipates poems such as "The Crisis" to come in the following year, rather than looking back to " 'Guido . . .' " and similar earlier ones. It might be termed transitional, or at least worth another look.

The reader of the earlier volumes, having shared his restlessness in New Hampshire, knows by this time it is not entirely Europe that has failed Creeley. Still, what he writes on November 22nd is as true for his life as for his poetry as it develops: "But I want, or I don't want, but wish only to be more simple, I mean, simply moved—somehow to get as clean as can be, to move on the most minimum means." Olson, too, recognizes the profound truth of his further observation: "The fucking world is such a density, a damn idiot-squeezed place."

The Olsons' child is finally born October 23rd, after much anticipation—on the part of the Creeleys as well. She is named Kate, after suggestions back and forth, in honor of Connie's mother, who had died unexpectedly in August (VII, 153). One readily imagines the infant held in the father's palm, a single palm, against his massive chest.

Even as he delights in his child, Olson continues as patriarch of an ever-increasing tribe of ideas. His rereading of Shakespeare, to which several letters are devoted (and whom he had reread earlier in relation to Melville), will continue over the coming years. One result is a ten-chapter unpublished book (of which the essay "Quantity in Verse, and Shakespeare's Late Plays" published in *Selected Writings* is a sample). For a poet as concerned with the "post-modern" and its sources in the archaic as Olson was, the reader may be surprised initially at the amount of time devoted to so familiar and traditional a master. Shakespeare, however, was always very much a source for Olson, like Melville, or Jung and Whitehead, Hesiod, Ismaili cosmological doctrines, or Taoist distillations. There are probably as many allusions to or borrowings from Shakespeare in Olson's writings as from Pound or Williams. It will be through continued readings of Shakespeare that he will be helped over questions of poetic measure he shared with Creeley and Williams in a sort of Triangle Trade of ideas in 1954, itself a basis for adding gains from Whitehead's *Process and Reality* and Hermann Weyl's *Philosophy of Mathematics and Natural Science* in the later 1950s and by which his poetics is advanced another step beyond "Projective Verse." Thus, the concern with Shakespeare here is no idle sidetrack or temporary enthusiasm. In Shakespeare also, especially in *Antony and*

Cleopatra, Olson discovers factors that can otherwise only find fulfillment in a Maximus: an "acting present," which is necessary for verse to "deliver itself of its maker's person" (November 26th), and "magnification" (November 27th). One only regrets, in the present situation, that Creeley couldn't get hold of a copy of *Antony and Cleopatra* in his desolate circumstances, to press or encourage the issues.

While Creeley is in what amounts to an isolation cell, Olson by contrast is in steady contact with some of the brightest and most creative young minds, no matter the "drainage" and "wear" of Black Mountain (which of course is as much the stress of a newly more complex domestic situation). He reports, for example, "the pleasure, of talking to a boy as open & sure as this Twombly" — Cy Twombly, the now celebrated painter — "abt *line*, just the goddamned wonderful pleasure of *form*, when one can talk to another who has the feeling for it" (November 29th). The stimulation is constant, with results shared here. He reports, for instance, a "breakthrough" in considering Shakespeare's methodology, how the Bard's "image system is the clue," arguing that the plays arose from a single dominant metaphor. The result, to the delight of Olson's own thinking, promises a reading of Shakespeare that champions the particular and rejects that "biggest turd of all," the "universe-all."

Olson's December 1st letter is yet another substantial one, in which he proposes metaphor as the "science" proper to human affairs and actions, as opposed to the generalizations of what he calls "species thinking": "For species thinking has two human lies in it: perfection, & progress." As an alternative, Olson argues for "a single human person's act," offering this personal testimony: "i have not yet known any example where any other imaginative act than one inside the particular person making the act has moved me sufficiently to change." The inescapable conclusion is that each man or woman is, or must become, an artist.

Thereafter, the Christmas season gradually absorbs both men along with their families. Thus ends the second year, actually the first full year — full indeed — of their remarkable correspondence.

George F. Butterick

xii

Charles Olson & Robert Creeley:
The Complete Correspondence

Volume 8

Notes to the letters begin on p. 257.

Dear Chas/
          Continue to feel somewhat bogged; the lift from that letter, & A/ — & then Fenollosa, got me a ways, put it, but can't now manage to pull out anything. Yesterday, particularly dulled & almost added a note, to ask you if you knew of anything back there, that wd be possible — job or whatever. Simply don't make the french life; can't speak the language & can't now bring myself to learn it — not laziness so much as it is deadness. No interest, finally; hate the tightness of it, etc. Etc., and I don't finally know what the hell I am talking about.
                    I don't honestly know what is coming; I can't worry, in some ways, but do get scared. Nothing now moves enough to get out, nothing holds but other men's work, say, and particularly your own. Angles to that A/ damn well help.
                    Another: the *daemonic* . . .   it has a strong pull, that feel of it you note there. I wish I knew more about it; and would be very grateful for whatever more you can tell me of it, i.e., perhaps 'instances,' uses, or how they had defined it for themselves. Not simply the gratuitous in nature? More the 'inhuman,' or the force which stays by itself? Would be grateful for your help there; I dig the emphasis, i.e., I pick up on that point ′ where Lawrence was sitting.

Many things, anyhow, both from this (comes to be a kind of ware-house for me) and insistences, that continue anyhow. I get to think that IN THE SUMMER is the one, holds the most potential for me. That is, the sense of "inverse plunging . . ." does hold for me, does seem to be something true; and likewise, the continuum as felt in the 'beer' passage, i.e., I think I was on thru there, no matter the slips in form, etc.
                    And really, want that to be it, in the novel; and why I don't find the present thing, what there is of it, very exciting, i.e., I avoided too much. That incredible separation,

15

one is forced against; so that, the ironic, in coitus one is more far, more inaccessible to another, than at any other time; what Lawrence called the 'dark river,'[1] river of incredible passage, into what, I mean, into what place? I wish I could nail that one, hard; and don't find much else of interest. I used to think he was somewhat bitter there, and have heard divers argue a sense of impotence in him, on the basis of his taking of this act — idiots to say that, incomparable idiots. One facing into that, feeling that extremeness, I mean, the real turn, does get it, and sees what the hell he is insisting on. Later : "the dark gods" of the blood,[2] and I think somewhat too much wobble in that taking of it, or too much crud apt to attach itself. I like the river, better, like how he had it, as that, in one of the short pieces — how he put it as, separate. That was very wise.

The 'I's of Rimbaud — another thing, — "je suis moi," or something.[3] Infinity of selves, which Valery so messes. Makes into a mechanism, altogether intellectual. I find Gide very shrunken, these days, going back to him; very small, and somewhat pathetic. That is, the Counterfeiters — reading BROTHERS K/ — could not see anything added by Gide, and surprised to find how much the one book contains the other. A comment on Europe, perhaps. Time, etc.

One thing in NH was the sudden way one would buck into all kinds of reality; jesus, I do miss that very much. Could never then tell, or anticipate, what next. Going into Lisbon, say, anytime — didn't really know what might happen. The way it went, then : one time we were going back, from there, & picked up a man, about 40 [Added: Ann says, he must have been 60 — but even as I say it there (40), there was that push in him, actual, & very powerful — in the real.] or so, very excited & happy, and said he was on his way to join his bride, a young girl of about sixteen, with a name something like Rhodesia, or that oddness to it, — she lived at one of the farms, one which had for a mail-box, a big wooden cow with the box stuck onto the horns. The man was a horse-trainer, i.e., travelled around breaking horses for divers farmers, etc., and had just come up from one of the southern states, & had with him, sort of grubby packages, etc. But happy, jesus, he was bursting with it, all lit up, and crazy to see him. Talking all the time, tho he was hanging on the running-board, but leaning in, going like mad, about this, that, & the other. We let him off, and saw him walk in, etc. Going back to Lisbon, three days later, met him again, & picked him up, and all different — said nothing, and when we did ask him where he was off to, etc., not much answer, i.e., simply moving, and marks, all over him, tho nothing to see, etc. One couldn't face the change, really; it was not at all something one can talk abt too easily — a crumpling, all the life out.

What it was, then : now, nothing of it, and only this placid landscape. Which is a hell of a damn nuisance, hell of a waste of space, from any angle I can see. But only language, I suppose, cuts me out.

Perhaps I damn well need to move around a little; I sit here all day, as it's gone. See no one, and when someone goes by, feel very shy, & sometimes duck back on the stairs, so as not to be seen. A time when one wants to have no one see him, or even just that calling himself: 'one . . . ,' i.e., wants no sign of himself visible.

> Problem of sincerity: I thought of it, as when *selection* is ultimate, gets to that point where it can *use* all words, can hold them in its *intention, confession* becomes impossible, even if that too is intended.

One of the horrors, in some sense. One thing that constantly gets me to wondering or asking, if I am saying what I do mean. If the words are not falling much too simply, or easily, out of my head, say.

Infinite intention, etc. What prose saves is some slip — some place for the accidental, which is, or has to be, some of one's character. Cannot be the monster of complete selection, etc. (What finally, only, interested me in Valery — his idea of this.)[4]

But he never dug the alternative; look what he does to Madame Teste.

Anyhow, *one word at a time.* The way Dave does it, never falls back on phrases — a delight.

Hope this mail will be it; seems too long now, nothing in from you. But do damn well know what it must be for you, there, and all the waiting, etc. Wish to hell we were closer; times when letters can't make it at all.

All best love to you both,

Bob

[*Added at top of letter:*]
12:00/ G/ back on; and things move — will get in more next letter. Ok. And write soon, for christ's sake/ and yr lad's.

[Fontrousse, Aix-en-Provence]
October 5/ 51

Dear Chas/

Yours in, and things look much, much brighter — can't ever make clear enough what they do for us here. Especially now, i.e., when there is so much to push thru.

Well, very damn good to read it, & to have all of it. The list: will I ever make it? Well, I will damn well try the first time I can ever get close enough to where they keep these things. I always get way the hell off, but I can damn well begin, anyhow, and hope I have, at least to some minimal extent.

(That library sounds the end, there : someday you will take me by the hand

and get me into one in a state, call it, where I am not so shaken I can't articulate what it is I suppose myself to be after. The last time I tried (Dartmouth, & you should have come along, personally, with that $4) I was led to the stacks, pushed in, and came out with a book I had already read. I could never get up enough guts to try it again. Well, a problem OF my own, like they say; just that they do scare the hell out of me : libraries — they are so quiet.)

Anyhow, anyhow — and where the hell to begin? One thing, G/s letter, & the high-lights — that they are keeping on, damn certainly. The next issue will have 2 stories by yr lad (GRACE & LOVER : his choice, & tho I was, at first, nervous, now get to like that juxtaposition) & critical notes on you. I think I scared him off the poetry by the way I was grabbing at it for the Am/ issue — if so, damn sorry, but you damn well WILL be there, in FORCE: sd issue. He continues to hope for an edition of yr poems, and, if the divers presses can't be interested, an edition of CMI (with, he suggests, the addition of the Melville Letter). They sound like it is not very easy there now; "I am sitting here in a bureau, tiping french texts and have just a little rest for a private letter. Life has so much changed for us all during these last days since I am sitting here all day, children and Rainer lonely at home. But that goddamn money. And must be happy to have this job and to have some money regularly to pay the rent and all one needs for that little bit of life. Two days before my job began we fetched little Ezra from grandpa in Buehlertal where we left him because first number of fragmente didn't leave us time enough to have him with us. He is well and a very well-humoured baby, but not quite correctly feeded during his absence; so I have little bit sorrow about him. But beeing the happiest men of the world to be now together — quand meme all in one room. Rainer is busy to be ready for his visit chez nous and very happy to start soon . . ."
He is
due here sometime in November — well, I damn well hope so; I want very much to meet him, and hope, if the car is set, etc., to figure some way to make that trip back with him, and to meet Renate & the kids, etc. They sound like very damn fine people.

He asked me to tell you he wd write soon; in fact, was going to try to that night, so perhaps you have his letter there by now. Hope so. I damn him very often, not hearing, but do feel so damn silly whenever the letters come in.

On the Gasp/ & all: jesus, IF he would do a decent job of any such SELECTED gig, I mean: too much. The poems SHOULD be now set, together. The scattering is difficult, I mean, is a difficulty one can get round by such an issue, now. By all means, think that Y&X material should be included; and continue to think, with all seriousness, that Pro/VERSE piece is very much the item to act as leader. You said it: it should be with these things. But I'd hate to see Gasper screw it up by making an UGLY book; the Fenollosa is, of course, nothing to judge by — but could you get him to agree to accepting a design chosen by yrself? I.e., one approved by you — something clean, & decent. As my mother wd say, when washing my face, etc. (Give me a little time on any comment, call it, re the new ones; hate to jump in without thinking, on them, & I have feeling now, all you note there could certainly hold their own — want to say something that isn't fatuous, in short.) (I don't feel very easy on the Gasp, i.e., hello MRS OLSON, but hate to see any damn chance missed for such a thing — & I can't damn well blame you for the feeling on E/ in spite of that 1st ride, there, on his letter to me, say. No, it would be too damn much to start all that again. I can damn well feel that. It is that I feel G/ may be pushing a weight he doesn't have; a comment by Rainer, to the effect that he had never heard of him, no letters, etc., makes me wonder why the Gasp/ claimed contact in that place, etc. Well, only that slight edge, put it, of a question: it should clear up in his letters to you there, i.e., you'll know soon enough what gives with him, etc.)

　　　But the idea of a BOOK with ALL the stuff :
tremendous. Gives one, will give one, the real damn hammer to beat on a few of the idiots, WITH.

　　　　　　La Chute: I was chanting it, I
mean, I was, just so, chanting it (it IS magic!) yesterday aft, when the wife was off, I don't dare to it when she is here, etc. She says: smug . . . and you are not, for some sympathy, the only one she

addresses that adjective TO. Myself, I feel that DH Lawrence would damn well enjoy all of this; it is something he KNEW. Anyhow, to crow: it is, male, distinctly, & will, is also, male. Or, to say it better: this is *male will*. Ok! One can't expect the ladies to enjoy it, I suppose. (Which I will never live down . . . forgive me forgive me forgive me.) But Ann has Con's way of it : she never liked THAT poem . . .' (Phew.) Like a bull, she says: maleness, like a bull. "Sure it's *male*, but does THAT make it good . . ." (This comes winding up to me, up the stairs, from: below. Ok!)

Anyhow, Dave saw it all, right off; he gets the credit.

Re Bottegha: the thing that scares me abt getting this copy off to her is that she doesn't, she says, return mss/ if she doesn't use it, etc. And I'd damn well hate to lose this copy. So if you have one pamphlet to spare (?) then I wouldn't feel that risk, and would certainly get it back to you, if I cd get it back from her; otherwise, I can type a copy, to send, if that wd seem cool? Or you cd SEND pamphlet, from there. Whatever is simplest; I wanted to show it, to G/, and if it wasn't for the loot, wd say: (now that I have word of his idea) to wait to issue it in this big gig he has planned (CREATION: but can talk him out of title?)— stuff to appear in original tongue.

You say, then. I.e., either will type copy, or send this one, or you send pamphlet from there; whatever way is simplest. I *did* like the map; I must have damn well got smothered in the *text!* NOT to have said so, etc. (I'm pretty sure she'd send back a book, etc. I could get Mitch, in Italy, to forward it, & put in postage necessary for its return. But cd you spare a copy of the pamphlet, to have on hand when G/ shows, or simply for me to have here, to live with like they say?) Again, will wait till I have yr word on it.

Will get directions off to AB/ today. Is there a deadline on it? (Thanks / thanks for this one; I get very excited at this point.)

THE MUSICIANS, still behind the door, but will trot them out, or will hope to, directly. Quiet, pleeeeeese. (How abt that!)

Wild,
damn wild to have you there to be reading any of these things; I
can never, can never thank you enough, honestly, damn honestly.

Abt it, for now; and will be back on directly. Ann off, this aft, to
look at a ex-pigeon-loft, where we might possibly end up living.
And at that, would be very fine to get back with such. I.e, who
knows but the next few weeks will see you getting communica-
tions, again, from: A HOMER. Ok, and if it weren't for the
memory of someone's having sd: people who live in round rooms
go insane—I wd feel it the greatest. (I.e., it is round, they say; but
one can lope, at that, about, with more logic? All life: O. Pleasant
prospect!

Write soon. Keep us on. Hope that it all goes well there,
and that Con feels ok. All our best love to you both/

Bob

Another letter from Aldington, & they are pleasant enough, saying
he will come sometime next wk.

[Fontrousse, Aix-en-Provence]
Monday Oct 8 [1951]

Dear Chas/
Two of yrs here: tremendous. And have time, to get
this off before Ann is gone, etc.
Very *interested* in the Civil War
biz; i.e., give me more. (Talking with Mitch, here, & taking his
very quick interest as any gauge, etc., do think you have it very
straight; it *is* the big item, if one can manage the way in, & think

there, too, you are on.) Whether or not I can be of any use : your say-so. I have the interest, but not a shadow of the information. I wish there were some way to begin here — perhaps the Marseille Library, once we can get there, might give me some of the more obvious texts? Give me an idea. I.e., is there any way I can start anything, here & now, put it??????????? Anyhow, it is very damned exciting; I don't have the slightest comment, put it, to put into anything you outline here. But do suggest — *do it yourself*, i.e., make it all *one* piece, i.e., all method & means, & don't let any publisher yank it out from under you, as I certainly think they'd try to, if interested in any sense. The danger: that they will not be willing to do anything, until this interest you calculate is actual, i.e., 1961–65. And actual is only there to say, unavoidable, etc.

But *keep me on*, & give me more on it; that is, very anxious to know. I have the old letters, on this; I was waiting for it. Ok. Ok. Ok.

THE LAWS: terrific this far — do see what you meant abt it beginning to wobble there, as you quit, etc. But it is very *clear*, the 1st part, & many valuable angles in this second, just as it now reads. Well, these:

p/ 2: "FIRST DIVISIVE FACT" — that whole emphasis — terrific! p/3: siding of T/ & H/ : wow! That middle para/ : wow! In fact this whole page is of obvious value — obvious! p/ 4: Para/ starting "Mechanism" to beginning, "II" — as clear as I've ever read it; damn, damn cool!

II : RHYTHM : that makes absolute SENSE to yr lad — it always did, does, & WILL. p/ 5 : "Of course I assume that art is leader . . ." : this is something I have never heard sd this clearly, this basically : I damn well thank you!

(And DO remember Pound's statement: Medievalism[5] — had damn well copied out that WHOLE thing, for Ashley B/ two weeks ago, and DID dig that dissociation. Wow!

(As against the clear light, the held, the being held of : out from, *not* : in to. It was something, that clarity in sd piece.)

Think the run-off is on, "coital"? Well, to pass on, more swiftly, i.e., to ride on, quick : (you have sd, for one thing, that 'art' was moving on this Gk/ logic, etc., hence wd involve the actions, methods, emphases, of M/ —I mean, not to 'drop it,' but to allow yr reader to move into, quick, the BASIC tenents of RHYTHM, i.e., simply whack in, just here, with the counter, the true face, call it : i.e., what yr outline proposes. (I think you ran here, ran off, a little, trying to line up the 'history' of this false gig, whereas it is, I think, sufficiently stated, at this pt/ for the reader to make his own summations.)

Move *out* from coitus, is what I dig; no parodies, or not the petite extension, or substitute. The straight out — going.

Multiple. Well, crazy. Give me the next, eh? This to get back, & all thanks: think it holds very damn tight, this much. Ok. Write soon; will do likewise. All our love to you both/

Bob

[*Added at top of letter*:] Just trying the Musicians, again, when yrs came. Moving a little better; will send you what comes when I get it. Ok.

Bitter fact, that Mitch now sits next to a library (private) having all these damn texts; i.e., man there in Sori—which I cd get there, to begin, etc.

[*Added in pencil*:] 4:00—no go on Musicians—simply DEAD—or can't make it move—put it down for now, at least. Perhaps later, or can hope so.

[Fontrousse, Aix-en-Provence]
Tuesday/ October [9]th [1951]

Dear Chas/

Hardly answered you yesterday, & hope that the doleful note wasn't taken as any indication of what the hell I *was* thinking. I was going down, over the story, & difficult to keep it out, etc. Again, the Civil War gig does seem damn acute; & anything I cd do, certainly tell me — will be there at the drop of a hat, etc.

Also, this present draft (to that point it goes, etc.) of THE LAWS seems, likewise, very acute; I take to it, honestly, more abruptly & more excitedly than I had to the HU, even tho that belies my liking of sd thing — just that certain pts/ here, as noted yesterday, seem very *basic* to me, & their statement here, very *comprehensive*. Please give me the final thing, i.e., very close to me — not a damn doubt abt it.

Other things, for a moment : trying to isolate, at least a little, reasons *why* a story like that one dropped yesterday, cannot come to very much. That is, it would save time, to have even a glimmer of such a reason before one started the work. I begin to see, mostly as the result of having bucked it, now, off & on for some time, that certain attentions are more productive than others, certain potentials are worth the picking up — others give only description. In this thing, yesterday, I had, briefly, these main things : man, who was coming *in* to a meeting, of sorts, with the woman; this woman, content in an arrangement, a kind of balance of her living, more or less useless but seeming to her, at least, adequate & giving certain pleasures in spite of other discomforts, namely, her husband; which man — isolate, and wandering in the sense of — no weights.

But my final headache was, that the people, as I felt them, had no intention, in any sense, to do anything more than make use of, what they could of the others involved. I.e, each relaxed into his 'possession'

of certain uses of the other in question; the result coming to be—a
static situation, or one, at least, that could give me no occasion
for any shifting, or any kind of movement in the base meetings,
between them. They were, finally, there; they were, damn
hopelessly, not really intent on anything but a quick use, etc.
                                                                    In
short, a situation particularly barren to any yng writer of 'short
stories' is one in which the 'people' cannot be taken as having any
intention, intrinsic, to meet, to go out or in to meet, the others
involved. I know it is the ground for the 'fate' story, i.e., that in
which 'exterior circumstance' can be used quite effectively, *if* the
writer really finds things like fires & rainstorms of more *basic*
interest to him than the tensions of the mind & body, say. When I
wrote those 3 FATE TALES, I was probably being ironic, or as
much as I get so—the climax, if that was ever it, anyhow, the
movement takes place in an area in which the mind, the full
expression, call it, of mind *as* mind & body, is involved—then, of
course, exterior circumstance is nothing else but just your
objectism—the final world.

In any case, I did think back to the stories done, trying to figure
what was their main pull, on me, in the writing of them, and why
I found them, albeit densely at times, even so, anyhow—ground
for a *full* movement. Mainly I think because : in each instance, an
intelligence was attempting to clear itself, to move most certainly
into an area where he felt himself to exist (& I think just of
Fenollosa's reminder : of his noting it means to, *stand forth*).[6]
Quickly : In The Summer—man trying to find his position
between *two* others, trying to see where he is, in that place
between them; 3 Fate Tales—3 instances of an attempt to find a
similar position with respect to, exterior circumstance, and as well,
and I figure clear enough to call it there too, the intelligence of the
writer trying to plot a similar place, for himself, by means of 3
'examples'; The Party—attempt to plot the allowance (something I
feel as close to, the slip, or play allowable in a steering wheel,
say) in a commitment to any one person, i.e., in that instance,
attempt to see how precisely a man can feel himself to be
involved, even tho his apprehension of that involvement is (in this

case) blurred by a variety of fears concerning it; The Grace—
something more close to 3 Fate Tales than are the others, but the
change in method is also a factor—but say it is the shifting of two
people, again toward a gripping of one another, over the broken
ground of continuity, i.e., of the simple passage of time & the
event time evolves, or it does not evolve so much as it *witnesses*;
and Mr Blue—really the best, still, of this way : literal attempt to
understand something which has happened, something which has
felt impact but which is, as yet, not comprehended as, 'what
happened.' I have always been damn well *cheered*, that of the
several objections raised by others concerning that story, *not one*
has *ever* questioned the *truth*, or better, the *appropriateness* (call
it, the actuality, the acceptable position, the seeming rightness) of
the 3 *observations* made on page one—even to my mind, they are
not apparently usual ideas. And yet I *know* them to be precise, in
the sense that they *did* spring directly from a considering of the
event in question. I am very damn cheered by the fact that others,
to date, have granted that same fact, at least they haven't kicked
about what I would have thought their first vantage point for
disagreement. I.e., read those 3 things again—aren't they
'apparently' the real ground for anyone's kicking? Don't they seem,
prosaically, the obvious thing to attack? And yet (terrific!), NO
ONE DOES—and what that does for me, for my taking of these
things—impossible, really, to get it out clearly. I felt that IF that
could be done, IF a reader WOULD see that, then nothing was
really impossible TO prose, or TO any other USE of language.
There is NOTHING that cannot BE SAID.

To get back to *sequence*, very briefly. The most basic thing I have
ever felt about any continuity, of reality, is that it could not be
anticipated; and yet I could see, anyone can, that the attempt only
to get this un-anticipate-able-ness into one's work, literally, falls
very flat. One sees that reality somehow manages a continuity that
is exact in every particular. One hardly says it, but even so, what
is remarkable about reality is that, nothing *else* could really have
happened—despite the certainly ridiculous comment. It is so, etc.
And so, what to do, to have a thing, work, of art, like they say,
of that same character? I don't think it can be anything else but

what we have figured, anyhow—that one is oneself the content, the SI, that form is the extension, that the conjectural method, as you have kept me conscious of it, is that one most useful for just this ordering, in one's work. Thinking of those half-dozen writers of prose who excite me—Stendhal, and who would ever have guessed that Fabrizio would come to end, preacher & dying of love . . . I frankly don't expect it, even in *re-reading*; and yet I am very much aware that Stendhal hasn't the vaguest intent to surprise me, or to figure out anything which I might not be able to anticipate. They usually mark the idea, of his, of holding a mirror up to nature, and that is ok with me, i.e., it is the best, perhaps, idea to hand to a reader, to get him to see that the *natural* continuum, with its *own* weights, is the most obviously desirable. But I prefer, for my own uses, that comment wherein he makes it: I don't use outlines, feeling that the work would then be coming from my memory, rather than my heart . . . His statement, in the Balzac letter, is so very *clear*; can one finally hand, to another, a more precise commitment? "I see but one rule: *to be clear.* If I am not clear, all *my world* crumbles to nothing . . ." An incredible intelligence that can damn, without any reluctance, that of another which has applauded him for the *wrong* reasons; "This astounding article, such as no writer has ever received from another, I have read, I now make bold to confess to you, with shouts of laughter, whenever I came to an encomium that was at all strong, and I met them at every turn."[7]

You know that thing that EP quotes (SERIOUS ARTIST): "Poetry, with all its necessary similes, its mythology in which the poet does not believe, its Louis XIV dignity of style and all the paraphernalia of its so-called poetic license, cannot compare with prose when it comes to giving a clear and accurate idea of the impulses of the heart; for in prose one can only impress people by clarity."[8] I don't expect very many continue to read "On Love" even tho that is its base character, i.e, the clarity of the above. I frankly have never read anything to make clearer the constant necessity for attention to *any* particular; a book I would damn well not part with very easily.

To get back: my first excitement, reading Celine, was my hope that he had hit upon a sense, of sequence, that was new, or at least, was a return to certain attentions such as those practised, observed, by the above man. Now, I doubt it; I find it more & more, thinking abt it, a masturbatory kind of exercise. Willful, even; or better to put it, conscious, deliberate in the sense of, off the beat by sd fact. When I took it 'moral weights' were absent, & delighted in sd fact, I had forgot that 'moral weights' are, even so, a world, make one, and are its most apprehensible characteristic, at least for the novelist. To cut them out means to cut out, as well, a good slice of the literal *air* the people are moving around in. Can't be done with safety, or even, intelligence. Well, only to correct, admit to, correction — Celine is not that exciting I take it now. Not anything to bother with, finally.

The condition of, conjecture : think of it, or I do, just now, as the note in yr yesterday's letter about how you & your wife had come to meet. A happening, very pure & very simple. Even so, the job of apprehending what did happen might take a good long life, etc. It could certainly make a 'novel.' Set any man out after his own reality, to find it, and why it is, and what : what else. The persistence of certain weights is very attractive, and, in this case, sd attractiveness is coupled with an *absolute* logic of attention — one can do *no* better, etc.

All this, perhaps, simply to bury yesterday's flop — I don't know. I have to pull myself back up, in any case. To remind myself, if only that, that there is one way to make it, and that it seems better, simpler, to hang on to that, than to force 'fictions' into a 'life' they will never really have. They remain, fictions, etc.
                                                                          What
is real is what happens; what happens is what can happen. I don't suppose it can be seen too clearly.

When you smash the sense of 'record' as an aspect of an art, even its main purpose to some intelligences, — you release us from all the false judgment now smothering any instance of same. Well, I don't

intend the eulogistic comment—even so, it is damn well a
considerable thing.

Which sounds like a very old man, etc. (Remember once, first time
I had shown Max (the Pigmy Pouter, etc.), arriving at the place in
Boston, a bench show, & one of the men whom I'd been writing
to, off & on, coming over to find me, etc., thinking to ask me to
judge, and then saying, without thinking: but I thought, from yr
letters, that you were a *much* older man! I didn't get the job, etc.
But always the curse of sounding so very 'old' . . .)

(Likewise, Ez: early letters, had said—are you 63 or 23,—referring
to something you say you have been doing for the last 40 yrs!)[9]

All of which adds up to the greyness, now. Raining, and rather
damn dismal. Can't go out, kids can't, etc. Makes a tightness.
Hope we get out of here soon, in spite of the fact it's a damn fine
village. Sometime this week I have to put back a section of the old
lady's (opposite) well (and you never did tell me, IF you found
water, there, in Lerma . . .), i.e., the front part broke off, where
you lean in for the water, i.e, the rope, and somebody will, I
suppose, take the long drop down sooner or later, if not repaired.
So I offered, etc. And now trying hopelessly to remember the
exact proportions for a cement that will hold stone, & not be too
coarse, etc. I only did one such other job, and it was only for
ourselves, etc., i.e., a frost wall back there in NH—& very fine &
smooth, if I do say so myself. Anyhow, anyhow. I wish I cd
remember the exact proportions, etc. I think it is something like 5
to 1 : thereabts. Or, 1 shovel cement, 2 shovels sand, 3 shovels
gravel, or something. Fuck it; will get her something up, etc. TO
HOLD.

Will leave a little room, here : hoping a letter from you will be in
soon. Cd sure use it, this damn grey day. Well, back soon,
anyhow. Letter from Bud, yesterday, tells of: "President Quirino of
Phillipine Isles arrived in Madrid. He & Franco ride thru town in
Franco's car : Special model Mercedes-Benz, only 3 ever made :
one car for Hitler, one Mussolini, third for Franco. Streets lined

with soldiers & police. Bayonets, swords, etc. Then horses come in sight. The Personal Guard of Franco. Moors on horses. Gold hooves, etc. Lances. Fantastic . . ." At the very least.

(Hope to see him in November; likewise Gerhardt. And also, Ashley sd be back then, too. Will be so great to have someone, more, to talk to, in the flesh, etc. Miss the simple exchange, etc., and sit on Ann too much, as it is.)

All our love to you both,

Bob

[Added in pencil:]
Chas/ A note in from Ashley saying OK on the poem *but* I take it he would like to do it *back here*; i.e., he comes back some time toward the end of November [*crossed out*] — will that be *too* late, i.e., December [*crossed out, with note in margin*: my mistake — October, hence sometime: November, cd have it]? Tell me — perhaps use Duncan's poem for #2? Say what you think.

[In margin:]
I really wd like *A* to *do* it, if at all possible. Travelling: hard to figure it, he seems to say.

[Black Mountain, N.C.]

ROBT: Tuesday, Oct 9 51 — nor can i stand you shld look, each noon, for a letter. So, let it be, that, only this burlyhurly is cause — if ever anything else (like birth of child, or trip, or anything) will let you know — will try to manage my will to write you almost any moment, the trouble is, to let any space in, i have to drift, in such an environment — not drift, but, seep

(2) & that, now, if i am crazy with discoveries i want to
shoot to you, you must excuse me, i do that, instead, of, for yr
rich letters, come back on them — on so many things you raise,
beautiful businesses

It is merely that i am on a beat again — & this
morning, i think i saw it fast: it is the ETYMOLOGY OF
THINGS, of ALL T's, to get to the ROOT of

language	:so, my wild craving for,
alphabet	a dictionary, an encyclopedia
THE CITY	history (OF SUMER, MAYA, etc)
man as OMNIVORE	the ICE, after it
NARRATIVE	PLATEAU
art	river valley

NOW

Crazy, really, so much to do — & offerings, here. And so, because i
don't see how i can tolerate this place any longer than to get this
child to first age to move (3 months?), I am not worried, such
wonderful things can be done: ex., yesterday, all afternoon:
FARM. Just squatting & talking & watchin neighbor farmer take
care of sick cow (afterbirth, calf-bed, 2 weeks, & torn tit, fr
barbed wire); then, farm house, warm fire, talkin & readin Mrs
Jones' encyclopedia bought $120 for spastic son (13, Benny)
Compton's — & impressed at what, such a thing offers, the folk: my
father bought me the then lousy thing, "Everybody's," I believe it
was — crap. But this one! Answer for me on CRUCIAL ? been
kicking around: ANY TRACEABLE GRAPHIC or GLYPHIC PAST
                IN PHONETIC ALPHABET AMERICAN WORDS
                MADE UP OF?[10]

Of such importance, I give you what I now know: 1905 Flinders
Petrie found, Sinai Peninsula (between Red & Med Sea)
inscriptions; no clues until 1931: American named Martin
SPRENGLING, Arabic scholar, saw same as language of Semitic
turquoise miners, a people called the SEIRITES, working under
Egyptians around *2000 BC* (so, suddenly, for me, earliest evidence

previous was Berard's news that stela of Mesha (MOABITE
STONE), 9th century BC (basalt slab)![11]

"i, the miner Shamilat, am foreman of mine shaft number 4"
(READ IT, LAD: it is the 1st sentence writ in yr language!)
how abt that? how abt that how abt that: Harlan,
KAINTUCK

what happened: these miners had words as sounds for things
needed, like "water" was MEM, "mouth" was PEH, "tooth"
was SHIN, the worker his mark was TAV — and when he
quit working he did rejoice — HALLEL(uia!)

BUT, no way to write, or at least no way to write so that
they cld make their Egyptian masters understand, or that
the Egyptian's orders could be understood by them, except
by word of mouth, I suppose, and gesture: pointing, a
tooth, twist, pain, communication, needs out!

SO: Egyptians had signs for each of these things: the head
of a bull for the idea of ox, or a little man with his arms
suddenly UP for the idea "to rejoice," eh? Simple-like, like
the drawing of a hand for the idea of hand (YOD, sd these
Seirites!)

But both of these people, there, the mines, were no priests,
& no more interested in graphology than any workers, or thugs
(thugs is short for bosses), anywhere, eh? So, between them,
they made NEW SIGNS, in this sense that, they used INITIALS,
like R C, or a round O, eh? to be quick about it, and at the
same time have some signs which would be common to both of
'em — like this:

(I'm thinking this thru, myself, to be clear)

For example WA-TER: the Egyptian sign for the syllable WA
was a picture of a water wave:

But the Seirite *sound* for water was MEM, in other words
began with what we would call since an M

Result, when the Seirites wanted a *sign* to stand for any first
sound of their own language, they arbitrarily chose pictures
out of the thousands of Egyptian signs available, ONLY, they
obviously started from the commonest words, like, say,
water — or OX

for M, they took the 1st sign of the Egyptian word for water:

for A, they took the 1st sign of the Egyptian word for OX,
their own word for OX being ALEPH

and when they had exhausted what they could figure out to
be the differentiable sound of which their words were made
up, they had a series of signs which could be always
combined to make a writing of *any* word! SO: AN
ALPHABET, the FIRST! And here it is, for YOU, RC, the
STORY, lad, the STORY! and it WOWS me, to realize that,
behind our

A, is a BULL
B, is a HOUSE
C, is a T-SQUARE

D, is a DOOR
E, is A MAN WHO REJOICETH, who YELLS — aiyii! eeeeeee!

F, is a PEG, H
is a twisted rope for a WRAPPING

I, is a HAND ("I am": YOD ALEPH MEM: HAND BULLHEAD
          WATER!!! — christ!! how abt that for,
          pig latin, or hog American!
K, is a leaf of a PALM
L, is a LOOP of a string, and N
is simply a SNAKE. (And this snake ate

the FISH out of our alphabet, which, as a sound, was so close to
S, that, its representation gave way to the other representation for
it as TOOTH: in other words, the TOOTH (SHIN) was stronger
than the FISH (SAMEKH). And this mysticism can be cleared up
so: a fish was so drawn in Moabite & Greek (XI) but died out of
   the Indo-European there

Continuing, a round O is
AN EYE! (Eye am O: AYIN ALEPH MEM YOD: HAND
                                    BULLHEAD WATER EYE)

P, is a MOUTH, Q is a TAPE (presumably, to cause a mouth to
                           shut up, eh: my old man used to
                           say to me (who was so like hisself)
                           "what you need is a jaw-tackle"!)[12]
R, is flatly a HEAD

& T (to cross it, & end) is, HIS MARK, literally, even then, the
EWIPETENS: X

   (Just read this off to Con, to see if it made any sense:
anyhow, tended, to DRAW you the thing. Crazy, straight. Jesus:
think, that, *before* the damned *miners*, these TURQUOISE
MINERS, it does not appear that *any* human beings had noticed
that the number of sounds which a human voice system can make
was LIMI-TABLE! that this small field of sounds could be seen to
be capable of reorganization by signs to stand for the sounds
themselves, instead of thousands of pictures to stand for every
conceivable differentiation of "a," or "e," or "t"!
               (Tho what I don't yet figure, is, that, it was only some
               500 years later — with the IONIAN GREEKS — that any
of this system became a vowel system: that is, apparently A, was
AL, in other words a syllable as H was HAL. But the Greek vocal
mechanism did not include these — what we wld call gutturals,
maybe — anyway, like ourselves, we don't have an umlaut capacity
in our voice mechanisms. So, the Greeks used these letters to stand
for the naked vowel portions of these Semitic sounds. They kept

the letters for A, for short E, for I, and for O in their old place in the Seirite order, but with these new "vowel" meanings

Also, a change in handwriting made the base shift you will notice below. The Phoenicians, like the Semites, wrote from right to left (as Hebrew to this day). But the early Greeks used a back-and-forth system, that is, the first line went from right to left, the second (in a natural rhythm I am fascinated by) from left to right, then right to left, etc. And in each line they turned the strokes of the letters so that they faced according to the first, or declaring line. Pix, here: [*Not included at this point; see below.*]

But by 4th century BC, top Greek boys wrote left to right only.

> (ITEM, again proving—like a kid sd, last night, "Olson only thinks there are two narrators worth . . . Creeley &, Herodotus": Herodotus wrote in his "History" that letters were brought to Greece by Kadmos of Tyre, and that sd K stopped 1st at the island of THERA, and then went on later, to found the Boeotian city of THEBES—and by god, if these scholars don't now find that the *earliest* Greek inscriptions aren't to be found on the ISLAND OF THERA—& that the letters there used most resemble the Semitic writing of the 13th century BC![13] I love, THAT! (me, & Frobenius
>
> PLEASE
>
> note: please ask GERHARDT if, he cld pick up for me any, & all F's works, there: especially, ERYTHRA[14] — & that if so, will get moneys to pay for same

(going crazy, to buy, books! which [*i.e.* wish] some patron or ess wld do for me what someone did for Ben Jonson—gave him a swag each yr for books only! Christ, the books I need are all 5 and 10 buck goes! One: Frazer's PAUSANIAS, goes 75$!

Ok: will give you LIGHT: here PICTURES!

[*Added in pencil:*]
Will be back on — I hope — tomorrow! Wanted you to have these,
while on it.

> One thing now clear: that the tipping of Sumerian 90°
> I once wrote you about is also here — only, most of
> the time, it is a 90° to *right*, where Sumerian went
> *left*

Ex. SAG	before	after	before
(Head)	3200 BC	3200 BC	2600

(Wld figure this means
Sumerians wrote *left* to   after
right, initially)   2600

DOES ALL THIS SEEM AS REAL GONE for you as for
me?

    O

[*A chart showing the development of the alphabet from
hieroglyphs to ancient Greek, adapted by Olson from the*
Compton's Encyclopedia *article on the alphabet, was enclosed with
the note*: FOR DAVE! another sort of CHUTE!]

[Fontrousse, Aix-en-Provence]
Wednesday/ October 10th [1951]

Dear Chas/

Notes, etc. Yr past statement: "art is perfect
control"—that lush picture, sometime back, of Jackson Pollock (in
LIFE) 'at work,'[15] i.e., as Ashley sd, incredible thing to do to *any*
man, to so show him in such an act. He squats there, legs
cramped under him, & leaning way out, over the work (spread on
floor, the canvas), to let drop some paint from a big brush, the
paint-can held out, too, in the other hand.

I.e, the loss : when the
paint *passes* from brush to work *without* the hand's control, it is
not art. At least, it seems to me, not to be so. The *gratuitous*
circle, say, or just blob, so got, will have gained its nature, its
character, from forces too free of the man. I know that some
argument might be made, from the angle : this character of the
blob is no less relevant than the character of the marble, say, or
of, even, the words—words have shape before you use them, etc.
The blob is *utilized*, etc. Even so, it does not convince me,
although, since I have seen one or two of his paintings, that I did
like, put it, I wish I cd see it, perhaps, that way. Not honestly,
however.

Ann had thot: directions on the planting of daffodils,
tell one to throw them out, on the lawn, i.e., just toss them, and
then, without moving them at all, plant each one where it has
fallen. 'This is Nature's Way, etc.' And yet I cd no more plant
daffodils, that way, than I cd any other thing. Ann used to laugh
at me, planting, i.e., at first I was so intent I had got a little stick
wherewith to sink a hole for each seed, i.e., I planted everything
one by one. Which was foolish, I know, but I had that feel of it, I
mean, it did literally bother me not to so do it. But it took so
much time, etc. Finally, I enjoyed only those things, that could be
planted so: potatoes, corn more or less, etc. The great pleasure
from the poultry (poultry still seems to me the more or less
'perfect' attention to go along with writing, etc.) was that it cd all
be deliberate; raising the birds the way I did, etc., each egg set

had numbers of both parents on it, each chick hatched: toe-
marked accordingly. One tried to *know* insofar as he cd, what
might be expected. Ira has feather-charts (feathers from each bird
taken from breast, back, saddle, wing, hackle, etc.) on *all* birds
kept, which date back, now, over 40 yrs. There were no accidents,
or there were no accidents that weren't *noticed.* Why, finally, he &
I (despite age, etc.) did get along so well: this same feel of it, etc.
He cd, certainly did, break down the 'Barred Rock' and put it
together again; I have seen him do it with other breeds, and where
his 'art' lies : in his ability, by means, literally, of his constant
observation, to select & couple for his own purposes, varying
characteristics that have no *apparent* relevance taken separately. It
was no less, I really believe, than the same biz: "Swift perception
of relations, hall-mark of genius."[16] I can't see that it was anything
else. Of course, poultry-breeding so taken may seem a gratuitous
art, i.e., a man like Ira breeds for a 'perfection' that cannot be
proven, i.e., it is only proven by one man's conception of it. Even
so, what else is a perfection, but just so, one man's idea of it? If a
man can breed a bird, any bird, to a type, an appearance, any
appearance, which he can *maintain* with a minimum of variance, a
minimum of accident : certainly he has done *something*; and if the
bird, say, isn't taken as very much by some people, even so that
man, & his attentions, are a considerable force in any 'place.' It
might rub off, etc., or one might hope so, etc.

I wish I had some here, damnit. I plan an old age with nothing
but chickens. I never used to have coops, enough, or decent
enough; — endless angles. Sometime you will have to try it for
yrself.

Thinking to yr LAWS— when you make that, 'art is leader,' &
emphasize that man *is* artist, or simply doesn't go on living, the
whole thing gets very clear, very much opened to *use.* The whole
thing being : a base conception of art, the job of. The two existent
controls are : nature & man. They are *not* the same; and making
that clear, you do, again, considerable. When one says, of
something, story, poem, etc., but this is an accident? — to answer,
it is an accident, but the 'accidental' is myself. To make that

actual, etc. When the man goes out, his intelligence (body &
head), nature comes in; the play between them, the constant
tensions just there, are, I think, of prime interest. (Again, yr citing
: 3 Fates Tales, etc.) When someone says, yes, but nature works
thru man? Etc? Man can, nonetheless, *do* things which nature
cannot ; he can kill himself with a gun, say, for an obvious
instance — nature cannot kill him, *that way*. Even tho she gives the
means, etc., — she could not *use* them, herself. Suicide, an instance
of 'art,' etc., tho pretty stupid to run off to that side. (One thing I
do continue to respect, very much, in Dostoyevsky is his making
use of these two disparates: the tensions a man may invite into
himself, the tensions that get in *anyway*.)

They are always there,
so: really the groundsense of yr 'objectism,' I think; I mean, that is
the way I apprehend it — these tensions, these forces so locking, so
sided, etc. The obvious reason for giving them attention, in this
relation : can a 'world' exist without its *existence*? What the
abstracters somehow never get round to thinking abt. You can't
get rid of nature, i.e., you can't write or paint, or sing, say, minus
it — but you *can* utilize the tensions, the differences, in the 'field' —
you *can ride* them hell bent, etc.

Method is, I think, so damned
important because it is the obvious place where the man most
comes in; his content is singular, granted, but his means are even
more immediate, even more himself than what he might say with
them. His means are, literally, that *moment* when he is writing,
etc.

Anyhow, I do think that EP's notes on criticism, heading MAKE
IT NEW (Date Line),[17] are basic, are mainstays for an attitude. In
all of his prose (and remember, I do now, yr comment that his
prose, no less than his poetry, represents, *is* of major use, its
method) I damn well find the *position* maintained with all *possible*
consciousness; it is pretty rare at that. The one argument for its
use, that people should be reading it : certainly that one. And yet
I can't imagine (and I don't know of) *one* college, or school, that
utilizes these incredible instances of *clarity* (simply clarity of
expression, of *presentation*) to show its students, call them, a

possible way in to the same; take that English A bk/ at Harvard, for one item; prose, almost all of it, *descriptive*—writers intent on the diffusing of 'impression,' men after 'color,' after 'feeling,' after 'intangibles.' Whereas, Pound's MR HOUSMAN AT LITTLE BETHEL wd give 1) *more pleasure*; & 2) more discernment of the necessary ingredients than any of them. "Saxpence reward for any authenticated case of intelligence having stopped a chap's writing poesy! You might as well claim that railway tracks stop the engine. No one ever claimed they would make it go."[18] Add Housman, & you have the dimensions of : 'a course' etc., etc. Levin: perfect example of a man who *does not know* what a *clear* statement IS; when he starts writing about STENDHAL, there is certainly cause for LOUD LAUGHTER. (I never regretted, as much, the excursion via Joyce, tho it was equally wasteful.)[19]

Ok,

& this, only, to keep on; you do same. All our love to you both/

Bob

[*Added at top of letter*:]
got me damn well CUTTING WOOD here—back ON directly. OK!

[Black Mountain, N.C.]

Friday Oct 12 51   ROBT—fucking cold in head. Anyhow, immense craving to be out (October & all). So, am trying this, in sun. (Trouble here is, anyway, all one's proper cravings—to work, read, walk, anything but to have to do with too many people! SO—immense craving, to be alone, *out*—yesterday, with Goodman's fine dog (left here last year) alongside (redbone & cur mix) over farms in neighborhood, merely looking, emptying myself of "head"—& delighted, & angry, to watch the dog drive calves in

on neighbor's herd, & then be faced up to by the cows, just so
long as he did not do more than bark, but, running in, they high-
tailed, yet, always (& not any biblical observation, maybe) but,
those hoofs (but hawgs are more bold & more intelligent?), made
so, make me ponder

                     (chance may go on bear hunt here after Oct.
15th, with Jones, the farmer, and this wld seem to be something,
no?)

Well. Don't mind that I shot off to you the little verse:[20] can't
figure a thing of that order, just, feel a damned fine pleasure that,
words go around like that. Yet, figure it as too easy—and in that
sense *not* clear (in that luminous sense you quote (two letters in
this morning) Stendhal

Thanks for ride on The Law: it died right there, as is, and have
not (the trouble, also, here, that, things are too broken up—even
to getting a meal, a price is paid I am not used to, or, believe in).
Have not returned to Law.

Had also to get off a couple of jobs to cid (one on his verse, The
Soldiers, and the other, a letter to him in answer to his news, that
he had overshot on #3, and had to cut HU: frankly, had no bad
feeling over that one (am patently sick with such discourse, even
when it is anti-d!) but did think it an occasion to pull cid up a
little on general strategy[21] (Con against my letter, but hunched he
needed a little righting, even in his honest enough regret: that is,
what bugs me a little is, any loss of the wonderful thing he offers
us, a closing of the usual gap between the writing of a thing and
its appearance—when he talks abt either #3 or #6, and so I
discover that issues #4 & #5 are somehow gone, six months are
gone, and that, for me, seems poor policy when you have two
such horses in your stable as thou & me. So I sd to him, taking it
easy but curving again at this business of planning such things as
"foreign issues," saying flatly I take it the Americans are still the
busiest & the forward ones, and that any such ordering (whether
we are or are not) is wrong, basically "what-idiots-do": that is, I
still take it you & I in any three months can make each a thing, at

least one thing, which he ought to keep a clear-way for. Organic
way to make a mag move forward: the men, not the mag, which
is paper, even when it is written on however handsomely, or,
otherwise. Plus the sort of ideas any such horses are bound to
keep also shoving out. That is, with all due respects, I don't see
any gain to cid in losing the very impetus I take it he gives us (by
getting us into print so fast & fine) by planning (1) a "foreign
issue" and (2) I suppose #5 is this Morse go on Stevens?:

that is,

continue to feature either A. MEN or B. A PROPOSITION, a
LIVE idea (in other words, LIVE men, LIVE ideas, but not a
stereotype, like an essay on Stevens or an "issue" of "foreign"
writers:

let him have a Kitasono issue or a Gerhardt or an Ashley
Bryant—but not a cover-all

Anyhow, just to tell you I have done this: suggested, for example,
such ideas as an issue of Origin "featuring" ORIGINS (e.g., the
etymologies of all things, and so, he would get in, other forms of
writing than the looked-for "narratives"—what does he think the
world is full of, Creeleys? I'd say an Herodotus tale, smack up
against one of yrs, without comment, ought to lay the narrative
proposition on the line. And if he wants critical pieces—

aw, to

hell with beating back over this—it is simply, that, I regret his
tieing up six months in a bundle which, basically, squeezes out
things you & I might be riding, there—and for no live purpose,
that I can see, that is, I don't see the "foreign" as a legitimate
device, or, do I think "pictures" (18 pages, the woodcuts, in #3) or
an essay on Stevens is worth a host of propositions you and I kick
around daily

But there it is. And I feel so damned mean abt it I wish you wld
just let me beef off, and not breathe a word to him, for, he is—
like they say—an angel, devoted like a dog, and certainly the only
place I ever felt I had a home. So, I see no gain in rocking the
boat at this moment: in fact, before he had received my letter, he
picked up from the go I gave him in critique of his Soldiers, to be

straight-on, and say, he'd like to excerpt from it for #6, saying that, he figured, just about #6, the mag wld need a clear statement of its directions! So, he must himself be feeling his way along similar lines, and there isn't anything to do now—as a matter of fact he seems still quite open on #4, even sd he wld like to try to run HU there, as well as the Answer to Gerhardt. So maybe Con is right, I am jumping the poor guy. In any case, it was an honest reminder that, he can string issue to issue on us—a sort of pointing, flagrantly, to the center field wall!

No answer, of course, to my letter to Emerson leaving the whole question open—what a scared shit he is! What in hell do you figure he does with his day—write verse after supper every night? Ho ho.

And on GUIDO: we are ready for it right now, but, if Duncan comes in with something (or Goodman, whom I wrote to, asking for several, to look at, to see—dangerous business, but)— or Kitasono's Shadow, if he gives me word—and WHAT ABT YOUR PICKING, AND TRANSLATING, A GERHARDT??? please: just get us Ashley's design when you can, when, you can

and any
other ideas? (I have this feeling, that, I make a poor editor simply because I am passionate and so have the trouble of not liking more, or enough, to give a spread—anyhow, not on a "contemporary" front—wld spread in other ways, eh? well, this one is a good beginning for me, anyway, though, I can see hurt feelings ahead!)

Will get off, directly, a take on all the verse you have sent me, & also, on that note on verse (which I did not, by my silence, pass by: it is always that, on such things, I think you take your clearance, and so far as I am concerned it's the works:

my only
feeling is a truculent one (and somewhat an embarrassment for me, that, I personally want no more than to tip my hat at EZ, these days, he is getting so damned much time—and I am so sick of this biz of comparison—all over the place, it is "like Pound" for me—

christ, it makes me sick: none of them honestly know that two
men stand forth out of the half century: he and DHL. In fact it is
not those who know Pound that say this easy business of, like
him, you, are like him, but, those who still pipe for TSE, always,
it is they—and the intent is, to beat me with that stick (as Ishmael
was beaten by the stick of Lawrence & Dahlberg!)

for christ sake,
just give me my air, whatever it is—the issue, anyway, will only
emerge in the issue

(i guess i am fucking testy today, and you
musn't pay it much mind—you see, I also was given the Corman
"pass-on" technique: he wrote me that he had called Levin (in his
good-hearted way) to ask him why doesn't Harvard ask Olson to
give a Morris Grey reading! and Levin says, he is only a "callow
Pound." And that idiot passes *that* on to me, at the same time that
he ties my hands by asking me not to breathe a word of it!

To be
in a fucking "college" and have to stand off such inroad! to be in
mud, and when one needs rock, one's own commitment as rock!

(And not a peep out of those NY bastards—supposedly,
they were to act on that grant—which would get me to
Guatemala, Honduras, anywhere but here—Sept 15!

by
god I can't stand the irresponsibility to other men of such
generalized things as such—the nerve, to let it go like this, to
make me to wait one day beyond sept 15—and me keeping myself
here basically to meet their condition of affiliation!

Fuck it all, let me tell you what's been interesting me:
PREHISTORIC CAVE PAINTINGS!

only Frobenius any good on
same, but these quotes, from Max Raphael,[22] just to chew on (he
is Marxian, & refugee, & stupid because non-practicer—only value
is, as, from another area, reports:

> "The paleolithic artists knew that the specific forms of surfaces
> and space are shaped by biological and magical forces, a
> knowledge which the Greeks made us forget."

((This bears on
your own important solutions of tension in the narrative
area—and why no one CAN do any more than see that
those 3 propositions in BLUE are INTACT))

The following is loose, & does not have enough geo-geological
density of, say, Sauer's fisher-folk[23] behind it, yet, as of now,
it is, I think, interesting:

"Let us return to the most obvious spatial experiences of the
hunters who wandered with the herds. Space as infinite
distance and emptiness separated man from the animals and at
the same time compelled him to wander further and further
along; the sight of crowded bodies showed him that the
animals could be attacked, and thus enabled him to anticipate
a period of rest. It follows that finite and closed space
acquired for him a positive value, practically and later
ideologically, and infinite and open space a negative value.
Under the influence of Christianity our values are the exact
reverse, but this was not the case with the Greeks who, for a
long time ((he is not specific enough, here)), as seafaring
tribes, were nomads ((one can't take this a step beyond the
Odyssey, and even there the older elements are a ready thing,
however much the general air is, precisely, this density of
MEN as against all fucking dispersions))
                                        "in their eyes, the
finite body meant salvation" ((clearly, the coital was a
degeneration from the magical,—in fact, a proposition surely is,
that, without this recognition all is biological)) "and rest" ((this is a
sort of a lie the general passivity of the figures in Francocantabrian
forces even Raphael into, he is a scholar, and is frightened at his
own boldness in attempting to show how much motion there is
inside the surface frame of those animals, those buffaloes, hinds,
mammoths:
            what really sends me, in all this, is, just this firmness
of stoppage, this holding, and then (as you so often) the motion,
inside, from, the personal act there as art, as so many lines and

spaces, and each, only there, for, the relevant and elemental force
they can be made to serve))))

                        "just as open space meant unrest,
hardships, dangers"

What I most wanted to tell you is, that, you must be within
striking distance of the best of this stuff, and do, please, find out,
and go, in order to tell me back, what this stuff is, straight, from
you, to me. Let me at least give you the names, and if I can find a
map with them located, will see it gets to you:

      LES COMBARELLES   &   FONT-DE-GAUME

  seem to be the two chief French caves

         & of course ALTAMIRA, there, Spain (in case
(the hot French bird, whose book might be around you, or
surely Marseilles, is the Abbé *Breuil*

And this most important shot against humanism, as it was
Euclidean:

    "The geometry of the paleolithic artist was not based on the
    human body but on the human hand and the play of hands
    and fingers"
                (isn't that beautiful — and an eye-opener? it feeds
                right in to what the Maya (and their hands, in
                red, as signature: me fecit) also, seems to me,
          were up to — that is, they had hands & the sun
      these, hands, and animals

    "If the world was conceived after the image of the hand, it
    was conceived as an abundance of forces. . . .

    "The hand is not a structure centered on an axis, it is
    unsymmetrical in shape, it has a one-sided direction just like

> an animal in motion, and its motions are free
> and independent of one another, because, unlike
> the human body as a whole, they do not
> constitute a single system of balance"

that last sends me — is a thing i have been waiting for, the
pertinence — what do you say!
    Or this, to close it:

> "The paleolithic artist knew those devices which were
> compatible with his fundamental attitude of not centering
> himself on man, and of determining all form by constantly
> changing forces."

Well. Not much of a letter, lad. Excuse it — just pissed off. Will be
on directly, on, your self and your things. Con may be under the
wire by time this reaches you: Oct 19th!   still can't figure it

Love,
Charles

[Note by Olson: c. Oct 15]

NOTES ON AMERICAN POETRY: 1951

The writing of poetry, and no one, perhaps, but an American
can realize the full implication, is not very easy. It is not at all
easy in a country which takes its poets to be some servile form of
loafer. The average farmer, mechanic, or doctor is, I think, in a
position to tolerate, even to understand, an art more concretely
than is his counterpart in the teaching profession. Poetry, in the
U.S., is often believed to exist as an adjunct, an embellishment, of
this last vocation.

There is a condition, then, to understand; it may not be of ultimate importance. Even so, the present reader will not comprehend the nature of present insistences in American poetry lacking a knowledge of their possible reasons. The universities have absorbed, in past years, a great number of American poets; thinking of the younger men, now writing, there are very few who are not teaching. This may seem, on first look, advantageous for all concerned; actually, it is not. The outcome has been an increasingly sterile art, an art based on trivia, on pedanticism, on motives too alien to the base intent to effect anything of literal use. A man likes to eat, etc. One can hardly blame him for that. It is impossible to support oneself writing poetry in the U.S. I suppose it is equally impossible in other countries. Hence, one teaches.

"Peace comes of communication." It does *not* come from a use of words in any sense calculated to obscure a motive. If a man writes verse to make *clear* certain premises, certain emotions, certain characters of idea, to the extent that his verse is conscious, is written with clear apprehension of the means to such statement, it will be worth the time of reading. Otherwise, it is doubtful. Two-thirds, at least two-thirds, of all poetry written in the U.S. is written to adorn a position, usually academic. Criticism has become a more prevalent form of writing than work within the basic mediums themselves.

All of which sounds very negative; there are, however, other manifestations. Receiving the somewhat specious National Book Award for Poetry, Williams answered:

". . . We are said to be dreamers, but in dreams, as W. B. Yeats has told us, begin responsibilities. The words are our responsibility, the government of the words; the nearest, the most to be valued, since it is of all governments the archetype . . ."[24]

The 'government of the words' is the most basic act of which a man may be capable; his speech *is* himself. Making that false, distorting it, he becomes filth, muck in human form.

The present selection is, certainly, neither very representative nor very complete. My criteria was this: 1) the speed with which one perception issued from another; 2) the concision with which all such perceptions were presented.

Beyond that, it *is* 1951, a [certain *crossed out*] number of unequivocal developments have occurred. Fifty years ago one might have written *about* the beauty of something or other; now he must either hand it over, direct, or simply shut up. "No ideas but in things . . . ," says Dr. Williams;[25] at least there is no further excuse for *any* generalization of *any* sentiment by *any* poet.

Form is an invariable headache; there is, at present, a tendency to treat it as though it were "a derivative of plastic shape."[26] Form is never more than an extension of content;[27] to consider it as an essentially external component is altogether useless.

Which is about it, or one cannot say more than the poems can themselves. American poetry is as sprawling, as inchoate in its bulk, as that of any other country. But there is, contained in it, the work of some men who maintain a basic sense of integrity, who do not allow themselves the convenience of distortion. Their work is all that matters.

————————

Chas/ a flash, i.e., PBlackburn just wrote, letter in, etc. Kasper turns out : "One of EP's newest, but he don't write. He taught at City or Columbia and got thrown out for some honorable cause I hope . . . Can quote EP's pomes, cantos and all, by the yard-length, and after fussing around for a couple of months promoting boys like Lekakis (a pretty good sculptor) finally ended up with this publishing deal, after talking to Pound apparently at length. The reprint is a good thing . . . Kasper himself, no editor, I'd say. Maybe a promoter . . ." [*Added*: Confidential, i.e. don't want to screw P.B. OK.]

Which doesn't say much, but gives, I guess, the main points. There seems a slight soiree atmosphere; i.e., discussion & all. Games, etc. Not very interesting, etc.

Will tell you whatever else I can dig up; apparently, they had you spotted as a 'name,' i.e., wanted that lift for the deal. It all sounds damn shaky to me, not that that's any reason to go sour on it—simply I don't figure they cd hold on either very long or hard. Laughlin is angry about the reprint; i.e., duplication of some material he has reissued at $1.50, etc. Not, then, much chance of any distribution thru his outlets, etc. In spite of the Gasp/s conjecture.

Honestly think you'll do much better to hold on to the gig there, to a possible move here, once G/ is in & settled, this spring. Likewise, what about Mrs. Crosby, she sd she was getting back in November? How abt her issue, say, of the A/? Well, time enough. This, only, to spot the Gasp.

[Fontrousse, Aix-en-Provence]
October 17 [1951]/ Wednesday

Dear Chas,

Yrs in yesterday to find me, likewise, with cold, etc. I hope to christ yr now feeling better than I damn well do at this moment. Dulled, goddamn head all thick, etc. This is shit—fuck it.

Also, was just doing another job on that gig for G/; I didn't much like that 1st try, either. The tone, finally. Didn't make it, albeit it cd have been declaimed, with gestures, like they say. Anyhow, this new draft enclosed, & say what you think; time for several more tries, if this don't sit well.

A point of contact: that is, I know that dog, believe it or not!
This hand has patted that head, etc. Do you know the Goodmans'
kid? There's a wild one for you. They used to be in this little ap't,
dog, kid, Mr. G/ & Mrs. A 'happy' family : wow! Leed is a good
friend of his; in fact, the one time I got up there, I did damn well
like him; I like the wit, & the shrewdness; I don't suppose I wd
ever really dig what he might do, or nothing, to date, beyond the
three novels, but anyhow—he is ok. The poems, however, I
thought horrible—i.e., that bk/.[28] Jesus, they were stiff things.
Stuffed. Don't leave me scare you, however! That prose is what
made it for me : 3 novels aforesaid.

Some hound, is right; she was loaded with fleas the last time I saw
her.

His wife is wild; i.e., very pretty, almost the college-girl ideal, tho
now too old, I suppose. But a *voice* that has you screaming, after
about 15 minutes of same. Sharp, nasal thing : a deadly weapon,
like they say.

Poor old Leed used to bed down with her; talk with Paul, etc. I
don't think he ever discussed even the weather with Sally. One of
the dumbest women I ever met!

And PG with this infinite theory! You should have dug them,
eating, the kid with this damn well satanic gleam, just doing
exactly what wd fuck matters most, most thoroughly, & P/ :
now . . . . , etc., etc., etc!

O well.

Cid: he had just written abt having to drop HU; not a damn thing
I cd say, etc. I.e., I get to feel he'll have to work out these things,
at least a lot of them, on his own. Matters of woodcuts, & all. No
good reason why, say, 18 pp/ of same shouldn't be the end—but.
I had my own doubts. At the same time—tho this instance aint
it—the main thing is the verse, to keep making room for that.
When he tells you *that* has to wait, then *do* shoot, etc. As it was,
THE PARTY don't get in till #6 either : I know what you mean.

If you cd meet him, i.e., get up there sometime after things cool, etc., I think you'll find consequent dealings wd go altogether simply. There isn't any question in my own head but what it is us, for him. That is, no worries on that score, at all. But he wobbles, even has to, a little. If he doesn't get it all in his own hands, i.e., can't get to hold it that surely, we will be the losers, anyhow. I expect he wants to widen the thing, some; perhaps feels that there is danger of hermeticism, etc. I don't share that, etc. I mean, Paul Blackburn, some of the Bronk, can be regular components. And one picks up compatriots in the going-on, etc. I wish he wouldn't get nervous on that score. But anyhow. Let him wander, if that seems necessary to him; no doubts but that he'll dig, then, what that does to the base.

I told him, anyhow, *everything* I do, re either prose or poetry, goes straight to him; he suggested at one point I might send that PARTY out, i.e., pick up, he thought, some loot by trying elsewhere. I know it wdn't go, but anyhow, sd, no: is for you, etc. Keeping the work on him, i.e., piling it up there, and granting it's worth issue—he can't dodge it, i.e., must dig what's up. Figure that's the coolest way to maintain the emphasis; avoids any ill-feelings, etc. I haven't, honestly, any eyes for tangling with the big-boys further; Kenyon never even acknowledged my return of their check, nor my first letter asking that that story not be used. Hudson strikes me as the only other possibility. But for what— shown their slowness re Blackburn's work, i.e., a year now on some translations of his, picked at them all the way, he said. It doesn't matter to me that much; I can make the point elsewhere, *if*, say, Laughlin holds on & very lucky to have J/ Hawkes in there, fighting, on that ground. ND is, I suppose, the obvious out for any novel that wd go with any publisher—this gig, now, and his willingness to use yr intro : some encouragement. I continue to feel that some kind of play, there, cd be made; how well do you know him? I mean, some of this material, both 'critical' & otherwise, seems worth the attempt to get out via him. Anyhow, Hawkes wrote a fine letter, in yesterday; at that, his 1st novel (CANNIBAL)[29] showed sequence beyond anything I know of, around. The 'historical' lean, i.e., that frame, is what confused it,

finally. He is a clean man, in any case; & a serious one. He was
digging the stories (In The Summer; et al) back two yrs now.

Ashley: a letter, also yesterday, & says he'll be back by the 1st or
so of November. So then things can move, for the broadsheet.
Very sorry there is this damn delay; but he was picking up there,
foolish to interrupt him, etc. He had told me abt the caves: sd
they were incredible, & once we have the car, will make it. The
one they got those LIFE pictures in, is not too far from where I sit,
etc. Over on the Spanish border. Fantastic, so A/ says. Power,
like nothing else in god's world : simply cannot avoid them. (He
sd, some kids found them, i.e., looking for a lost dog, heard the
barking, and getting a light, went down in, and suddenly, flashing
this light around, SAW these THINGS : I wish I had been ONE
OF THEM!)[30]

Well, will get there, & give you first-hand acc't. On the spot, like
they say : ok.

Aldington due here tomorrow; with Australian. Don't know how
that will go—feel so lousy, at this pt/, don't much care. Cannot,
in any event, get to shake off what he did to Lawrence[31] : well,
time to see, etc. Will write what happens.

The quotes: very damn interesting. Will be writing G/ today, &
will ask abt Frobenius bks/. Ok.

Casals plays, I think, not far from those caves; a pleasant
juxtaposition. AB used to sneak in to all rehearsals; goofy, i.e., no
one else sitting there but Schneider,[32] et al. C/ was too much, he
sd; his one adjective : NATURAL!
                    Ok, & this, to end, for the
moment; will make copy of this new draft, of notes, etc.—give me
word when you can. Hope yr cold's done by the time this gets in,
& mine likewise. All our dearest love to you both : & keep us on/
                                                        Bob

━━━━━━━━━━━━━━━━━━━━━

[Fontrousse, Aix-en-Provence]
October 17, 1951

Dear Chas/

Yr two just in : very, very great. The alphabet goofs
us both; heretofore, we'd been leaning on Kipling's exegesis, viz :
JUST SO STORIES[33] — that, will goof you. Anyhow, wild, wild
stuff, & keep us on. Will nail this to the wall, this thing, &
ruminate. Ok.

The poem is very, very lovely; very fine, fine-boned, I would have
said, very light & tremendous *grace*.[34] I do like it, we do, very,
very much. How you manage to get these things out, what with
the pressure, I don't damn well know; myself, I couldn't have said
a damn thing. (Rhythms, crazy here; love the lightness, the way it
rides : very much like those little sail-boats one wd launch — to see
them ride out, with this freeness, so very fine.)

Rain stopped, & feel less swamped than a day ago; dulling effect
of it, kills attention, we huddled, etc. What I did want to get off
to you, notice of a letter in from EP; it seems the ice does move
out of that river, etc. Cannot say that I am anything but pretty
happy it does. I think the Kasper move is the same biz; I noted,
for one thing, that K/ wanted the Western Review poem (T/
Granger) & that you say, in one of these last letters, was one of
those EP liked, etc. I wonder how else sd Gasp/ wd have located
it; he doesn't sound much like an explorer, frankly.)

Anyhow, anyhow : text as follows & as usual, strictly
anonymus:[35]

The Creel prob/ not see current Hudson/ but isn't time fer Creel's generation to revolt against the dead hand, dating from Dial or before / backwash of aestheticism /

vid Tate in current Hud/ Tate's morality:

"if you see a child about to fall into an open well, DO NOT make an unseemly noise to prevent it."

Whether Creel has observed ANY élan vital in all that almost three decades of so called "literary criticism in the U.S." I leave to Creel to decide.

BUT if Creel and affiliates ARE bursting into argument might be good "front"
              or BACK to fight on.

Glad R. Ald/ well disposed/
hv/ also given him address of good guy named René Laubiès, 33 rue Rossini, Nice.
translating by feel and got the makings,
minor howlers of no importance.

                          in strict anonymity
                          4 Oct

Half a dozen basic issues ALL idiotically ignored / and does NOT strengthen ANY poetic quality, to ignore 'em.

Mrs P/ adds : "So very glad you are noticing the light. V. Gogh also — !"

Which, all of which, may mean nothing; even so, hope it indicates we got in there. I think so. I.e., he had both issues — hardly think he wd have written, at all, or bothered to put RA on, etc., if he did not dig some of it, etc. Etc., etc. Who can say, like they say. But will keep you posted, in any event. It continues to seem ridiculous, to have him down on anyone like yrself — anyone who makes what you do. (My letters to him: one on prose; one on the Fenollosa, etc.)

I put it out, directly, re ORIGIN in the answer to this one; i.e., sd what it meant to me, if to no one else but me & yrself.

I was also thinking, other things, that, picking up on yr earlier comment about what he had done *in* prose : (if a copy is handy) viz Polite Essays, pp/ 144-5 (certainly others, etc.) — how the *sequence* is managed, or is not 'managed,' is, in other words, *found*. Anyhow, I don't know of any other prose-writer who was making this base sense of sequence at the same job, etc. Stendhal always had it, however. I mean, he never wrote but what he *was thinking of*. I wish I'd noticed that a few years back.

Soon, I want to rewrite that note of G/s Am/ issue; just too much left out, too much echoed, too much not said, etc. Will send you on what comes of it; I thought, reading it again a few days back, was altogether too sure, in a harmful sense, call it.

Otherwise, hauling wood back on the bike this morning, had got to a curve in the road, big log of sorts balanced on the carrier & handlebars : a lady drives by, neat small car, beautifully attired, red, red lips, ec. I thought of, back in NH, working in the garden while the trains rolled by, etc. Certain fear, I guess, in being mistaken for landscape, or there is when one wd have, perhaps, it otherwise. Anyhow, sit here, log now in stove beside me : we make out as best we can, etc. Our day will come, no? One hopes, etc.

An old friend sent in a picture of herself, stretched on the lawn in, not much. For what, eh? For why.

Check me, on this one : arguing with S/ Lawrence, per usual, had it that, "It turns out a humanist is one who takes the human act to define all others; even a country doctor could correct him . . ." I wanted to lay it out 'fairly . . .'; I mean, to give them all benefit —

was it too much? Even so, I can't but think there is a basic error
in *position*, even giving the ground as above, say. The human act
does *not* define all others; it is not the prime gauge, etc. By same
token, I can't really think that there is such a 'prime gauge' lodged
in any one category of, act. The only endurances are structures of
activity, etc. It could still stand better statement, in any case.
What happens *between* things : you sd it.[36]

Cid writes, with great excitement, of how you did a job on his
SOLDIERS. Was tremendously happy with it; never was, I very
honestly believe, a more conscious reader than yrself. In that dep't,
I sometimes think I read, literally, with this one eye. Or only
occasion when I wonder if the one eye is a limit, ho.

I dreamt of Ez last night; i.e., I dreamt I dwelt, etc. It was a boat,
or about to be, a boat; that feeling of people so got together.
Divisions, etc. It wasn't till it was over that I figured he was, at
that, in the 1st class. I thought, dreaming, that was the insane
asylum, i.e., why there were fewer there, etc. I had the face from
his picture in the beginning of the Cantos; but really, now that I
think of it, was one that Paul Blackburn had shown me, cut from
some newspaper, he wears a floppy sort of hat, is smiling very
damn beautifully. Sort of wistful; anybody's old uncle, etc. I was
let in, i.e., passed thru some division of gate, or level, and
walking over, could know him, then, without any real sign of
'introduction'; he somehow began to include me, or to make notice
of me, in that fashion. I.e., I was in the conversation (and now,
again, that I think of it, it must have been a monologue, i.e., no
one else close to him) whereas, a moment before, I had not been.
(Taking leave, later, I think we did it at some table, having tea,
perhaps; some simple displacement, in any case.) All the talk had
to do, I think, with categories of attitude; it was lodged in how
the thing was seen, or said. There was no subject, that I can
remember; unless some air of a murder, of something one would
face into as, *how*. I think he left it as, he trusted me, in some
sense, to see certain ways, i.e., to have some hold on the divers
attitudes possible; but he more approved of P/ Blackburn's
intelligence, i.e., he thought he was more himself than I was

myself, etc. He moved, again that I think of it, apart from everyone; even so, there was a wake, i.e., he had strong position.

If you got yr dream-bk/ there, give me the word, eh? I think I wd honestly faint dead-away, face to face with him; I can't think of one relevant word I cd say, i.e., trying to think of it. PB told me about his meeting, i.e., arriving he was sent from the entrance over that lawn to, the door. Ringing the bell, no one answered. He cd hear voices beyond, some room behind it. Stood there, etc. Rang again, etc. Nothing. Abt that time a voice comes out, real loud : For god's sake, LEAN on it . . . , & he did, then heard someone coming, door opens, & man appears to show him in, etc. That room I guess, EP, wife, & [Dallam] Simpson. It seemed the privilege of going out on the grounds had been given one of the men there, & all morning long he'd been playing with the guard; ringing the bell, that [*i.e.*, then] ducking when the door opened. Myself, I never wd have got over the lawn; they cd have buried me, where I fell, etc.

Achilles Fang noted, how Mrs. P/ wd pick up on his conversation, i.e., he wd stop, Ez wd, and she would come in with almost the same *thing*; he sd, the same. I.e., thought so moving, etc. Is that right? It sounds reasonable to me.

He is the only man, finally, other than yrself, that I really want to meet; Williams doesn't have any of that pull on me. Something as simple as being, 'Bill,' pushes it off. This last letter he starts, 'Creeley' & then corrects it, to, 'Bob . . .' Something damned irritating in that; & not all the 1st 'lack of familiarity . . .' I felt much easier making it, Dr. Williams. I hate the jumps, when they aren't actual.

In any event, you remain the only one I do believe I wd have something precise to say, to. Otherwise, you would have got only silence on, the telephone call. Sometimes I damn well can't speak; no matter, etc.

Not much moving, otherwise. Haven't got anything done, haven't really tried anything. I feel very restless, at the moment; hope G/ gets here, & that the proposed trip back to Germany with him works out. I need some kind of change, I figure; very stale at the moment.

Sawing wood with a pruning-saw; trying to sharpen it, can't find anything able to hold it firm enough. Damn wood goes quick; tried to buy some but too green, just smokes, no heat, etc. So I trot out twice a day to the ridge back of us, and gather the faggots, etc. Can't work up will enough to get in a supply; so I was out in the rain, etc., pulling up dead trees by what roots were left.

That poem is very nice—just stopped to read it again. Terrifically *fine*. The right adjective, if there is such a thing.

Someone wrote, in fact, was that man in Swampscott,[37] so it does pay to hold on : I begin to see there's not much difference between explanatory words, & descriptive, once you've unhurriedly read a few things. Or words to that effect.

> Can't think of much else but yr baby : any day now.
> Should be. Hope to hell it isn't bugging C/ too much.
> Impossible to think anyone could ride it, coolly, like they
> say.

And, reminds me, my mother wrote that she was sending on a few items. I.e., I noted same back a bit, or that I wd see abt it? It seems they have some things (shirts, etc.) which you can't have too many of, etc. So, figure they should get in there, sometime soon.

Dave now FOUR; what I damn well forgot to say. We put off his birthday a few days, & suppose I got guilty. Was nice thing; happy damn day. At one pt/ he sd: I'm so happy, happy, happy, happy! (His companion statement, the opposite : all unhappy & sad . . .)

Things move, without or, with me. Nice to
think of that.

SO. Write soon, let us hear what's up. Will do
likewise.

All best love to you both,

Bob

G/ is doing some work on you, I take it. Notes, or something. For
something there; he sd he was writing — has it got in? Hope to god
he *does* get here.

[*Verso envelope:*]
If a man named Louis Dudek, Canadian, sends you anything for
broadsheet — this to explain it: saw one very nice poem by
him.

Do you pass on Blackburn [*lines, asterisks drawn around*]
item like *The Birds*, say? I think he's got very, very *cool* rhythms,
handling, etc. Let me know.

[Black Mountain, N.C.]
thurs oct 18 51

Robt:

you are a life-giver — & at a time i needed it — ur two letters
in, & break a vise of a pattern been on me since i last wrote you:
a week in bed, with flu, or, whatever: figure, myself, it was the
toll of this place plus the last couple years, & that i've been doing
a simple act of rejection, keeping the hell a way from people,
sleeping, reading, gnawing: & it's been fine for con & me, to be
without people (tho they have a habit of coming in at night, and
throw me back a day!

anyway, this to tell you. am still not much
good, and figure to stay put a bit more: the only good occasion i
have to shake it off is the imminent birth. And Con is
unbelievably splendid, rosy, and full of a very handsome
happiness (crazy biz, this, anyway, of a child, there, in that taut
skin — we were just watching it swing its kicks, or whatever the
sudden squares are which show on the skin — and Con yells! and
then it's over, like that, from the side to the middle — so much like
something working under ground, eh? old mole!

                                             i figure myself,
not the 19th but 21, or 22nd, whatever was three days from the
sailing New Orleans: the Gulf, or probably Vera Cruz (which
seems to me a proper thing to be [able to] tell the character, that,
it was conceived *off* the mainland, out of these hyar states! of or
near water! like, element, hoho

                             the point is, that, what you write
here, your words, and their fall, are life, and raise love in me as,
always, such, eh? damn moved, and figure that you have it there,
that, the only endurances are structures of activity

                                     & more &
more take it, that, ourselves, it comes to the act of narrative, &
that such act is the act of language anew

                                and that the endurances
now are those which restore resistances (such cloggings) to
whatever in order that force (the rude thing) is allowed back in (

  anyhow, that there shld be no surprise that language, now,
need examination back to root in two directions:

    (1) as it is hieroglyphic, that is, as it was *first* sign, the act
        of *pointing* (even perhaps preceding *naming*, in the sense
        that — so fucking completely obscured to the moderns —
        that experience is so strong, and so personal, that, one
        can well imagine these inventors were trying, in the
        sign, to leave the thing superstitiously unvoiced, as
        though any word would dissipate what they recognized
        in the thing (that is, when you had it, as of Ira, that
"swift relations" etc, that, such are exactly such recognitions):
GESTURE, somebody sd, each act is also a gesture.

what i am trying to stay on,
and yet not allow in these traps of concept — magic, mana, or all
these sinkers — is, this difference between the act of recognition and
the act of representation, that is, something which exists in space
as extricable from time, eh?

for (2) as language is *phonemic* (and here, too, sound, which
is time is not simply such ((((here is something crazy happened, as
of EP's poetics, a couple of weeks
ago, and no time yet to get back at it
for you & for me, but, suddenly,
read him on rhythm, & something is
wrong, something is cento, in, his
idea that rhythm is a cut in time,[38]
that the block is time, when,
palpably, it is not so easily time
(Boulez, again, and why, I want
to inscribe In Cold Hell to his 2nd Sonata . . .)
sound also has
gesture, or plastic act in it by way of *the hands*
that is, (here i
must elaborate more, when my head is less stupid), i wld argue
that the hieroglyphic holds in itself an implicit respect for
experience outside as non-aesthetic and magical, say, and the
phonemic is both (because it is inside, the human, act) aesthetic
and non-magical, in the sense
(which comes home to what you
have written me) in the sense that man does not conceive himself
as magical just exactly when he recognizes that all else is. On the
contrary: he thinks of himself as instrument, and as he is force of
work not as source of wonder
(the death of god in modern life is
this fucking confusion of wonder as human versus wonder as
extra-human: both propositions are only possible when man has
lost touch with the reality of, any experience
which implies, i
guess, that the death of god *and* man of man as definer (as prime
gauge, you had it) are both to the good!

((am most struck by when this notion of "god," "Lord," Father,
came in—

> before him, but, Augustine, is fantastic measure of a
> terrific lad who went off precisely, on this point of,
> insufficient grounds in the concept to support him in his
> wonderful African passion for things, and so, he goes off
> half-cocked, into this swelling, toward, god

BUT, he had
one thing, the sense, that *work*—that the only endurances are
structures of activity—and this is beautiful in him

> so, to get back, as man is force of work as instrument, then,
the wonder, stays over there, outside—or rather, as you have it,
just that outside where the inside meets the outside—IS NOT
HIM

> all a man admires is what he accomplisheth

art is the only
measure of his capacity of accomplishment

> so he stamps his HAND on things. as he does in his
greatest act, language, even in its coming into existence

> (((I'm afraid I'm leaving out several steps here which ought to be
> put first—as of THE LAW, or, THE DRUM—but will try,
> soon, to get them down

> Just, that you wopped me, with,
> these letters!

The news of Ezripuss, on, puzzles, still—& i watch (as another
member of the cat family!) for the jump! but it is sweet to the
senses, that man, eh?

Crazy, too, just before yr letters came in, a tremendous hunger, to
be together and to talk! ((Riz up Monday and

> whacked out a Fulbright application—just to give myself a
> play, a chance, to get the hell out again, next year: figured,
> this place, was a ground I'll not have long, to act from—
> and want to go Mesopotamia! So, no offerings in Iraq, put
> my hand out for (a) position Istanbul and (b), position

Tehran! for next fall! so figure, if you still there, will cross, eh? Wild, what?

"Never wrote but what he was thinking of" — beautiful

Damned nice, that, yr mother, will send — it does give me delight, to see Con, ahead of time, putting her hand on things (like the blanket you people sent) in passing — and the other thing, two weeks ago, she rearranged the bedroom so that she wld know where the child wld be put! told her, it was straight like that wondrous cat we had, Washington, who, would put Con's mother out of her bed, she had decided, days before the coming of her cats, where she intended they should be!

      ((You see, I begin, to feel this thing coming! And maybe (as Jala, the sharpy, had it, that, I am myself an African, and have took to my bed to prepare my wife for, her, confinement!

      Please keep writing — much need same — and terrific, what you have in here today

         — all love to you both

           [Charles]

[Fontrousse, Aix-en-Provence]
October 19, 1951

Dear Chas/

    To keep on : I don't know, the only relevant question or comment seems, IS IT BORN YET — don't keep us hanging, for christ's sake. Tho, anyhow, do if it gets forgot, etc. One understands! Ok, and when you can.

The weather is so damn dulling here, at present, it saps anything I might, otherwise, be managing. Just can't beat it, at the present; wish so damn much we were into a bigger, easier place. I have to shift this damn machine upstairs & down, etc., about 3 times in the course of each 4 or so pp/. A drag, in any case.

To report : letter in from M. René Laubiès.[39] And he sounds ok. Offers all help possible re Cid, has an in with les Cahiers du Sud which could help move things here in France, or, anyhow, that possibility. He says : "very glad to get your letter and the review. I like very much the review and your works there — I am quite willing to help M. Corman with any french poetry, etc., etc., etc. Do you know les Cahiers du Sud at Marseille (about half-hr/s ride from where I sit, etc.) — they may help you — and they could publish something of you, too — I am going to see them end of this month, etc., etc., etc." The upshot being, will see him then, when he comes there; can find out what might be forthcoming, etc.

He is translating Pound; Leon Gabriel Cros[40] is to write preface for him, sd man being, I take it, one of those on sd les Cahiers du Sud. Voila, & shall keep yez informed. Just fired my other barrel at him, viz: Rainer's 1st issue, & stapled a note to the p/ with yr Praises, saying : watch him! Gave yr address, fact of ISHMAEL publication by Gallimard, etc. See if some of the poetry can't be moved out there — but hopeless to anticipate, as they may all have very long grey beards, etc. Anyhow, shall soon see, & then : will let you know how it looks. Voila.

On to England : that seems the die-hard. Writing to [Peter] Russell, about getting bks/ etc., there, also sent a copy of the 2nd issue; more or less dull answer — he proposes a swap on some stuff so hellishly involved I cd never make it, — he even encloses an invoice in the event I am interested. Wow!

IF, say, sd les Cahiers du Sud (I heard of it, but only with reference to activity circa 1890-1910, say)[41] cd pick up on the poetry, there wd be position for some leverage on Gallimard for further issue, etc. But again, hopeless to anticipate. These french, etc. They fool me every time.

Wd have no objection to Cid's idea re foreign work, etc., IF it wd only be issued as the continuance, i.e., whenever it's too hard, whenever it has that bearing, etc. To make 'foreign' issues : well, not the greatest. It seems to predicate a once & once only gig; dulls everyone.

Meant to go on, more, re Paul Blackburn that last letter, but that damn cold had me. Now better, and hope to god yr likewise; hate them everytime, etc. Anyhow, with Blackburn : I have to insist on handling, that it is damn well fine. The content is, to date, negligible, or is nothing close to the handling. I know they can't be spoken of, as compartments; the point is, his value is the fantastic control he somehow manages at 24 yrs of age, etc. His translations are also, something. So, just to note him, I mean, to suggest him as an item for the broadsheets. I met him, there, NYC; I haven't the slightest doubt, myself, but that the content deficiency is most temporary — such a thing he's working out of, home, mess, etc., he has to do it *this way*; otherwise, he'd lose his sanity in a matter of some very few minutes. You wd like him; I mean I would take that risk of assumption in this *one* instance. Matters of simple clarity : he has that.
         Writing this, say, does predicate a seriousness, if only in terms of, how can it be done:

> "For miles run
> rails rusting in the sun,
> stretch town to town;
> and dark to rain the highway tangles down
>   between these places.
> Yet over these the message passes."

From poem he since threw out, etc. Sounds, sounds there : you can see what he's trying for, what he wants as, control, etc. It is not your own, not mine, etc. It is, even so, pretty crazy, and *if* he could get to dig yr preoccupations—this man would be incredibly *good.*

Well, anyhow,

This, from a letter from Mitch, re prose : I thought it just what Mrs. Ainsworth letter was—you can't turn it off.

"As for me. This seems to be my rhythm: if I don't learn in this alley, I'll never learn at all. I'll never be able to afford to give it up. I've got to go on working it because as far as I can see now it's all I've got. It doesn't, thank god, obliterate or dull me. There have been times when I've lost all my confidence and with it all my impetus. But that's temporary I've found. When it comes back I can go on moving, and learning. Something new continues to happen. I've never been as curious as I am at this moment to work my way through it and see where I come out. Only from that far side will I be able to see where I can go next. The least it does is to give me a window . . ."

He is a crazy man; as clear as I've hit, as honest. Talking with him, one gets an incredible weight, I mean, there is that actual weight of attention; it all gets heard.

Well, this for the sign; wish to christ this weather would pull off, and give us all some peace. The house shrinks very much, on these wet cold days. No place, really, to go.

Write soon. Tell us how it all goes.

All best love to you both,

Bob

[*Verso envelope*:]
Have written Renate G/ about possible po-em for translation—will keep you posted.

[Black Mountain, N.C.
ca. 20 October 1951]

Rob't: Taking the Greek mythological system as as interruptive as the Greek metaphysical system (I can't yet find out any other villains for the piece), what follows is more & more clearly wider, each day, and determinable, thus:

(1) that the act of logic did cap perception that side of where it can be capped, and, by so doing, knocked off a bloom & head which, once, & now again, has to be readmitted — and so, for the phrase of it, to work ahead, let's put it that the act of logic impeded serious parts of the act of magic

(2) that the act of classification (whatever its original apparent advantage as a method of clarification — by separating parts & so naming them ((this was as much an act of the mythology as it was the metaphysics — this I don't think is sufficiently seen — and, equally, the god-demigod-hero divisions were, as statements of causations, & progressive causations at that, allied to logic, and so, each of them, logic & classification, tended in two time directions, the chronological & the superficial (in the sense that the demonstration of classification, as it is necessarily deductive, spreads the thing out from its round to a flat surface of statement)

       that this act *partitioned reality* (the clue, here, is your own phrase, and is light)

(3) that both (1) & (2) must have behind them a shift of men's attention which caused them:

it is this which I propose to keep trying to run down — nor is it easy, to figure, what would cause such divisiveness in the face of the overwhelming fact, that, reality is this instant & me, and that any discourse about it is only to enable any of us to state or to make an equivalent of, this fact — FACT, the SINGLE FACT, from which all LAWS have to follow

:so far, I take it it was some *loss* of respect for rhythm as METHOD — and perhaps the truer oppose to the act of logic is the act of rhythm?

and surely it is a respect for rhythm which impels *act*, in fact that one clear reason why action has been so long askew is, that it goes, has gone, and still will go out without any law of rhythm on which to depend — so, form, FORM is neither understood or worked for. Thus content degenerates to no more than *agitated material*, which is chaos, and immoral. Form, then, is the only measure of the moral, and rhythm is the only mechanic of the moral?

:(I am now most suspicious of the Ionian physicists as possibly the beginners of false inquiry, of false discourse — that the rot has to be pushed back from Athens this degree — for example, I would hunch that, so far as verse & myth go, it was Pesistratus who put the ice-box in — and he & the physicists are, I think about contemporary

:a thing that seems to go with this is the coming into existence of the master-disciple biz, of, the "great man" not as leader of the state or of society but as leader of ethical, metaphysical, intellectual & religious sects or movements — and I have this feeling, that all this, too, is WRONG — that one of our jobs is to strike as much at Confucius, Buddha, Lao Tze ((all circa 550 BC)) as at their descendants, Socrates, Christ, Paul, Augustine, & the one who sluiced the whole business down to now, by way of his monastery, Cassino, Benedict

: which I guess is why it comes out quite simply that, art is sole leader, simply, that act as rhythm is the only excusable one in the face of the going on, that all other acts of definition are discursive, necessarily, by law discursive, that, they set out to be!

so, *system*, instead of action, & pride (which I now take to be the clue to humanism, that, man overrates himself once he lets his conceptual power escape the act of form he gets so pleased with his ability in discourse that he thinks himself mightier than his instant

And so

conceives himself as somehow separate from, & even greater than, the "nature" of reality. Thus he is led subtly along to the idea that the splendor is his!

And so so, three, he comes out with the concept of GOD – I am impressed by two things about the "saints," one that their secret battle is with their pride (that their will has come to stand up as a separate thing from the floor of things, like a stalagmite, and that it is *with* this icy calcium that they do battle, and against it) and that their overt demon is SEX (woman, when you come to it, the thing they must degrade: she is the shape of the devil that torments their hairshirt battle with their pride – a huge confusion here, in all of them, especially from Christ on, but note, that such wonderful passionate men as Gotama and Augustine have to leave their wives to take up the struggle! Even they – that it is not the hermaphroditic saints alone who are tempted, it is also the realboys, the lads who have had it – and come to the notion that they must reject woman in order to take on god! (The quote of em all is Melville, the poor latter day of em, in the poem "After the Pleasure Party":

the sexual feud clogs
the aspirant life!

Nor do I think I am being simply simple—I do take it that
at the base of this huge raised structure we call theism or
religions is, this simple avoidance

and that the reason is the
departure I am getting at thruout, here, the going away
from the instant as the immensity

so (4) that the immensity of the instant and you (because the
understanding that it can only be dealt with in terms of
itself only and that all conceiving of it is only preoccupation
with it—that a step away from this durable, this durance
will lead to what has been known, for, since, at least 500
BC

and so, i am as elementary on the posteriori of it as the
priori: that the invention of the god biz is inevitable as
SUBSTITUTE for the immensity, that man cannot sustain
his pride in himself, and so pushes it off on to the
"creator"

the very word a chronological one, and so sad,
history immediately following, & discourse, & and all
deductive forms, or false forms, like Dante, Virgil,
Shakespeare

For the act of substitution is as eating an act (all
substitution is devouring) as there is

It *will* go horizontal as surely as it is
a removal from the round of what bears on us

The proposition, then, comes out this way:

that either any of us
face the immensity as inevitably involving us too in creation on
that instant (for so any alive serious posing of oneself to it is)

or, the race will end up with a slide, with, a creator, who, instead
of being examined as of the instant—as being "life"—gets put back
to that false thing, cause, or beginning, explanation (so ontology,
& teleology—for the other part of it is, that, beginning implies
end, and so you get judgment day and the immortal, all futurism,
as the dribble of the leaking faucet at the other end

poles, & the
whole ugly birth of the "either-or," instead of the multiple, which
is the real biz of reality, that, it is multiple, and does not STOP

the going on, that's what has been emptied out of both mythology
and metaphysics — and man's ugly little will to stop things ends up
always in products, those dirty solids which clutter, and deprive
him, of space

so, it is, time, that whores space, but only because they
interlock, and are inseparable, are, instantaneous, and only go
apart when man goes part from their action as the harmonical
[*i.e.*, harmonic] system of reality

that is, that space-time is the
syntax or weather in which reality is declared, both the inside
one (man's) and the outside one (however you call it)

and that
biz, of, the meeting place, exists in space-time as the
environment of it which cannot be redisposed by man either
chronologically or materially

(note how all saints are involved
in two ponderables, the pre-existence of god (so the Trinity,
or like problem) and the resurrection of the flesh, that ugly
horrible butcher notional things, that came one [*i.e.*, on],
when?

again, H Melville, Pierre, "to glut the damned Cyclop in
the trencher of the grave"[42] — when did man construe
burial as an advantage over the worms?

when did flame go over from the instant to the likewise filthy
notion of consuming so that the "spirit" might be made clear,
the body burned off!

when was the Holy Ghost depressed to
3rd place (note that, that, the Creator or Father is 1st, the
Son, or Adam, or, Who Takes on the Body, and by so doing
cheapens it to a temporary "house") and that the HG (who is
even called, in the Apostle's Creed, the "Lord and Giver of
Life") runs a poor third!

It's crazy. But is not these lights
right? It seems to lock up only too neatly. Yet, I don't know:
in fact, isn't this also one of the LAWS, that, the direct
always is that simple? It is, certainly, in the experience of the
instant — otherwise, not a poet could ever have existed. For the
act of metaphor is "neat" — swift relationship, eh? So why
should an exposure of the negatives which came into being
then, whenever, not be clear, direct, and this apparent? Even
more so, surely, than the illumination of the positive, what
bears?

For here the devil is, what Bill sd, that, there is no end
to, desire[43]
For desire would seem to be the real human condition equal to
the going on (the old question, what makes us want to?

We desire
or we die, are dead. Life is desire, so far as the human participates
in life, so far as it is life. The other "life," what goes on; must, I
take it, have its condition comparable to desire. What it is, other
than its coming at us, I don't know. Nor do I think it matters, in
this sense, that, to unravel it leads to all that I take it is wrong,
simply because I don't see how the human can be so assumptive
that it thinks it is capable of understanding another order of life
except as it penetrates it for and by its methods, its, conditions —
and for its ends.

So we come back, that, nature's nature is not to
be easily intruded on (all science is such an anthropomorphic act,
however shrewd and impressive its experiental method, its shifting
of the mechanics from the human organism to the machine as
recorder and calibrator — as mischievous and falsifying a
substitution as god, in fact both of them "machinery" *in the place
of* DESIRE

art, again, clears itself of the two
other major systems — religion & science — which, each of
which, is, I am suggesting, a removal from instant, just to
the degree that it admits only one mechanic, the
human
And so finds no need to transpose man's system and

condition over as equally valid measurements into the
examination of nature's reality

Thus, both
anthropomorphisms are, by that very fact of anthropos,
wrong, useless, and based on the partition of reality

I mean, we come back, in this sense, that you or I has to behave
in the face of that other reality modestly, to this degree, that, *we
don't know*. Nor is it of the matter that we should know except as
our desire is our knowledge. There is no knowledge without
desire, anyway. And so no action (it is here, I think, that the
intellect gets properly restored, that knowledge only can come,
once desire has disposed us, by this other simultaneous function of
our organism, the intellect — and not as an agent of discourse
(which is what it has been separated off into, another stalagmite in
Plato's filthy Cave, as the will, and the soul, and all these phoney
deductive & demonstrative "partitions" of us, parts — jesus, I have
hated that word, parts, exactly, usage, man and woman, as,
exactly making sex also separable from the going on, our own,
going on

((here, too, i am led to think that even DHL got
confused by the enemy into an overstatement of the phallic into a
part — in his honest attempt to start to bring sex back into the full
play — that is, that, it is now necessary to be as chary of separating
the phallic as it has been the custom of the enemy to separate sex

: in other words, that Dionysus, or Priapus, is as suspicious as are
Confucius & Gotama, to our statements, now

which again curves
back to the mythological (I guess that it is what is leading me,
throughout)

that the act of mythology is being reconstituted from
the ground now as surely as the metaphysical: in other words, WE
DON'T KNOW NOTHIN — or better, WE ONLY KNOW WHAT
WE PURCHASE IN THE CLEAR, BY ADMITTING OUR OWN
METHOD, no previous one

and this is a way to define THE
ARCHAIC as the condition for which we can be thankful as our
present one

so i can now come to some grips with that word
magic: it is a poor word, and probably also comes to us from the
time of discourse

Coolly, the other reality is so huge (stretches forward and
back before and after man so hugely—as well as out from him as
it is the universe) and stays SO HUGE just as it bears, as it is also
ORGANISM (what i am trying to be clear about is, that one can
distinguish the features of that other reality as definitely as I can
distinguish your face & eye from the man inside, and can
differentiate those features—the shape of the thing—from its
"life"

it is its LIFE, which invokes our DESIRE

and this is what
involves us properly in mystery: I dislike this word too, as, of the
vocabulary of discourse

again, a created thing, say, in our minds, a
story or a poem does have a life of its own

just there is what we are required to recognize: that it does. And
that how it does (so far as it exists without necessary reference to
a man's own capacity to make it—his own puzzlement, that he
"made" it) is something one flatly *does not know*

so, *awe*
(whatever) comes to be as sufficient a word as desire:

there is no
end to awe

That granted, I take it one can deal with the notion of the
magical: it is or was only another system (earlier than religion or
science, preceding both) for registering man's awe (as action is his
only known registration of desire

and i have this suspicion, that magic is the lower order of art,
that magicians come into existence as priests do when the
people crave to satisfy the urge which only art satisfies

that is,
one may make this trope: a golden age is describable as one in
which *all* citizens are as active as creative men *must* be, that all

act as though act were only relevant as *art*

and that the original sin is no such thing at all, is not even stupidity, but that the race is not capable of *enough* desire (however much each may have some) to pay the price of the act of desire

so only two alternatives follow: (a), either men then (and I think they have, and can) keep dignity and fullness in their life together by permitting only artists to be regarded as leaders

or (b), they give over their own function to some other invented system like magic, or religion, or science, or the state — and allow such leaders to make magic for them, to give them some frame (instead of the only valuable thing, an organic thing) in which to continue a paltry recognition of *what they are in the hands of*

That is, man *cannot* give up either awe or desire. He can only cheapen them — and he does just that to the degree that he allow[s] any other notion of act to stand in the place of art

(If one were to make a fiction of the narrative of man one could possibly argue that such a golden age is alloyed not by man's declining from his pitch but by artists declining in their responsible function. It is interesting, for example, that the painters of the paleolithic caves are considered to have been magicians!

In any case, you and I know that it is exactly individual responsibility on the part of a creative man which does declare the relevance of his art — and that this is the only moral force which matters (both to him and to society).

"Holyness": another phoney word. And surely a concept which came in in a silver age (or maybe damn well exactly in the Bronze Age!). For it is a misconception (and as such leads to the "notion" of the validity of god). And it must come from men finding themselves as outsiders to the personage of artists — and noticing (from the outside, alas) the *intensity* that a life of art writes on a human face and character

For desire, acting with awe, has this effect on the creator of
things which we call art: it *intensifies* him.

I, for one, would
stop there, so far as vocabulary goes. And it is far enough.
For it only proves what is the law, that, all things, all effects
feed back in (do not go "*off*") or they are not true effects.

Intensity is only the degree of desire. And its effect is only
more desire (and so, *more* awe). So, the same thing is only
more of same. In other words, *more* life.

It is so beautiful,
that, we are involved in a thing which is only itself — is never
anything outside itself except as man makes the error of trying
to describe it, to ex-pose it — to place it out

it turns into
paper, or a net layed in a field to dry, to get the salt out of
the twine, or to make the tar stiff

in other words to do
anything but ACT [*revised on carbon copy among Olson's
papers*: TO FISH]

O, Robert, all this seems so clear I get scared. And yet I am not.
For, getting it down — getting down, I think, altogether too long a
mistime or misman — is only getting the trolley car back on the
tracks. It is no more. It is only a correction of NEGATIVES.

The
irritating thing is, that, there [are] so many negatives, that it does
seem so clear that all that has come since "history" seems to have
been so false

(I am even worked to the persuasion that one of the
reasons why we have such few records of the so-called past, or
prehistory, is, not that man was not "advanced" but that by the
very conditions above described as previous state to discourse,
there was no reason why man needed to *record*: he acted, instead.
And this was his glory, this was what made him more man than
he has been. Simply, there was too much *life* to be wasting it, in
texts!

In other words, what we do have is enough:: look at rock

paintings, and all the clay, the worked or written-on clay! Look at the Venus of Mentone![44]

What else do we want? And had we not, ourselves (I mean post-modern man), better just leave such things behind us — and not so much trash of discourse, & gods?

Well.

Over the sea. And all our love: Con & I just came in when I started this from a long walk in a light and foggy rain: the apparency is, that, the child will be born — I say — in the next 48 hours!

It is like a chasm, for me: on the other side, is another life! So this letter feels like a terminus too.

Love,

Charles

added note:

stay troubled over this Emerson biz, with you, on poems

figure he is using you for a parlay

(1) the fact that he has never answered me on the proofs — or even sent me a copy of the gg issue — and now knows i never saw either!

why does he cry on yr shoulder when all he has to do is say, look, olson, 100 bucks, for, you damn well know, i'd not have him spend any such dough — if i were sure he had

(2) i want to call him a fucking liar, and, like you sd back there, jump all over the little prick, with both big feet —

and if he has yr poems, he is in position to laugh, the little bastard

(and my question is, isn't that exactly the reason he is making this offer to you?

and when the

use is over, what likelihood is there that he will then treat you
any differently than he has me?

                        it bothers me
                              he is a very dirty
guy
     & very tricky, like, such usually are: they take advantage of
our innocences, our goddamned honest wish to be published
                                              well,
            let me know: i wait (it's three weeks now, since i
            wrote him saying, i had never had proofs, why
            not send them, and let's get back on:
                                     my
question:
       DID HE EVER HAVE PROOFS?
                           (for example, as you
pointed out the "printing" of the verses in gg are vibra-graph, or
some typewriter system
                     how come, if, July, he sends me "proofs"?
(the whole point of his supposed expenditures of 100 bucks, was,
to have the plates used in gg ready for the pub book?
                              i think he
lies to you, as he has faked to me, all along

                       for, if he had proofs,
why not SEND EM? SHOW ME? eh?

christ, it makes me sick

[Fontrousse, Aix-en-Provence]
Tuesday [October] 23rd [1951]

Dear Charles,

Ann just off for Marseille, to meet Bud & wife; and
is abt 6 or so in the morning. Light just breaking in here, sky
more or less clouds : a fine look.

And think, myself, this is the
morning to have a baby, but Ann insists, it was yesterday, etc.
You, for christ's sake, say just as soon as you know. Ok.

Enclose another story;[45] it was damn good to get it out. I work
very much in the dark these days. It strikes me, this has bearing
on all this in the last letter from you—even so, too dulled with
this rush, now, to get it out. But what you say, of wonder—that
edge. There continues, anyhow, the point where all things break
out, into some other dimension. One goes for that. Not a trite
magic, but some other kind; and it all rides me back to, "where
space is born man has a beach to ground on . . ."[46] I've always
liked that, have always used it for a hold.

Well, pretty cold here; what with the 3 rooms, & the 6 of us,
now, I suppose things will be more or less wild, like they say,
these next weeks, but I'll damn well enjoy it, much too much
isolation these past months. Hoping to land a bigger house,
somehow—very scarce around here, any house, but somehow.
Have an eye on a chateau, that could be swung jointly, perhaps
Ashley, say, and will be looking into it directly. Will keep you
on.

Jesus, I can't see why you can't land a Fulbright. Simple
matter of yr background, of the 2 Gugs/, of the specific you have
to put in front of them. And to think of you moving thru here—
wow. And pick me up, I mean, invite yez to carry me off to, the
desert! Likewise, wow!

So, about it. Re Ez & all : it remains peripheral. And frankly,
very few ever get very close, it seems. Yrself, one or two others :
that does it. Otherwise, he does goof me, this criticism, these

poems, etc. It is a clearer, or as you put it, once, post to touch, the cleaners of, the shit, etc.[47] Clarity: a simple ingredient, etc. And too, the contacts he can direct one to, these are usually helpful, or are when they are people like G/ & all. I hope this Laubies turns out another. Simp/ & cohorts simply dull, just waste, & I never said to him they weren't. I remember writing him a letter against poor old Simp/ on the occasion of that damned silly preface to Bunting's poems,[48] which I don't honestly yet manage to 'understand.' No matter. Allons, etc. All one can do.

Sounds breaking in now, a few, & always goofs me, these mornings this early. I don't however make them very often! But could think of, in Burma, along the roads, the jungle, waking up to all the odd cries, it was something.

Ashley due back any minute; have written him in Aix, to get out here directly he gets in. Will see, then, about the poem, etc. He is a man wd dig all of this; his face is rather damn fantastic, thinking of it, it manages an infinity, i.e., is multiple, fractures, is never the same to say it that tritely. Sometimes the eyes are all there is in it.

(And now think of the lady, back of us, who told Ann she went out doors once last winter and saw the face of her husband, who she left, filling the whole sky!)

I do so hope it is a boy, not that a girl isn't nice too, certainly. But with the boys, it has a necessary fierceness under it, an area of a continuum that isn't, I think, possible in any other way. You find them very strongly there, I mean, they feel you, very soon. And you them. Dave will allow Ann anything, but with me, he works with an infinite subtlety, a care really. I admire it very much, & like, more, the way he has, finally, a very strong head, a clear one. You can dare it, etc. I mean, you find it catching you, not tritely, but picking up on all yr pieces.

Otherwise, when they are very young, better almost to be animal, and stay away, or only make it, the little thing, etc. They don't come out, really, until they are 8 or so months along, but you'll find the first signs come soon, first times you see them watching you in a sense not wholly expected.

Reading any definition of time, in the dictionary, gets you off to a somewhat abrupt recall — time came after sequence, etc. That 'time' is a matter of something other than passage, that, like the image, it has its wanderings, actual — speed having exact relevance — in this way, almost plastic? Time certainly a variable, in any case, odd as it wd sound, I suppose. But sequence, the hinge, since it gets back in, juxtaposition. That time occurs in terms of things, never abstract. Variation of time, even Ez' irony: we do not all of us inhabit the same time.[49] We literally do not, all of us, inhabit the same time. There are speeds in it, deeper roots.

The animate wd create any sense of time, certainly. The act of breathing is a second, etc. Something passing, but that passage, always an instance of relation, that it was present. Or is.

A good musician can reverse time, even in a somewhat literal sense. Even hearing a drummer, like Max Roach, you find it riding in on you from anterior points, although it may be illusion? No, but there has been an odd precipitation, and Bach, sometimes, declares lines without any 'time' weight. Which is interesting. A line in a sense not time's.

What they call the spatial arts, etc., if the workmen were better, simply *more* conscious, that wd be the obvious place to look, I think. But this is back to yr Hieroglyphics. At some point a balance was conceived of in other terms, than those of time. Our present see-saw, etc.

If I put :
/) **** #, say, that line, of sorts. The Painter, or myself, for that matter, can see it in a multiple of directions, a 'time' in each perhaps, but it is not the main weight. Something else is. Similarly, a poem, or story, can be such a deliberate passage, in terms of other weights. When Ashley sd, I can read yr stories *any way*, i.e., from this end to that or the other way round, or, of 3 Fate Tales, beginning at the end, and reading back again, etc., he sd what you said, and what continues to hold me: I had broke thru one aspect of 'time.' It cheered me very damn much. When

they put, in Liberty, say, reading time : 3 minutes, etc.,[50] they are
destroying a dimension I don't suppose they really are aware of.
Ashley, also sd: spatial—that again pleased me. A dimension of
weight beyond 'Time.'

And to get this new one copied, ok.
And do write soon, yr letters are tremendous help, and get well
TOO : ok, & Africans ALL!

All our dearest love to you both.

Bob

[*Added*:]
Re Emerson: my own poems don't honestly matter; we have
GERHARDT come spring—like give E/ just that damn little extra
ROPE. He can HANG if he wants to.

[*At top of letter*:]
Thursday/ Ann forgot this yesterday—but anyhow. Bud now in;
thing[s] quiet, and will have you one off tomorrow. Do let us hear
how it goes there—the baby! Ok.

[Asheville, N.C.]
Tuesday Oct 23 [1951]

Robt & Ann:

A *daughter*, and this day, 1:30, so—Vera
Cruz!

Have just left Con, coming out of, the ether, and figure you
two are the ones I want to have the news first

"a girl—how terrible," says Con (& surely, figuring, I wanted,
a boy—just because, I suppose, it is still assumed a boy is more
important?

Actually, as I am suddenly relaxed, it seems very beautiful — I saw the child first (that is, before Con), brought straight from the delivery room, and it is a very pleasant thing (I notice most sort of big feet — my hunch is, it looks like her mother, the skin, and, the *head*

And the Dr (whom I met for the 1st time) is very good, in the eyes — & none of that fat (capon fat) I abhor of such —

The thing is, Con, again, ether, had her mathematical vision of three planetary worlds, & a cruel god, a Conspirator!

What brought me down (beside her being in there) was, that, coming out, she says, "I love you . . . with the utmost *motivity!*"

And then, "We *can* move, move, MOVE!" How abt that?

I must tell you, the thought of you both, throughout this biz, has been enriching of it, I suppose it is your love, it is also your own joy in this sort of thing

And that seems rare, is unique, for me:

You enable me in my own quietness about it (our Greeks, Washington, sent us their last precious KONAK, brought from Greece last year, to celebrate this event — & Con's & my 1st drink will be to you two, & yr boys

"What *is* the *end*," she also said, definitely in the context of the *conspiracy*. And, again (as the time before), she lets out a hidden valuing of the vision, by saying, "*I can't* solve it. I'll leave it to future generations." Curious, curious thing.

Another — "It must be why people talk of God"!

(What a figure he comes out, in her "satellites")

She seems to have done it strong & direct — started slowly about 2:00 AM, losing, a very little of the water, & a first pain, an[d] irregular small ones thereafter. She washed her feet in the bowl (an old trick of mine, hating, baths!) — & the 1st time I ever saw her do such a thing). Has not wanted to take bath for days—& did not wash her hair. We drove in here (Asheville) without calling doctor. So, all told, she was inside 12 hrs.

She looks wonderful—& the Dr (who sd *he* was slow, which I liked) says—& none of that medical goodness—she was straight, throughout (She was proud she only let one scream go: this appears to be a point of woman pride, Ann?

                               Well. I'll take a turn up to see if she is asleep as she wanted to be. And pick up something to eat.

                (Am curiously reluctant to go anywhere, or to let anyone else know but yourselves (strange feeling of closeness, & singleness, in this biz: the three of us—now!—here, & you people there

                (dare say, neither of us having parents left reinforces such sensations

                (I feel little touch with Con's 2 sisters)

OK. And to tell you, what, you two put around this thing. And so another & abundant statement (kind) of love for you, sitting here, with this thing

                (The other sense is bewilderment, how *I* can raise a woman!

        Love, Charles

                                         [Black Mountain, N.C.]

wed rob't: oct 24 [1951] (the kid's birthday, therefore, is TWO-THREE, 2-3, 23

crazy. so much. & always go wild: so many things loosen my tongue. can't stand to be silent long, when, such things racing, eh? Want to talk, after, a certain isolation (like, that note you people, from, the hospital, alone with, the whole damned biz). Then, shot out, after, a little more time alone with it. And today, it's women, anyhow (did have one nice thing: came back here for supper, and, driving in, figured, the one i could choose to tell the news, was Jala. So, drove to her house, straight. And there damn well found (1st time i ever found anyone there, when i called) THREE WOMEN — and the three of all i'd choose: this gal Mary Fitton, and old Dehn's younger wife Toni. And Jala was pleased it was a daughter. So, they toasted "me & my women," and of course I, with the sherry, toasted "women." But it was all right, because it was such — women. For Mary's somethin. And the other two are Europeans (as, basically, were the women whom i have always been running away from, the sort of my mother, my godmother, etc, eh)

The payoff was, much the same group wanted to go see a free movie in Asheville last night. So, as I was going back to see Con, took em. And after, figured, some sort of celebration. Well, Ann knows Asheville. But there is one place, a store, wonderful Wop foods, Mrs Mascari. And one can stand in the back & drink beer. So I took em there. And dug provolone, and french bread out of Mme. And South African rock lobster (55 ¢!). It was ok, & the 1st time I ever got a chance to take Jala out! ok. Or rather, fit, eh?

Stuck on naming the d.. You see, if you have an immigrant name, & it is (as it is) an AngloSaxon frame (not the chief immigrant, Mediterranean or Scandinavian system, of, names as family or Christian, and all composed to disclose son of, daughter of, patriarch-matriarch, records), it is a puzzle how, to be homogeneous. Besides, just because my business is words, desire to be, dry about it, to leave her without such overlay. Flat, yet straight

(Vera C. — & the C to be Constance, might, do it, and at the same time — knownst only to you two & C — give a fact of some conjuring to the likes of;

tho i imagine Con

wld like (she so liked the aunt she takes her name from — as well that it gives her clearance from, Olson, which, not only, but,

Olson himself is something to clear yrself of, eh?) her own name
for, her daughter, and, I wld have no objection whatsoever, I
liking Constance Mathilde

> ((The Vera has a hidden other point, in that it is a sound
> of my father's people: my grandmother was Ida, her
> brother married a Linda, my aunt was Vandla O, etc:

Or flat Mary O, both my mother's and my other aunt's. But this is
not to my liking, simply, that Mary was, whose!

Well, to hell with that. Wanted, to get off to you, some thoughts
further along letter to you Sunday:

> (1st, small, a sudden sense,
> yesterday, that one further reason why the Jew comes all the
> way through to now with force & strangeness, is, that, the
> more I work the backwards of the Near East, the more it is
> apparent that the emphasis on Abrahama as hailing from Ur
> of the Chaldees needs to be seen for what it is, that the back
> of the Jews needs to be opened as fiercely as the back of the
> Greeks. And if this is done, one sees that the Jews, whose
> homogeneity is the most pronounced of modern peoples, have
> thus passed on to now one of the longest pasts, and not
> theirs, so much as the ancient, the, Sumerian thing:
> > just one
example (and suddenly realize you have yet to get that SUNDAY
LETTER OF JULY on the Jews—coming out of the first sight of
Shahn again: so, put this in your hat for the coming, one day, of
that letter to you! Have had it out for three months waiting, to go
to you!))

> one ex.:
> > the oldest wind instrument known, is the 7 note
> vertical flute of the Sumerians, older than the pipes of Pan
> > TI-GI (other names,
> > IMIN-E for "7"; GI-GID, GI-BU, GIS-SIR for
> > "long"; GI-DIM for "large"

played joy, was love-flute (*mon-aulos* of Greeks)

Now, this was
the UGAB of the Hebrews, and is mistranslated "organ" in the
King James. And was scorned by the H's: as the instrument of
Sodom & Gommorah! (Jewish Puritanism).

AGAB, means
(Hebrew) to BLOW[51]

And there is a flock of other *closer* etymologies, disclosing, how
much of Hebrew life is taken over straight from pre-2000 (Abe's
going away from, UR)

This is something also to get on the back
of, eh?

* * * * * * * * * *

But the thing I wanted most to put down, was this: (and I
have to skid over to Asheville, so, will put it, and maybe take it
further later)::

it strikes me it is another necessity of PARTICULARISM to
face up to just in what way one can say that REALITY
CHANGETH—

I am thinking mostly of how true it is that
the reality which bears on us is *different* from the reality
which bore on the fathers (even on Ez & DHL, say)

that, each
of our acts *changes* total reality, *moves* it so that it is to that
degree *different* for another, for others, for the *later* ones

And that the *recognition* of such *movement*
of reality is of considerable importance

At
least this way, that, giving *Change* this particularism intensifies—
densifies—two crucial "eternities":

(1) life is eternal, does not stop,
and is, to the degree of its
admittance, not! dogmatic

Yet (2) man does stop, and because he does, is involved, at a
      certain point, in declaring his own dogmatism — that is,
      he does take a stand, he does, however much he leaves
      the thing a flowing rock, makes a rock for his structure,
      for, the structures of, his activities

                              Accepting this (I'm
too new to it to be sure I have posed it right, or phrased it right),
suddenly the "choice" of eternity (which I dare say is, at root, the
finest way to give saints & the god-people their "act") must be —
(even their visions come out that way, are, involved with
immortality & the eternity of a home for man: a permanent home,
the very idea of PARADISO)
                              it must be a CHOICE dictated by a
wish to avoid the stoppage & the dogmatism of the very sort of
action which does change reality
                              a wish to enter into other waters,
in fact, a "preference" for fluidity as against rock, your rock, mine,
the rock of THE MORTAL
      (in other words, I am back again on this idea that the divinity
      kick is a surrogate way to deal with the immensity — and i
      shld say a "wrong" way, a false recognition of, a *man's*
      problem
            (figuring, that the condition a man has to hew to is, that,
            he does stop & so he is involved in a "stand,"
            willynilly —
                        that to take "God's side," to choose
            "Eternity" ((the word, in this context, rings of the N.E.
            nun, Miss Dickinson!)) (((and how many others!)))
EXception:
Bernard, & at least one woman I knew, who, make the Christ
wholly sensual, sexual actually
            (Bernard was praying to the Virgin one day, and was
            giving a heavy emphasis to that part of the hymn which
            says "Show me you are the Mother." And by god, says
            the miracle, if the damn statue (or herself in the vision, I
            guess) doesn't pull out her breast, and let the milk flow
            right straight into Bernard's mouth!)[52]

Or Bernard's biz, of the three Kisses, the one of the feet of
Christ (humility), of the hands (illumination), and of the
mouth (even, by god, to the tongue, going, in!), the mating![53]

This seems to mean another VIA, and a tricky one: ultimately
the most offensive, yet, I'd not follow the pathologists, that, this
is insane (however much it is!)

in fact, it would be better to be
most slow about attacking, at this point, simply, that, the act is
a blind way (in lieu of other necessary clarities) to maintain the
mortal in the spiritual

that is, I can never jump any sexuality
too easily, knowing, the pressures, eh?

Anyhow, that (to get back), until particularism discloseth that
ACT as ART is SIGN

that man has no eternity except as he
changes reality

(the gimmick — the old word is paradox — is, that, he has to
give up the notion that he has any choice, any way to take
on those two aspects of "life" which he is denied (non-
stoppage, non-dogma) except by using his two conditions
(stoppage & only one openness, his own, and so, his own,
rock is all that is open — otherwise, you get Gide, & all
the Disponibles[54]
Les - - - - - - - -

all hermaphroditism

(I am distinguishing the androgyne, as (Mao, autres) organic, as
doublebacked beasts)[55]

anyway, that the recognition of these areas — of *this* area of
recognition, that reality does change

— makes for HUGE
CONSEQUENCES?

Anyhow, let me have yr responses on this

crazy stuff, no?

        crazy, to be so fucking metaphysical, but, i'm
just wild to get this stuff sort of out & done with, just, for the
straight of it — & the ride?

        the thing I keep feeling is, that, there is
a ride in it
      that it does not dry up (as such always, for me, did,
does (except when it is theee & me!

   shit. wish i was born to do otherwise. but

        anyhow maybe my daughter will
dance!
          and fuck beautiful
              and have
     a great heart!

         yrs,
         Randy (that, by
god, seems to be the mark of becoming the father of a daughter!!
old Tom, we'll have to call Olson now!!) ok, Ann, pay no
mind!
     olson

[Fontrousse, Aix-en-Provence]
Friday Oct 27 [*i.e.* 26, 1951]

Dear Charles,

The wonderful, wonderful news in — I hated this christly distance, that couldn't let us even get back to you, fast, any damn sign of the joy. It is very wonderful, so very, very great that it all went simply.

In fact, do envy you, that it is, a girl; all the shit to the contrary, boys & all, they just don't know. To hell with them. Ann immediately jealous : ok!

Anyhow, anyhow, anyhow, I couldn't say it, honestly, in spite of now wanting to so much. That it is there, that it all went without trouble. Anything now possible.

Here, a fine warm day, & yesterday much the same. I thought of it, Tuesday, it must have been, and it was, that same morning I was sitting here thinking of it, with the sun just coming up, and all very finely quiet, and waiting for Bud & his wife.

Con will be home by the time this gets there? Will hope so, and all our very greatest love to her, & your daughter. Again, fuck them all, they just don't make it, even at all, at times like these.

So much to get to, with the letter with this crazy damn news, the one just before it, and it is very, very clear. Give me time, and you will now need it too. But, damn it, I want you to get here, somehow to get on to Teheran, those damn magic places, truly — this is next.

A night back, pulling out some of the earlier letters, to read some to Bud & his wife, and it is all there, take my word for that. Soon, once you've had time to sit down, etc., and things quiet, I will get them off to you, i.e., all these that matter a hell of a lot to me. But get them back, i.e., could not honestly let go without knowing I'll have them again here. I didn't bring them all this way for nothing, like they say.

Thinking about that story—now a little dull on it, & look for whatever word you'll have time for, if & when.

Anyhow, to hell with all bisnesses. Just this.

All love to the three of you, all that damn well matters,

Bob

<hr>

[Fontrousse, Aix-en-Provence]
Monday Oct 29th [1951]

Dear Charles,

So damn little time, at the moment; either cutting wood, or talking, & tho I make it, still wish that we were not so very cramped, & that there was more ease to it, to make it that simple. But Bud & his wife are very fine, I haven't anyone but yourselves who I would more want to have close to me.

Yesterday, horrible biz with the landlord, horrible man, & not knowing, finally, even ½ of what was going on, simply flipped & did, quite literally, kick him out the door, and I don't suppose that was very intelligent. He had come to threaten us, more or less, was going to put his mother-in-law into these 3 rooms with us, & all similar shit, which declares him unequivocal bastard. So did finally shout that one word I am sure of, avoir [à voir?], and went for his throat, & pulling him round, I could shove him thru the door, then booted him, to the street, etc. He'd left a package, & Ann took it out to him, to find him wanting to begin it all over again, smiling, etc.

Luckily, I didn't jam things, & find that we are

secure enough; but hardly pleasant. It dulls the works & makes us
wish, even more than usually, we were anywhere but where we
seem to be anchored. Impossible to find anything else, as it goes.

Etc. Dull with that, & think of you 3 there with what little
happiness I can damn well muster at this point. The name. Well, I
don't know, you will have it done, anyhow, & names : shit —
anything that doesn't kill the kid later, doesn't pull him or her into
idiotic relations like they say, etc. Fuck it. Constance, I like, i.e.,
the Constance Mathilde, etc. Vera, not so much — but it is her,
anyhow — a damn shame she can't speak yet!

Very much like the things here, this present letter. What it seems :
all 'ideologies,' or really better, systems of conversation, sprout for
the purpose of 'stopping,' of holding onto to the one pleasant, or
anyhow, 'point' — all lean to that.

      (An item : that a man is usually
most interesting, at that time when he attempts this arrest, & finds
the passage constant — sometimes nightmare, etc.)

Reality *is* change — I can't see another way to define it. But so put,
perhaps as dull as I honestly am, just now.

      But it does hold in
with yr premise of, the contest of reality. It is how one goes into
it, to make a part.

      Another world, well, it does avoid the horror
of killing this one, perhaps. Even so, what interest? I want to die
completely. I don't want anything left.

I feel you under all these *words*, & it is something, I wish I had
even the vaguest way in, I mean, to be riding this with you, but
you do it for me anyhow. It is very exciting stuff, very damn
hard, I think. I think this would explode, so hit & opened — it wd
certainly mean death to certain things, fixes, now ridden like any
pot-top, etc.

Reality does change, change is reality — perhaps to get clear the
divers emphases there.

And feel, by that, just by that, that damn
sweep, coming in. I mean my own reality, my corpus, myself. Wd
you note me, for one beginning, what seems to lie back of this
same word, *real*? It wd help me some here.

Anyhow, I think of it
as, field, multiple forces, the constant shift. So that what one says,
if he's yrself: what does not change/ is the will to change.

The *one*

constant.

The real : phew. It is something. Perhaps best to leave 'change' in
the qualification of? But change, too, a basic, even if not, say,
substance? But it is anyhow an interpretive, or, say, willful word.
We take it as it has happened; we rarely sit on the act of it, etc.

That religion : a damn weird flower, all of it. There seems no
religion without this root, in any event, I mean, the sexual. How
else, to find a man, or any way into him he can hold to?

(Mind,
etc., being via, & of little, or almost useless, 'permanence' —
without, that should go in too certainly — what it is the mind had
worked on, etc.)

Etc. I wonder, I float so much. The one constant, oneself: they all
die, but to say that, I have not died. It is what matters? No, but
to begin there — it seems no other instance of position can grant
you that base logic? Something like that.

And certainly a world,
here, as you have said it: the 38 doors to the body,[56] and I must
know only one at all intimately.

"man has no eternity except as he *changes* reality . . ." That makes
it, for me.

I suppose they just want to keep it, i.e., will not ride out, and
beyond any fear of any particular pain to one's body, it is also
hard to hold yr mind, to whatever its attentions may turn up.
Hence, most boats are empty!

Anyhow, anyhow—this to get
off to you. Figure that I raise my own murderers, like they say!
You tell me how it goes the other way. At that—it is crazy to
have them so very close, to witness any act, put it, to know at
each turn, the logic.

Dull, damn dull, & forgive me for that. But kicking that idiot :
you don't have that every day. Ok, & write soon.

All our best

love to you ALL/

Bob

[Black Mountain, N.C.]
Tuesday   Oct 30 [1951]

Robt & Ann—

All's well—just beat for time
Name's KATE

(came out fast, between us, just
when leaving hospital. Am pleased abt it—gives her *chance*,
eh?

And is fine—much sensation, to hold same—& figure to make
speak!

Con mending rapidly (no dough to have woman in, thus,
I'm busy bringing food, sweeping etc

by way, yr 50 got the baby &
ma out of hock—bill was 92 bucks! Jesus!

OK. Just, to keep you on—to tell you all letters, including *Jardou*
in—

Love
All of us

[*On verso:*]
   Will be back on—the hope is—tomorrow.
   Also trying to do biz here is what loads me   OK.

[Fontrousse, Aix-en-Provence]
November 6, 51

Dear Charles,
            Haven't honestly wanted to load you with my own
dullness—simply that I am all off these days, get black with all
this miserable weather and the absolute inability to find us any
other house. At present, six of us in here; it would be cramped
with two.

            The main thing, anyhow : Cid. I get to feel like a
hell of hypocrite, there being, now, no other damn way to answer
these incredible letters he writes me. All manner of idiocy,—'praise'
as dulling as anything to the contrary. Or listen to some of this:

            "I don't know anyone that comes near you in this
kind of amazing, objectiveseeming, pursuit of the inner
character . . ."

            "my handshake on another fine piece . . ."

            And also (which drags me to seeing just what it *is*
all about): "But then, after three days with you, I felt very
strongly that I've never seen a man react so sensitively to his
children and so well . . ." Which is, simply, blah—more than that,
none of his goddamn business.

In short, a damn monster—I figure it wd be a hell
of a lot more honest to drop out, I damn well mean it, altogether.
But wd it be too fucking cute? You say. Or to hell with it, i.e.,
don't let me load it on you, but much more of this drivel, and will
damn well start looking elsewhere. This man *is* an idiot, and any
attempt to 'believe' him otherwise leaves one feeling very damn
dirty & dishonest. Pompous inflated drivel of this present letter, all
the damn bullshit, his 'activity,' etc.—fuck it, I mean I damn well
do *not* want to hear about it.

At the same time, time-lag you had noted on the
things of yr own, now same on mine. I thought this was going to
be quick turn-over. Suppose that consideration now gets buried;
these adjectives apparently offered as alternative.

Have you seen that damn 3rd issue? I haven't got copies here yet.
How does it look? I damn well think he's on the skids, judging by
simple list of content. Fuck it, I get not to care a damn thing abt
it, all pleasure of the first of it, that potential seems drained out in
all this christly flurry.
(Did you hear abt his goddamn ARS
POETICA?[57] Shades of Ralph Waldo!)

IS all of this shit on his part simple vanity??? What I begin to
wonder about—to hell if it seems, 'unfair . . .'

Abt it. Bud reading the stories, etc., I was damn well happy.
Simply, that content. Yrself & him—only ones I cd ever trust on
such things. It comes out the same. He put, likewise, PARTY at
head of the new ones. It was damn well exact.

Well, fucking
bleak, useless to say it's otherwise. Seeing Laubies, yesterday,
could hardly listen to whatever it was he was saying. He was very
nice, etc. I damn well felt an idiot, being that he was that nice,
etc. So fucking heavy, rough, helpless, at present : should sit in
this damn room & not go out at all. Wd save all of this damn
bumping.

Anyhow, will see Gros shortly; some hope for an out for things over here, & will do all I can. Is there anyone, *there*, who can make passable translations? L/ is painter, feels, I think, the translation wd be back-water, or matters of time in any case. I don't know anyone else who cd translate; I think he wd be agreeable to polishing, say, anything we cd get a rough draft on. He will see Mascolo (i.e., gave him sd man's name, & having Pound's ok on all french translation, i.e., rights to same, now, perhaps that will add weight. He sd, Gallimard very, very slow on all items taken; matter of yrs in each case.)

Well, — write. I hope it all goes well there, it is the only damn time. I envy you three, but hardly reason, or I have two here too. Ok. Write soon. All dearest love to you all,

Bob

[Black Mountain, N.C.]

R CR: Monday November 6 [*i.e.* 7, 1951] — & all expletives it has been so long: of course you were right, how, such, throws one off — this moment is the 1st one in two weeks I have walked in, a coffee in my hand, on time, to set to a day

Best waste is just looking, at, the daughter. And that surely wld do, & not eat up the rest of time, if i were not in some terrible slump, grim & tired (like the mimic i am, i sleep like the daughter — or want to, all the time). And take no pleasure in much. Figure it's simply I am real stale, that (with Con over it, & out of it good, & the baby here) I suddenly just let down

(The drainage of this place is beyond belief, the wear of it. Was somewhat relieved to find that Litz feels the same thing, & for like reason; that, it has to do with some false form of

questioning of these creatures, students, that, because they do
not know what a person purchases by work by their going on
with some seriousness abt their own business, they subtly
poison one's own amour propre. It is most curious, how
ignorant (not of knowledge but of plain life & its decencies,
the immaculate, say, of a person's insides—

it is one's dignity

that seems always under attack

The devil of it is, that, one is mostly aware (of most of them)
that, they don't know any better, isn't it, the way, it is put? that
most horrible of all indictments, and the one which exposes the
race most, that, they don't *know*

one knows it anywhere, the
only trouble with such as a collegiate community, is, that, one
is hired, actually, *for* one's dignity!

At least, certainly, Litz is, I am, and Lou Harrison just his
bit: he's a wobbly fellow, all gifted nerves, & real crazy,
like an old fashioned genius (Katy tells me he complained to
her, "They want me to explain things I don't think it's any
of their business to ask"

And this is also true, that, most of the things which
matter one cannot say, or define—at least not to anyone
but someone one believes in—& how in god's name can
you believe in people in a group?

There's one or two (Kalos, & Cernovich, say) who give one one's
space. But the rest—

Well, to hell with it, with so much else piled up, eh? Origin 3,
e.g., in: I did not take such pleasure in this one as, of course, in 2
& 1. And so shall not write to Cid with the same relish, however
much I still like his composing (though less) &—to my surprise—
Boyce's blocks[58] (though, again, they are too "nice," for the likes
of, me—

the whole issue seems too such; Bronk & Morse, too,
and this Hatson dame

        [Harry] Smith's another matter, glad he's
there

      For me, of course, it's you, the Wilbur poem &, damn it,
my own[59] (am soft on that one, like, what goes on, however much
i damnwell don't know how I came to write it

           Actually, Rob't, Bronk ain't got the brains for his
           usage, & Morse so cuts himself back to the local . . .

The whole damned issue has a limpness of the record of life's
going on—jesus, it is so dull to see critters thinking, that, it is to
throw light (singular) when, surely, it is *lights* only that anyone of
us can throw. And so, it has to be fast, fast

                     how they drag, by
going over, going over, trying to drag out into the light what
won't get illuminated except by flashes

                     just poor brains, & so, the
nerves, however good, aren't present, enough

          I miss passion, therein: just that. And a passion
of *language*, a pleasure in same, not, this dreadful business of
mixing it, diluting the egg with milk, of human philosophy

                         (my
god, I'll even take Morse for an occasional rime!)

                 Smith has an
ounce of directness, only, he takes interest in the dullest of people!
He shows himself to be more interesting. Only, why don't he stick
to himself?

It just dragasses. Morse & Bronk won't stand that much of either
of em—& I for one am unhappy that #5 will be *all* Morse

    In short, figure, now, we'll always be somewhat dubbed by
    that epigraph[60]

             & I'll always be crying, Get out of that bed, bo;
             & for crisssake leave wisdom to those who move

The thing abt the datter is, the mother even sez so, it, looks like
an olson, god help her — only, to olson, it looks like the Hedges
and that's hard, my cousins, my father's sister Vandla, who had
a goiter made her a hen[61]

NO, that's not fair, this one is quite
lovely (neck, cheeks, and steady good working eyes): it's still the
feet & hands

And not so much the little animal like you say. Or
maybe, the 1st one (the curiousness of nature, etc, to turn out,
in 9 months, etc) seems a curiosity & a pleasure and so, an
individual?

Con nursing her, & tho the breasts cracked for two three days,
all's well now. And both healthy. (Con got jumpy once, that her
feet, were cold, and there by god were the blue boots you people
shot over, USED! Laugh! I killed myself! But it was something
wonderful, to see! Those large small pink feet with boots on!

* * * * * * * * * *

My interest is JARDOU (have just spent one hour finding the mss,
the house is that wild from the BIZ!

and all the time, kicking my ass, that, so long, here, you have
not had from me anything like the order & directness on all
that you have sent:

PLEASE, Robt, forgive me, and let me
again promise to go back over all correspondence, and give you
the satisfactions you deserve on

(1) the several verses
(2) the NOTES ON AM P
(3) JARDOU
&   (4) sundry affairs (as of GUIDO, as broadside, with AB's
design, we await yr word — have now
also an excellent [Robert] Duncan, the
Song of the Borderguard)

[*In pencil:*]
Back on, as soon as possible
          —just this, to keep
things moving—
          excuse these damned
          pressures

                              All yrs
                                        Olson

KATE

or did I get the word to you?

                              [Black Mountain, N.C.
                              8 November 1951]

By god, RobT;   you see, I take JARDOU by this handle (&
GRACE, to the degree of its locus, & the moon, too): the
idyll
          And there i am abt to write it down when, Gerhardt's, lines,
pile out of my mind!

                    die idylle   unsere schwachheit

Crazy, real crazy
                    (And now, equally suddenly, it comes at me
that you quote from Trakl, via G, that,
                                        und leise tönen im rohr
die dunkeln flöten des herbstes![62]

Which wows me, that, as you'd know, neither of these are as much to me as your more "American" stuff! How abt that for narrowness!

No. Not that simple — that is, this more than that. Or surely I'm not one to leave it at that. For the thing which needs investigation is the degree to which "nature" as olive trees or as moon & fields, is usable as frame in which to exert your own pressures —

I come at it this way, that, in JARDOU, just because you are basically attempting *more* than in GRACE, it is not yet *done*

What excites me about J is, what you are setting *out to do*

I of course rise to such, that, you are getting at *placements, & sounds*

(I am again exhilarated, as, say, in the snow-blood-cat-mouse of 3FTs

But what I raise up is, this question of, the wavering, which anything but the most one-to-one management of such huge elements as olive trees involves

(for me, at least — and, as I say, I am ready to allow is wholly a marked armorican bias

((GRACE, e.g. is most loved in print by Con, and obviously by Cid — who, on the phone from Boston paid by Shoolman, from her room, 387, the Copley Plaza! called, a week ago, and said, GRACE, that's the great thing in this issue, and (something like) "the best, of Rob'ts"))

But goddamn it, no: I wld go in this way, that, *no* thing can, in your hands *ride*

that the secret of your art is the bearing, the constant sharpness to *all* inside any given go

and that the most obdurate of all is any such fact of nature as olive trees or moon, simply because they carry with them a host of association which, allowed to ride, *spreads*

give a sort of amnial [*i.e.*, amniotic] cloud
which is another sort of environment than the one *physiologically*
proper to your advanced birth

I say you must peg *anything*—even
such—as fiercely as you do the crying of the child, the passing of
your hand near the woman's breast, the position—& certain
weight—of the husband

And that any proper noun has to be given
the attention you give to any proper person

OK. Damn big order.
But, for me, you are the only damned one I believe can execute
any order.

That is, these loci are frames—& I wld press on you that by
yr own law of form ex content, there is no frame, that a frame is
a death

Now this is not, of course, to say that an idyll is not possible.
Au contraire: the fact that you are doing such is proof (if there
were not my own recognition that exactly the idyll in exactly the
sense of the return of the art of ornament (I think a yr & a half
ago i had it, "decoration") is wholly crucial business for thou &
me

that the answer to the arts of caprice (which underlie all
essential bohemianism, Pound, or Robt Duncan) is triangulatable
exactly in this area of which idyll is one expression

Which is why I am so excited by JARDOU, that, I think what you
have put your hand to here

(what Provence seems to have worked
its ancient "Greek" way on you as)

IS CRUCIAL stuff

And I wld urge you to go at this specific thing
with the same methodology that you give to the killing of your
birds by a hawk—or gathering iron of a winter day down the road
some piece [*Added*: THEOCRITUS, the measure, not Horace, or
the anybodies else!]

bring all your natural guns to bear: don't let
any allure of nature come in except as it strains through your
language

For I am of the conviction that
the question ultimately is your pushing the prose (this new syntax,
observable, surely) *harder*, forcing your own immense *clarities* in
as shims to level this old nature lying so heavily (fragrantly, I'd
have sd) over you

CUT in. Be the blue knife, without oil.

That is,
there is a wild sexual thread moving through the sounds &
placements of this story which isn't wound enough to make the
bobbin you are

(my hunch is, the whole story is done too fast, is
not yet done, is either in need of clarities introduced carefully by
the prose or is in need of longer treatment?

don't know (no man ever can
know, no? what is actually called for, by another's, law)   but, my
feeling persists that huge things are here

(has the excitement of
verse particles, the electricals in this thing

(but "draggled," and
"left a trail in the wet road" is of a tone not tensed enough to
support the materials

Actually, what you are after here, is more
than such, & more, by the way, than the barrier of [*added*:
french] language for the teller, the he

Even your lovely use of "I
love you," falls, by the absence of a bearing in of the language

Let
me take this guess: that, in this case, the experience which
provoked the story has left too much of its autobiography
hanging, that you stumbled into an immense cubism of sound &
persons & a day, and have not yet cleared it of the causations. So,
the CENTER, the THING, is not formally revealed

                                                    (It seems
almost a problem of Cezanne — taking off any history from the
metaphor — and requires his sort of longness of either,
concentration or paintingness

    That is, I'd either remove the language problem (as causation)
or make it very simple & clear, stated, so that your reader is free,
at every point to move in the greater ambiguities of, this
wonderful mystery you have here got your hand to again
                                                  (as in
BLUE, you have, here, yr hand on just the *intervals*
                                            — only, shall
we say, *outside*? —

                And isn't that sort of exactly the difference of
an idyll from, whatever is, the other thing?

Anyhow, I am damned excited at what you are cutting away at,
by such a *move* to outside as (for me), Grace, & Jardou
are
    (contrast, the PARTY?)
                        And JARDOU argues, to me, that you
are tackling what — implicitly — the novel (it now seems to me) was
moving toward
                That is, I rather think I am hammering along the
same lines [*added*: as I did on the novel], no? but, that, now, with
this insight JARDOU seems to me to give to your advance, I feel
your purpose and the problem is much clearer, is, this huge
question of, how, does what impinges so exactly as such things as
these hands picking olives, these kids, the shiftings, the sound of
running, the women's voices, yours, and the man's, counterplay of
silence, and then, this phalli[ci]sm

                    And if I were to speak of where
I'd strike you in, it is, to say, *any* description
                (moon's light — the beautiful, & most successful
                moment, is, when, the he feels it at the back of his
                chair — the *recognition*, rather than any description

(as, say, in the bedroom, that, it is passing down,
has passed down the sky

((the problem of, the
"poetic"

(or such as, the trees were very old, the branches filled with
the fine leaves, fluted, and still wet from the rain — my
question is, is this *functioning*, is this doing anything but
framing?

In other words, I don't now
take it it needs so much emphasis on a one-to-one *human*
concentration as it calls for — what you always are giving, by your
nature — *a* concentration, at all points

a sort of *action*, like, say,
implicitly in, the last "incident," of throwing the twigs at the kids
in the trees — only, there, for me, such a phrase, as "the little
things" weakens, is, somehow, soft — as, damn it, nature *unless she
is as investigated as* you investigate anything

Even, there, the exactness is
not pushed enough for me to be quite clear what is the cause of
the man's "fear"

[*Crossed out*: that is, I don't mean that I should
know, but I should not have to wonder what I know — o shit, that
is obvious, needs no such stupid statement.]

(Have just gone over mss, enclosed back to you)

Ok. Can't say. You let me know.

By the way, suggested to Corman that, now that you & G
may be together, why not ship off to the two of you the crazy
attempt of mine to translate G's LETTER — Jalowetz gave me what
help she could, but, all these Deutschers here are unaware of the
usage G gives his tongue, and I'm sure there are holes, holes,
holes

between you & G you could make a translation which wld be
wonderful. Why don't you do it, from scratch?

And ought to be
something, wish I was there, to work it out!

And I suggested it to Corman, because, plenty of time before he
sets up #4

Well. Otherwise, am still pounding to get the fullest
sort of picture for myself of what now seems to be the upshot of
both THE HU & that fragment you have, THE LAW

that is, what
gauges of the mythological as a via can be discovered back of the
Jews & the Greeks?

And I am most excited at what
turns up by starting with those cave businesses Bryant has seen —
and you must see for me

((I say that the more, today, that, yesterday, I got the
NO from the Wennergren, Viking creatures. Just NO.
No explanation other than those fucking euphemisms
they use — as tho we were kids, who had to be tiptoed
to, the bastards — plain evidence they haven't the guts to
expose on what basis they make grants, eh?

So I am full of gloom about getting out of the country
again — even the Fulbright seems slim now, by the token of no
where near as natural a claim on their attentions as I had on
these bastards.))

That is, Paleolithic already had fine things, plus a woman sense
(Menton) solid enough (herself as animal, not as earth, fertile,
that, distributed business comes in with agriculture & herds

Then what happens with emmer wheat and six-row barley ?[63]

(7000 BC — say, 4000

And is it abt 2000 that man as god gets to be boss?

Ok. Well, will be back. This to get us moving. And

all love to you all, the four of you—and best to Bud, who seems

close, through you. And Bryant and G. You are now having it,

lad! Wish I were there.

Kate howling in next room (yesterday, from 1PM to 11, poor
thing—looks shaken. Maybe it's my machine: what abt your
experience on this?   Love, Olson

JARDOU
[*Creeley's typescript, sent with his 23 October 1951 letter, with
comments and markings by Olson throughout in ink, from
November 8.*]

Clearing, the wind left, and the sky was very light, and
walking along [*Olson suggests by square brackets and new
capitalization that the preceding be omitted and the story begin
with the following*:] Behind them, he sang, but softly, saying, you
want to pick all the olives, but I will pick them all. And sang,
again, feeling very good, the sky now altogether clear, and from
behind the high house in front of them a single white light
climbing down and falling all over them in one heap. [*Note by
Olson: This is, for me, a proper force of nature, that is, what is it,
except as sequential to our experience of it?*]
    But she was in a hurry, pulling at the little [*square brackets
added around* little] boy's hand, and behind a rope draggled in the
dirt, tied to him, and left a trail in the wet road.
    We are late, she said, but knew the rain was an excuse, and
did wait [*note by Olson: this may be rime (to late) but, it seems
softening, & so, loss*], taking his hand [*note, with line drawn to*

he *of opening paragraph*: because the "he" here is so strong, the boy is not clear, immediately] as he came up, then let him lead her to the small [*bracketed*] gate, waiting [*underlined*] while he opened it, then went in behind him.

I love you [*note by Olson*: This is too good not to juxtapose more exactly (by his, like, his song, above) to the wonderful shout], he said, and stopped to shout [*underlined*], hello, and heard it echo round [*underlined*] the building to be answered from the field, another shout [*underlined*], and they started out [*underlined*], calling the little [*bracketed*] boy running in front of them.

The trees were very old, the branches filled with the fine leaves, fluted, and still wet from the rain. [*Noted added*: This I would locate *after* the action. That is, to *lead* with nature is to give her altogether more than she is — her force is *on* ourselves.] He had expected some diligence, to put it that way, or some aspect of determination. But he now saw them almost finished, the mother by the furthest tree, reaching up and pulling off the olives. There was no hurry, he thought, the husband was too quiet [-et *underlined*], sat off by himself in the wet grass but did not seem to mind it [*underlined, with note added*: and this "it," is floating, for a moment, & so, loss of moving for reader]. Listening, he heard the first sounds of their speech and felt himself left [*note*: Same vagueness here on language question], but liked it, and went to join the mother, saying, hello, again, not caring that she would not know it.

I love you, he said, but to the other, coming up now to join them, and she made a face back [*underlined, with comment*: lovely!], laughing, the woman standing still nervous, her skirt held out to catch the olives which he began to toss down. Straining, he raked them clear, then dropped them to her, not looking, and saw the olives above him he could not quite reach.

Those, he said [*note added: Wonderful!*], and pointed at them, and his wife explained, the fine [*bracketed*] speech wavering, breathy, and expounded [*underlined, with comment*: works powerfully, backwards to "breathy," but forward, to "things he could not understand," is too big a word, no? And so the sentence falls on face for me], he supposed even things he could not understand. Bringing the chair, they both held it firm, and he got up on it, quite safe. Stretching, he picked more, leaning back to get them, and found himself on tip-toe [*bracketed, with question mark and note*: That is, figure myself, it is just in such phrases that I want them more "worked"—why, I suggest, the thing can stand *extension*—to get its (*form? focus?*)], balanced, and picked what were left to give them to the woman.

Getting down, he put out one hand, and did touch the woman, his hand quietly there, and slipped off by the breasts, to come down, his feet again on the ground. [*Note added*: And surely, here, no? That is, I assume you are exactly trying to keep the action in a sort of unraised evenness, yet, the difference of the tactics, in each case, *cannot* be left out. That is, this is wonderful in itself—but its placement?]

Once there, they all sat down, and he lay back against the tree's trunk, not caring about the wet. The father still sat past them, over to the side, and seemed caught by the children, or watched them with an almost peculiar intensity [*underlined, with note*: why, left, unexamined?]. At first they did not think to bother him, then called, and getting up, he joined them.

You don't know, he said, what you think you are doing? [*Sentence bracketed, with note*: This question I'm damned if I can figure out.] And laughed, as he might, because the man could not know what he said, and his wife looked back at him, smiling, and felt no uneasiness.

[*Line drawn in margin along next ten paragraphs, with note*: This is solid.]

They grew quite content, under the tree, the father stretched out by the women, an old hat pulled down to the back of his head, nearly reaching the ears. His hair fell very straight beyond it, curling slightly at the neck.

But he was not, even so, unformidable. There was a very precise weight present. The younger man might not have budged it, he thought, but thought then of the woman, and looking, saw her dress almost worn out, and pulled tight about the shoulders.

I love you, he said, and echoed it in invariable silences, saying, each time, I love you, but never feeling very much.

Shall we begin again, his wife said, and translated it, to them, so that they both stood up, waiting, but the father was not very interested.

You are not concerned, he said, but could not think of the right words, and his wife repeated it, to the man, smiling, and he shrugged in answer.

I had thought to pick olives, he said then, to his wife. This doesn't seem very close?

And laughed. One didn't care. And got the chair and brought it to another tree, placing it under the high branches and then climbed up on it, to stand there. Following, both women took hold, so that he might have been their own, held there, in some attitude of attention [have been their own *and final phrase underlined, with note*: beautiful].

Still the children ran by them, shouting, and played, very happy, the boy tagging after them, joining in. Above them all, he looked down, thinking to pronounce any spell, perhaps, saying that it could be that way, but they waited, and he went back to picking. [*Added in margin*: solid.]

He gave it, now, all care, parting the leaves very carefully [*phrase bracketed*] with his fingers, and trying to find all those which might be left. It was difficult because the colors were too similar, and hiding in all shadows, it seemed there was one more. But, below him, they pointed, and following their hands he saw the olives, and picked them, dropping them down.

All done, he said, but asked, and looking down, saw them pointing, and he reached out, to get it, then tossed it down to them.

Are you tired, she said [*opening words bracketed, with note*: This throws me off, as more of, a softness], and he got down off the chair, falling down beside them, then took the bag from the woman, smiling, to see how many he had picked [*phrase beginning with* to see *bracketed, with note*: & this?].

Back of them, the father came back, and stood in a tangle of brush, and lifted a camera, holding it steady, to point, the hands very quiet. But the children would not hold still, and all crammed together until the father shouted at them, something, and they stopped and grouped themselves nicely, the grass brushing against their legs. He took the picture, then bent to wind the film, and went off to the house to leave them, there, by the tree. [*Added in margin*: This is *real* crazy!]

Released [*bracketed, with note*: too easy?], the children would have run off but the mother held them, pulling down the youngest to sit on her lap, and he saw the cloth pull tight [*last six words underlined, with note*: nice], and called to his own son, loudly, to come.

Sitting him on his knee, he stroked his head, the boy chafing, but held quiet there and let him do it. He would have spoken, but couldn't, and looking to his wife, wanted to push at her, to explain, but did not know what he wished explained. [*Note in margin*: solid.]

But she knew it anyhow, the woman [*opening words bracketed, with note*: again, too "loaded"?], and watched him even intently, smiling, he thought, or perhaps she smiled. Behind her the other children stood all looking at him [*underlined, with comment*: nice], and he wished very much to say something, but knew no words to.

Turning, she spoke to his wife, and listening, he heard them now wander into sounds so very distant he could think of no words that they might be, and said, stop it, and hearing him, his wife stopped, to smile, and getting up, he pointed, again, to the trees.

There are some left, he said, asking, and the women came after him but then were gone, somehow, or he didn't see them go, still looking for the olives [*in margin*: who?]. The voices, behind, were too alien [*underlined, with note in margin*: ? It seems a question of the *texture*—the cloth of—the language—that a careful homogeneity is asked of you, throughout], now, to keep him and broke too far away to make him listen. Some wind, returning, did make the trees whisper [*bracketed, with note*: what I mean by poetic], but still passed out beyond them all [*underlined, with note*: non-poetic].

Filling his pockets with what olives he could find, he turned to see no one but the children, still running among the trees [*underlined, with comment*: nice]. He watched, then brought them to him, calling, then sent them up into the trees for no reason [*underlined, with comment*: beautiful prose], and they brushed past him, climbing up and over him into the branches.

Waving, he began to toss up bits of twigs, and old bark, and anything he could find, almost dancing, his hands busy in the trampled grass, then throwing up the little things [*bracketed*] to see them fall, past the children, to the ground. One, now above him, did sing, and he looked up to see her there, braced tight against the crotch of the limbs, and white along the ankles and up the legs to only that small skirt, and wave to her, crying out.

But the careful voice followed, now sounded gently behind him, and turning, he saw the man there not even looking at him but up, and white, with fear, and calling.

Etc., etc. G/ sent me a poem by Georg Trakl, not finally very much, I think, but this line, which I now see is echoed up there :

"und leise tönen im rohr die dunkeln flöten des herbstes . . ."

or, something, something:

and on the reed *the dark flutes of autumn sound softly* . . .

: what

I liked.

[*Final note by Olson:*]

Don't know. Am bothered. Maybe I have missed your intent?

It puzzles me, this one.

Am I crazy to want it *worked*

more?

Anyhow, will shoot this back, for what, if anything, it's worth

It troubleth me

[Fontrousse, Aix-en-Provence]
November 9, 1951

Dear Charles,

So caught, at present, I get no time for a damn
thing I wd want it for; it seems we cut wood all day, etc. No
matter but that it kills everything else. That 'matter' certainly.

Anyhow. A letter in today from Laubies, who I'd seen, as noted,
this past Monday; fair enough. Do think that he will be one to
count on in this damn swamp, etc. He notes that he had found a
copy of Williams' DREAM OF LOVE which I'd told him of in a
letter Tuesday, says he would like to translate same & see abt
getting played in Paris. I mean, perhaps this one will move. He
went to Gallimard with the EP work (a selection of the Cantos),
they apparently want it; he had another publisher who also
wanted it, but wd not move on issue. Anyhow, he'll have that
lever with them on consequent work & has Ez' ok on all French
rights, i.e., to translate.

So, sometime soon I do want to line up,
or have for him, that work you might figure for a French edition
of yr poems; certainly use, then, the PRO/ VERSE as header?
Why I note this now : to get moving *now* while this thing is to
hand, & tho it will take time, the sooner one can walk into
Gallimard with the poems *in* translation, the sooner one can hope
for their issue in this godforsaken country, etc.

Do you hear
anything from Emerson? (I don't, & do suspect you damn well
right on yr figuring, but again, we have him if only by being able
to back out, i.e., I have no damn stake in those poems, Gerhardt
can be counted on, to some extent, for an edition in *english* of yrs
come spring, & we cd, perhaps, lever something thru Cid's lady as
a last ditch biz. In short, there is a good chance of out on yr
things, there is no damn rush whatsoever on these first tweedles on
[*i.e.,* of] my own. Voila, if one can damn well keep cool.
Anyhow, tell me what's up, if anything; the longer this silence
continues, the more it looks to be the same old slide.)

The thing, then: to start setting up a text for a French edition, that I can get on to Laubies, not to swamp him, but to show him what wd be available. IF that damn book was out, we cd hand that to him, etc., but failing same, texts will do certainly. I told him of the CMI, it was Mascolo he went to see there, but ended up with the secretary, who he sd was most charming. Anyhow, damn well *push* this one, I think he'll hold on. Have to figure the Ez' Cantos (or this selection) as his first objective, but figure that to slide ok, i.e., he's got the work done, now a matter of getting set on the publisher for same. Free, I figure, to translate new stuff & figure too, what with the CMI at G/s, that's the obvious move now.

Hope to see Gros soon now; that will be another angle, possibly, or I am hoping. Goddamn dulled, but shit, this biz is what never gets but work anyhow. Christly finagling, etc., I wish to god one cd run some other way.

Still burned with Cid, or he *is* an idiot, & can't it goddamn well BE (someday . . .) some damn ONE it doesn't have to be this shit with. You tell me; I haven't the energy to rise to it at this point.
But always to have to sit on it, etc., to damn well keep sliding it, pushing, — it kills the whole deal. Now he sounds like any damn tout, I feel he sells us by the pound.

Etc., etc. You damn well *are* there, fuck the weather.

Have been reading over yr letters, to Bud; soon will get off the bunch to you, i.e., those continue to push me. They damn well all do, I mean, I cd begin at the beginning, it would be that way. Anyhow, will hope to get to this soon but if it takes a few weeks, will know it's this horrible biz we now buck. Haven't been this dead for a very damn long time, only get angry as it now goes — can't handle it at all.

A thought: if you have any copies of the Apollonius left there, to send one to Laubies, a sign, or something that he can look at immediately; it wd make a tremendous introduction, to put it that dully. Anyhow, his address: 95 rue de Vaugirard, Paris 6ᵉ.

Not so much to put this before the poems, I don't, but the thing wrapped up, etc., what he can spend two hrs with & come out *different*. Likewise, might be the smartest way to present it to Mascolo, i.e., *thru* Laubies, who will be there in the flesh, etc. And also speaking a most liquid french, etc.

(Mitch has the copy we have, should be back soon, I have done nothing re Bottegha Oscura, but will, certainly, if you say so, i.e., I did not want to lose this copy, to put it honestly, I want, damn frankly, to *hold on* to it. Ok.)

Gerhardt should be by here, or he said so, but now have dictionary from him, sent from Freiburg — don't know what the hell is up. As usual, I suppose, but I get, at long last, etc., to trust him very much. So damn deadening for them there, I don't see how these interruptions can be bypassed.

I will make copies of all material I have here, i.e., IN COLD HELL, MOVE OVER, (i.e., ones in GG), likewise Preface (Y&X material), Sappho — but am missing some, and also suspect GG *lining* may be faulty. Anyhow, give me what you wd want there, i.e., we can begin to make up copies between us if you have *any* time, I damn well *don't* expect you to! Anyhow, anyhow : will make it per usual if only because there is no damn thing *else* to do, one lives, etc., until one dies, etc. Gloom, gloom, gloom!

Which makes me feel considerably more happy, like they say — I wish to god, as always, you *were* all here — last night we said, we could put them THERE — 'there,' being some 5 by two feet STILL unoccupied some 7 feet from this table.

Hope I don't jump on this French biz; still can't see how to lose by being set for same, i.e., Laubies *is* decent, the only doubt or hitch wd be his free time, i.e., how much does he have, etc. Painter, etc. I wish sometimes I were too, etc.

Kate & all I don't say anything of, I don't damn well dare to—too grey & superstitious, or what the hell, about it. I think of you all; we don't let go ever. Please write soon, it would make so damn much difference in this dismally grey place. Really, no place for any two people, etc. Life for *one* very distant man at best.

Where, goddamnit, I *do* wonder, *is* ORIGIN #3??? I suppose the bastard sent it 4th class. Fuck him, finally, for the fat blow-hard he *too* often is. Voila.

Write, for simple LOVE/ we HOLD:

Bob

[Fontrousse, Aix-en-Provence]
Nov 10th [1951]

Chas/ Yrs just here, & so great to have it. I am way down, useless to put it otherwise. Well, to hell with it, but to put in here, Cid's latest:[64] it shows you what he now shoves at me, & I can't honestly keep on eating it. Hence, have written him, and asked for out, called him what names I could think of, just told him nothing more of mine in any damn issue from now on. Not clean: not worth it. I could have got this biz with Kenyon.

Note comment re Ashley: 'covers.' Sd man walked over here today in a pouring rain to talk over this thing, how the hell could I ask him to do anything with C/s pompousness in my hand. Simply to hell with it. Laubies (who he includes, I expect, with Cahiers du Sud) had found 3 bkstores in Paris to take the issues, also biz of translation, & I'm damned if I'll do anything, now, to get sd issues into sd bookstores : worth my damn nose in this damn instance.

And Gerhardt : he is always eating at G/, & certain enough, or clear, it's me, too, he hits here. I hate all of it, I can't honestly take any more of any of this. I thought we wd get some cleanness, some decent turnover, some action, simply, with a minimum of bullshit. Now we, and it is *true*, get mouthed by him in any place his fat ass comes to rest; I want none of it.

Wd you give me Duncan's address? Cid obviously figures me incompetent, etc. I wanted to see if Duncan cd not go into this German issue, i.e., American; this is what I get as answer. Wd you damn well help me here? I.e., I do need him, I do know his verse somewhat *better* than Cid does. Well, fuck it, but that this is how I get it played back whenever I want something, say, from him.

Etc., etc. I haven't seen that damn #3 as yet, only thing I wd look for anyhow, I know, to wit: yrs. Why the hell bother with the goddamn magazine, etc. Shit, shit, shit.

Honestly, can't make it any longer; will hope that something might be got to this spring, say, even another damn magazine. This one dirties too fast.

Clear it all/ damn well do tell us more of how it goes there; so glad that Con & Kate are making it so well. All love to both, wish to god we could see you all. Times like this one.

Otherwise, it's grey as hell, but sunshine, etc., wdn't change much. Just thinking: 2 damn yrs work, on sd character, just gone down the drain — but play with an idiot, etc. Obvious enough.

This to keep you on, i.e., abreast like they say. Do tell me if you think I'm way off on all this, i.e, I'm not really cool reading such letters as the one here. It makes me see red first line, etc. But anyhow: am out now, DO feel better.

All dearest love to you all,

Bob

A/ moving on broadsheet now, will have info on what he can do
this coming week. Really stories he wd like, sometime, to do; wd
be crazy, well, dream to think of single issue of same, series of,
with such as him in too.

[*Added in margin of first page:*] Figure to set last page of Jardou,
again; now it doesn't feel straight, etc. Too bloopy, etc.

[Black Mountain, N.C.]
Monday November 11   51

Rob't: Yr plaint on Corman in, & know no answer other than yr
own to me on similar complaints same kerekter — that, the good of
him is encased in shit, & that the shit will, inevitably, be thicker,
the more he is apt to think ORIGIN is *his* success.

I'd suggest our
only hope is to keep at him correcting his errors, being straight
out with him on where you or i take it, he is letting down, or
letting in, shit — or even piss — or even round spit

The real bug, is, his own
work, that is, this is the point where the circle comes back to
what you are striking at, that, he is a fatuous, lazy fool,
downright awkward & stupid time & time again — & exactly, as
you have it here, where, he is *presumptuous*

Coy. He has that
fucking American disease to the utmost.

You will imagine, that,
when he told me over the phone that he had written some notes
on verse, & that he is planning to use them as a forepiece to my
answer to Gerhardt (his outline of issue #4, is, Gerhardt's BRIEF,
1st, and, at the end, my ANSWER) I felt gulled.

Yet this puzzles
me, and I'd like yr advice back: that is, now we are beginning to
pay for our subtracting ourselves from any control other than
persuasion on the policy of ORIGIN. And surely he hoped to buy
our indulgence in his use of his own stuff by so pushing us,
eh?

That is, I take it this ARS POETICA (I did not know *that*
was what he would call it!) is going to be the occasion. And I
hope I shall have no hesitation in cutting away at it. The point,
tho, is, that, I don't see how (if he does not take the step to offer
it to us first) that we can get at him *until* he has published it. And
then the damage will have been done.

There is this, though, that
he is palpably bad. Anyone reading him is embarrassed. I have
tried (& especially in that letter of warning three weeks ago to
him, on, tying up either of our things) to lead him to a
recognition that his gifts are administrative, that he has no rhythm
fit for verse, that his "compositional" force is in such composition
as the disposing of materials in his magazine. And joined to the
long go on his SOLDIERS, or whatever it was, it ought to have
made something clear to him. BUT, you shld have seen the answer
from him! Trying to weezle out, on the basis that, I'm asking him
to write like me! Christ, that stupid dodge. Surely, I have not
purchased that sort of sight, having been imposed on, myself, too
often, by those who, wld have any other man like themselves, that
most stupid and subtle of all presumptions, that death wish which
goes against all my sense of life. He is simply a bore, Corman, in
his responses.

Well, he ain't worth the time. ORIGIN is. And my
guess is we'll lose in the end, but, that, we should stay straight
with him not, in personal involvements but in values. And that we
will not be able to wink again (as I did perhaps by ignoring,
completely, his published thing to you & Ann: he has now gone
and sent us a verse for Kate! good god, what shall i do with an
answer to that, mind you! O shit.

To what is better, life these days. The child is a pleasure
unknown, a delight, she seems so alert, and hungry for company,
to be amongst us! She is so damned non-baby, in the alertness of

her attentions & her palpable loneliness. She craves to be out of her own room and sitting with us. (Our dear friend Riboud came in Sat for an overnight on way India-Paris-Houston, and Kate would have nothing but sleeping here in the kitchen where she could hear us!) And Con has taken to taking her into Con's own bed at night. And tho it is probably very bad, & somewhat dangerous, I dare say, yet, the two of them make such sense lying there both sounding off — Thursday night I came back from a go, & there Con was with her back to the baby, and the baby face to her!

I like her very much — and it's her eyes. And that couldn't be better, eh? But like you say, it is sometime before one can engage her, eh? But I have the obsession we will talk together any day: the two of us have a great business in that direction every time I hold her, looking at each other. (Nick dreamed, he tells me, Saturday night, that, Kate & I had already engaged in a big conversation!)

Continue to be more active conceptually than creatively, and I am not too nervous over it. Questions of value keep coming up, and outrunning verse. For example, last night heard OTHELLO, as recorded by Robeson, Ferrer, & Hagen.[65] And it gave me again the chance to dislike that play, to look upon it as the most offensive act of Shakespeare's.

I cannot tolerate his pitching love-lust-&-jealousy in such a low pulp plot as this one. It raises again the whole question of his moral nature on the subject of passion. It is such a tacky play, actually, despite his talent, his dramaturgy.

That is, gullibility works where money, say, is the matter — Jonson's VOLPONE, e.g., has much more dimension than OTHELLO simply because Jonson had the accuracy to place it, there. And it is curious, how much the matter of sex *is* present to the matter of OTHELLO. Yet, Shaks won't let it stay there (Cassio-Blanca, or, Iago's wife's observations on sex). He has to plug it with lust, and give us Puritan doctrine as measure of the matter

(The triangulation, within himself, is MEASURE FOR MEASURE, & THE TEMPEST. I take it, in OTHELLO, he gets caught between the Elizabethan as it was exotic (Drake, Eliz, America, the lighting of the Age of Migration coming on: THE TEMPEST) and the dirty little esoteric England which made Cromwell & Milton masters within 35 years of OTHELLO. And M FOR M, where he lays sex into the Catholic box & system exactly, works: it is that he has no container for his own fear of lust in OTHELLO: mark, sonnet 105, is it:

> The expense of spirit in a waste of shame
> 98   Is lust in action, and till action lust
> Is perjur'd, murderous, bloody, quick to blame (etc)[66]

Or TROILUS & CRESSIDA (written, the point is, just *before* O: the order is damned important, in here: HAMLET (1601, I think), TROILUS & C — and one of the tragicomedies, PERICLES?, 1602-03, then OTHELLO, and, in the one year of 1604-05, LEAR — AND Antony & Cleopatra only *after* all this
  & MEASURE FOR ME   (1606-07)

He was sick of the infidelity of woman from 1601 on — and I'd guess until he found the content of A & C, he could not free his horror from the only known measure, the Christian system (why LEAR gets it off into depth psychology, & why, on the other hand MEASURE FOR MEASURE gives it a proper rigidity, say)

                                                        That is,
one can't find Shakespeare comfortable in normal big city license. Yet Elizabeth's own maidishness on this question (if one of her lords — say, Oxford — got one of her ladies in waiting pregnant — as Oxford did, Anne Vavasour — both of them landed up in the Tower).[67] And between these two he fluctuated (in his own hurt) until ANTONY & CLEO. M for M is Elizabeth's device; OTHELLO, is loaded with, license.

In any case, playing with it, last night, led me into the damnedest investigation of the metric of one sonnet which is a huge puzzle — 125, I think it is, anyway, if you happen to have it handy, the one around 125, with the 1st line rime canopy to the 3rd eternity. It opens

(approx)   Were't aught I bore the canopy
. . . .
And laid great bases for eternity

What puzzles me, is, that, the metric, thr[u]out, is curiously
different from

(Baby just woke to bawl, and her mother not here, so, i am
   proficient, eh? have changed diapers, and all clothes, etc, plus
   (is it "receiving" blanket?) — what a mess

                                   and yet how very
   beautiful they do look *after* they are fed or cleaned, eh?

                                            And
   trying this machine now to see if it is substitute for pacifier,
   and, she does seem to pay occasional attention to its going on,
   and so, a let-up, on, the lungs!

                                   Enjoy so much
   getting rid of Con so that I can do a few of these things, and
   she & I can have some private familiarity!

                                   ONLY! — can't feed
her

I have just put on one of YOUR shirts — that is, is it, Tom's
stuff, came in from Axt? yr sister? Wonderful, anyway, and
Con most happy to have all of the things — several: a box
full.

      You both shld also know that the original blanket — the
   white wool — is so delightful to the ma that she has trouble
   deciding to put it on the baby or wear it herself as a shawl!

Anyhow, will study the sonnet more — don't have it at hand — but,
the point is, the metric is cranky, like, say, TROILUS &
CRESSIDA (as against the slickness of OTHELLO — even the verse,
there, seems to me, smart, a solution, probably, for a season of
his company, or something, pot-boiler

BUT jesus, to fool around with such material in a pot-boiler raises
up his responsibility, eh? Don't like what concepts he sets in
motion on that spectrum of lust-sex-jealousy-love in O

In the sonnet, the 1st 6 lines are such rimes as

canopy

eternity

a couple of antiantipenults

in ing, then,

shifting to antipenults savour

flavour

& then running on in mascloines

But the same quality backs up through the line.

Also, last night, by the way, heard, for 1st time, that PLEASURE
DOME recording[68] of TS, EEC, MM, BILL, Eliz Bishop (who, by
the way, if Corman insists on women or even on such women as
Morse & Bronk, is their superior, all of em, Hatson, etc — dry, yes,
but her FISH, & THE MONUMENT —)

Thomas (who, on the
record, delights me, with, his 30th Birthday

BUT it's BILL — and a
two-liner, which wowed me: the biz of, you give me courage,
ancient star
. . . no par*t*
(that movement, star, to par*t* — such a joy, that feller, in such, eh?

But the overwhelming impression, of all of them, after — straight
after, OTHELLO is, the smallness of these contemporaries'
preoccupations!

Nor do I mean this easily: not that usual shit, abt,
the universality — not at all. Merely, that, their sense of the
particular has no more essentiality than their own perceptive —
their own personal system

no grasp of commons

OK OK don't hit
me with a baby!

Miss you very much. These few letters not
enough. Keep coming at me—anything.

Also much delighted reading Jay Leyda's two volume documentary
life of Melville[69] —and inscribed, finely, to Eisenstein, as, his
"teacher"! (You know how much I take it ISHMAEL proceeds from
the same source)

Leyda has done a day by day record—a LOG, he calls it. And he
has such extraordinary material—stuff neither [Henry A.] Murray
nor I turned over. The details on M's income from his books, and
the movement of the critique of his work) vicious, in ways modern
reviewing is not (and his response to it (the pressure of his
economics, supporting, some 4 children, plus unmarried sisters,
plus a mother & a wife! christ, there must have been ten people
on his hands, at times!

what a man. his sister Augusta is such a
pleasure in her passion for him (she must be intricated to the
incest of Pierre, as well as the illegitimate one Murray & I figure
we know the identity of[70]

well, these are dull things, maybe. but
it interests me, to look at him again, mostly, in terms of, how he
faced to his materials, how he jumped on what seemed to him his
possibles
        (ex., the way they jumped him for writing Moby-
Dick!
        More, of course, Pierre

And how in each case it is sex
which provokes the attack—he wronged domesticity! How abt
that, and the guy, pouring it out, for his own domestic
establishment, never, poor fool, taking it on the lam!

ok ok & that one too—no bricks

say hello to Bud, et al

and our love to you & Ann and
the boys

all firm, if not passionate
these days

yrs,
Olson

───────────────────

[Fontrousse, Aix-en-Provence]
Tuesday/ November 13 [1951]

Dear Charles,

Very grateful to you for this reading of Jardou;
much more than just the one thing, certainly. I am very unsure,
these days; not so much re any way, call it, tho that is at bottom
too, but I don't sit with any sureness, anywhere, and get, now,
either to have to go much deeper than I even suppose I can, or
simply slide off, which I can't do either. I have really no
distractions; just this one thing to sit with.

I just got back from
seeing Bud & his wife off, had been mulling all this over in my
head all morning—almost not seeing either of them, honestly. A
mistake they did come now, but hardly any way to have known
that.

I have hated the loss of my own language ever since we got

here; I can't get used to it or find the slightest means to get in
another way. I wonder if I don't put Cid down really on that, that
I cannot stand his english, it is damn well obscene.

Mainly that I
want to put everything else down, just now, just this point; I want
the thing clear, or clear of at least that [which] I can clear. New
Hampshire was, always at this time of year, god knows how many
miles straight in, a sheer damn drop. And I loved it more than I
have much else, it was peculiarly, particularly, my own way.

Cid
& all : am I capricious on this? I thought, last night; this means
no more of being there *with you*, I mean, to be so, that place. It
isn't at all easy to think about, because I've depended on your own
reach, to lever mine many times. I don't feel any wish to publish
anything anymore, or right now at least; tomorrow I suppose I'll
feel as cramped & as shit on as I must have back one year before
all this had got moving.

But he shifts the damn ground miserably,
and dishonestly, and I can't take it; I am so damn well *balanced* I
cannot allow it *if* I cannot trust it. I can't trust him; it was
invariably figuring, etc. I can't make it anymore.

Really, there *is*
no decent language, but that of the whole thing, the continuum
which the stories damn well have to be, or to hell with it,
anyhow, nothing that can allow this present sense of uneasiness
without a too neat label. I really don't know what, or just what, is
coming; but even in such a statement I've severed the essential
progression. I don't know, I want to be *here*; I haven't yet made
it.

And so, or perhaps so, at least this last story; man comes to
balls? Perhaps. Or he would use that failing other via; he always
does, if he is one. I hate their world here so much, so damn
completely; I *do* loathe them 24 hours a day, and how can I make
anything out of that? I have to, but *how*; what kills me at
present.

And damn well *yet*, I can't give it up, I want this edge so
damn much, this fucking perspective, or what the hell to call it, I
want, damn it, to come IN to my own progress, and I suppose

that is rather ambitious. I don't suppose my head, what there is of it, has even got to le Havre as of this writing. Goddamn horror (immaculate) of being, so, in pieces.

Anyhow, am going to go into this one again, i.e., this damn story; I don't know any more than you do, what the hell it is. Or what is it, like they say, etc: damned if I know, *but* something. Etc. I.e., not gas or contrivance that I can spot. Perhaps an attempt to slide *round* them; I note what I seem to damn well edge for *is* their fucking 'nature' & can see for my damn self, as you can too, what the hell they cut out, to get me on that biz. Universals! I'll be damned!

Yr goddamn narrowness, or what you damn well call such: *is* the *one* rope, and don't let go *now*, & you won't, anyhow. You are exact, I think, to nail this 1) as idyll, 2) as leakage of nature, 3) that I am after some damn thing here, even if I don't damn well know, *what.*

    I tell you, what I know, etc. Is, or is it, I don't know, but *have to* damn well get them *all*; continents included. My fucking *attack* on 'Europe'? Something that will allow me *full* position here, allow all of this biz, *without* language. And I damn well do not know if I won't sit here, at that, for the next 2 years *without* language; I loathe the sounds of this one, I *am* hearing it, but I am *only* hearing it. It is an odd thing.

       Why nature does crowd in. BUT to take it on, again, as thing, as, as you say, what one is on, & *only* then usable.

Cid is, as usual, full of shit to figure GRACE 'greatest,' etc. I mean, is that any damn pleasure, etc. When, in his hands: THE PARTY. I didn't get any pleasure, I can think of 5, & more, changes in sentence, etc., I have already made in the copy here, or will. Beginning with that thing on moon sliding, i.e., to cut, & have it go: "The moon sank, the crest reached, and he watched it, catching the edge against the window, to try to hold it, but felt it pass . . ." Or something, there. Likewise, what Bud hit: ". . . until they (the dishes) were done. Then left them to dry there, *by themselves* . . ." To fuck off that last; is the loss, etc. I can't figure this as, *tight*. Needs cleaning, in any case. Pulling in, & will do it, along with the rest of it.

Jardou: will get what I get off when thru it, and give me another go. I am very damn grateful for this one, I cannot damn well ever make it enough or thanks enough, for what you do on any of these things.

Honestly, the only communication I really damn well want, or think I will want, for the next 2 years : yr own.

Other damn things: sorrow, that the bust is with Cid, anyhow, i.e., I feel silly, or vicious, or damnit, I have to let go now. I have notes on his ars poetica, coming up now; further he says he wants to publish Party & Jardou together, *possibly* in #6 (6 months) and then there is no assurance. Further, he wants to put another poem 'to me' against J/, & I don't like that biz at all; I don't really like the man, I feel this is almost obstinate. More, I feel like a horse, etc. Shit on him & his affections.

"On prosody. I probably wont send you the essay, simply because I dont have time to sit down & copy it. Same reason Charley wont see it, either." Why couldn't he simply *cut the shit.*

Well,

this off, quick; damn cold in my damn nose, etc. Fuck it, and will be back soon; things quieter, etc. All damn love, *all of it*, to you all,

    Bob

[*Added in margins:*]
Hard to figure on the type-writer bothering Kate, but they have to get to take the basic noises, are inevitable, etc. I.e., if you pamper, or simply try not to make any noise, etc., gets horrible — a pin sets them off, etc. Type while she is going to sleep, may work, i.e., to get her used to it; ann's idea: turn her on her stomach & put a hotwaterbottle under it!

But DO NOT EVER give up typing — it really isn't the main thing, put it, she'll pick up some other noise, etc. In short, keep 'em flying, etc., & she'll make it too. (*Sudden noises* :what is the bug.

If you have a radio, cd let it run low, say, all the time, as base noise, etc. Tho might have *you* moaning yrselves!

Fuck *all* schedules; C/ will *not* run out of milk — feed *whenever* hungry, or any peep.

Talk *loudly* to her, *play* with her — they get *very bored*!!

Lousy abt that damn *Grant* — *idiots* all. Still don't see — why not: Fulbright.

[Fontrousse, Aix-en-Provence]
Thursday/ Nov 15th [1951]

Dear Charles,
        Somewhat better weather now, or simply cold & no rain to speak of; and quieter with Bud & MA off. I felt very bewildered, seeing them — I hadn't for some time, or for no time to speak of anything. It was not very much what I had hoped, though, the saw, etc., these things rarely come to one's hopes, etc.
    But I am, in any event, a very damn muddled man at present. I wish I could keep that distance, even of that sentence. I begin to run into several problems, call them, I hadn't expected or certainly wish might be kicked out.
        I thought, back some weeks now, the base problem of 'sincerity' got hung with the companion one of

'selection'; the more able one is, the more conscious, the more his 'selection' *is* conscious, the more difficult, almost impossibly difficult, becomes the question of 'sincerity.' It is a diffuse thing at best, this qualification; one wishes me to speak sincerely, etc., and yet, even in speech, I come to be almost too conscious of any word used, or of any arrangement. Living off here, like this, sounds, or words, fall into a more or less *clear* place; even the simpler directions, etc., become some occasion for
meaning.

Which gets me a speech, perhaps, for myself, but I feel so often, talking (as we were the past two weeks) that I am much too deliberate, and plan, sometimes, a point that may take two days to get to in conversation. And yet I try to, and sometimes do manage it.

But I feel, in any case, 'sincerity' is not really in this, or not the thing which might be seen here. Making something, Slater would cut all his pieces to fit, say, and making them so, would be working toward something, just then, perhaps 'insincere' in the shape, or actuality, of any one board which might be in his hand; he took it only as the means to the continuum, the thing to end, etc. Which I don't much go with, or don't, pulled into this context.

Anyhow, I have a hunger for speech, and yet I know almost noone with whom it is any pleasure to speak. Ashley, perhaps. But that is some 'newness' and also, some play in the positions; we circumvent certain insistences in a way that makes them clear enough but is capable of keeping them in place. But Ashley does have clarity; he speaks with great care; sounds, in his mouth, are very dear to him. The voice is rather deep, that under-warmth a Negro so very often has in his speech, & laid, always, very carefully against the 'thing' he wishes to hand over. Bridges, of sorts. I like that aspect.

But, but. Etc. Dave has this beginning, usually, these days: "Yes, but . . ." I know who he gets that from.

Laubies: we were too subtle. At points, I could break in, saying, even, I feel like hell, etc. What a damn miserable place, etc. That made something, and writing, after, he remembered, I think, only that part of our conversation—only part, in short, which came from any actual wish to communicate.

There are those times when, a thing so put, will lever out a distance not got before, or simply a place; but, too, it may be altogether false, or simply shock or excitement, etc. But there is, I think, no other way to say anything.

Talking with B/ & MA : there was some continuous resentment against our having children, and seeming, by that, to posit a superior 'experience.' But he had been saying, earlier, re the fights: things one cannot communicate—the act of love, the feel of swimming, what a bull-fight is. (From Hemingway, etc.) And I could answer: here is another.

It did seem to me, when the children came, I had been thrown, or put, into an actual gratuitousness. Bud objected that a too close analogy, say, with the animal kingdom could be ridiculous, and yet I felt some existed; the way the male usually does not have to do, specifically, with the offspring, etc. The way he seems an 'agent' beyond any such involvement. Surely, or I do think so, there is a great 'sadness' in this act of birth, because we are left behind; the woman, wife, or woman, is carried beyond us in that, and continues at that distance, afterwards. Having broken, once, or twice, say, to then sink into some security of emotion, of even an amorphous sense of 'join,' this splits, breaks off, in this act, no matter the attempted closeness.

And yet it is *that* which delights me, deeply. It is this reassertion of the separateness, the damn important isolation, which seems gain. If I can't come, even ceremoniously, each time, 'new,' what is the use of bothering with it, & why not, finally, jerk off behind the barn with more purpose?

Having nothing, in that—there, coming to no place which is not, so, declared each time : a stodgy damn dead business, a filthy one.

Anyhow, I felt, when they came, I was again out, not 'free,' but pushed out, and if I don't get pushed out, if I am not kept out, clear, it's not very much use writing anything because I am nowhere, etc., I am too dulled.

I wanted to ask you what you had felt, perhaps; but I hate to interrupt. I may have, here, only my own feelings, etc. I have no real way to 'compare' them, and certainly, no wish to but with one like yourself.

Etc., etc. It's a big 'place' here, I feel small enough. But get to hope that such 'size' means little; the circumjacence, etc. Perhaps there is something to be hauled up.

And most 'acts' are so *in* the body, corpus, self. I hope I can keep my own in one piece.

Something happens anywhere, etc., etc., etc.

Still not on the story again; this cold has kept me off anything the past two days. Nearly a luxury at this point, or I can now indulge it, if only a little. Satisfying hack, etc. Also, what I manage to blow out of my nose. Peeking, after, etc. These being the delights!

Still nothing on a house; Laubies thought there might be one open just outside of Nice, but in a village there where the prices would not be affected, i.e., tourists kill Nice as might be expected. But sea? Too damn cluttered I suppose. Any house, at this point—this one is miserably damp now.

Anyhow, this to keep on; do tell us how it all goes. I have felt this distance very damn acutely, the past days, I have damn well hated it. But someday. Write as soon as you can.

All our love to you all,

Bob

[*Added in margin:*]
Have just got a copy of DHL's STUDIES IN Classic Am/ Lit. That should haul me out. First damn time I ever managed to get my hands on it. Ok.

[Black Mountain, N.C.]
Thurs nov 15 51

Rob't:

Damn fatheaded, last letter, to say not nervous — now i am, with everything piling up: (1) card yesterday the Gasp, saying,

coming here tomorrow, Saturday!

So that will tell, eh?

& (2), letter in fr Hatt (guy who did Apollonius, & Letter HM), asking me to record I, MAX, and make it the title of a collection of poems, finely printed (he says) AND WITH LONG-PLAYING RECORDS in envelope with book

Also (3), Corman's good news some dame sent him 100 bucks, & so, he's in the clear to #6.

Yet my mind won't look on these things, or, my will. And can't blame no baby. On contrary. Stay stupid, and reading (which I always only do when I am stupid?)

Miss, very much, yr letters. Have got so, they tense the string, eh?

(By the way, when you get a chance, take another look at that wild one i got off to you the Sunday before Kate: that is, October 21st, the long go on the gimmicks of la vie. I'd like yr gauge of it. Well, like I say, when . . .)

Apparently, I'm in one of those returns, to Mister William Shaksper. They happen, every so often, he being the man who opened language for me, a summer, reading, his plays. Nor was it Othello tipped it. Had been talking abt him, previous. And now have read again Troilus & Cressida. A very stupid thing, with only one line (almost), and it tells the

story: "All the argument's a cuckold and a whore." Yet it is his,
demonstrably, and so, evidence, eh? Actually, what a holy cow so
much of he is. What gets me is, this, universality, his readiness to
have something to say on anything.

Well, off with that. I figure,
today's the day to start cleaning up my back biz with you. And
1st, the one you must be on top of, now, or soon, the NOTES
ON AMERICAN POETRY, 1951. My impression (from the two
versions you have sent me) is, you are trying to say too much.
That is, if you come at it from the other end, from yr own sight
of the necessities—how you had it, in that little note for me, in
Montevallo, as a starter—you will jump on it.

That is, the last
version, gives the societal the advantage—you bother abt America,
when, actually, you naturally do not think of societies, or such
undertakers, as, professors.

> TIGHTNESS: that's the enemie, the pattern rather than the
> *movement* of its sense—and is also a sure way to get at the
> pedants, the eliotics, and
>
> WITH THAT AS YR OPENER, all
> of para #3, in the 2nd version, gets placed, securely placed:
> viz

"Peace come of communication." It does *not* come from a
use of words in any sense calculated to obscure a motive. Two-
thirds, at least two-thirds, of all verse written in the US is written
to adorn a position, to be "pattern," to exist "poetically." And so,
the only sort of honesty, or clarity, turns out to be criticism, and
that of the safest sort, literary criticism. (It is safe, as is the verse
of tightness, because TS Eliot, and the Lord Jesus Christ makes it
so.)

The other side, is, such as Williams, the anti-poet, or Pound,
the anti-State. And/or Stevens, who is less demonstrative than the
other two of the "fathers" but who has damned tightness by
implication: "There is, however, a usage with respect to form as if
form were a derivative of plastic shape." That is, verse has a

matiere which is as differentiable as a painter's paint or a carver's wood: sounds, can be alive or thin, played with or taken very seriously. And once taken so, they become the medium of a man who writes to make *clear* certain premises, certain emotions, certain characters of idea. And if he writes so, uses sound so, in other words to the extent that his verse is conscious, is written with clear apprehension of the means sounds are to such statement, he'll be worth the time of the reading.

((And do, Rob't, leave off that Yeats, abt dreams, & responsibility, even tho Bill lends it his authority to it, simply, that, it is an Irishism, such dreams, and is the refuge of Delmore Schwartz, not, WCW.

Even the govt of words (in fact, except for, "No ideas but in things," does Bill ever lay open? that is, by definitions? He does, with, We have bred, dug, no end to, desire[71]

And I'd leave the rest, as you have it, from "The present selection is, . . . Which is about it, or one cannot say more than the poems themselves."

(leaving it there, leaving out, the last 3 sentences, where, again, yr title "Am Poetry," leads you to a survey

FUCK

such:

what you have to say yrself, fr yr preoccupations, is all there is to this fucking country — or any other, at any time, anywhere

In fact, given FRAGMENTE, and Gerhardt's own evidence of the state of German practice 1951, I'm not sure you'd not wedge in most clearly if you hammered on two lines most natural to yrself (that is, sort of ignoring any representative statement):

(1) NO IDEAS BUT IN THINGS, for surely, this is the great hammering of Bill *and* EZ, and is, without underlining,

most Amurrikan, & most an offset to German practice
(Gerhardt *or* Rilke, Gerhardt notwithstanding clear that
R is shit: that is, his BRIEF, & fondness for Perse, are
signs, the abstract is still a ghost of Greece haunting
those poor, never civilized, only Christianized people

&   (2)   FORM IS NEVER MORE . . .   and that, this law, in
verse, involves

TH E LIN E

                        (and you might take a care to spell out
"content," in the light — again — of G's misunderstanding of it as
"material": that content is the *things* which the poem contains, and
that things in a poem are ideas simply because things, there, are as
things there, totally content in the ultimate sense, not, as
matiere — matiere is sound, but Mont St Victoire[72] is the content,
eh? and *the painting* (the finished thing) is the form

Look, Bob: if this thing is bugging you, you need not give it
another thot, that is, yr ORIGINAL NOTE, seems to me wholly
sharp and on the button. By all means add Duncan (will send if
you need copies) — and subtract? Emerson? Bronk? That is, this
sounds damned personal, but, neither — o, christ, just pay me no
mind on yr selections:
                        I hate the lot of em, & figure only Duncan
acts like a man

  Let me be cool: one — two ;:

  yr ORIGINAL note is wholly good
                              but if you wanted to give
it any more time, I'd say that 1st version cld get a little more
presentness, if you added to its tone, yr own careful distinction
between tightness, &, the lines as new, fresh

And yr idea of opening with BILL's descent,[73] is impeccable.

                                   So far as I go, THE K'S, is the
case, eh?
            (Now do you have a copy?)

OK.

[*Added in pencil:*]
Will keep on top of this one, now that the
time is coming — or is it?
did G get F#2 out yet, or no?
Also, will try to get off copy of
Apollonius   expect Kasper to bring
back to you:
                  did you, or no, decide
to ship off one you have to
Botteghe Oscure ?
                  OK. Rushing to a damned go by O on — what?
William Shakespeare or
                  G. Herodotus?
                                   Yrs for
                                   freedom   Olson

[*Verso, in pencil:*]
Con sends love, &, now that she is beginning to see over the edge,
wanted me to tell you both how damn well much you & yr sister
did get into our hands — & how pleasant it is to have the Kate
covered, & accommodated —

    the diaper biz. sd, hoy, it is as it used to be when we were
swimmers (not having been a warrior): how high a sign of man
the SPHINCTERS
                  are,
                        eh?
Do keep me on — all yr visitors, & biz

The publishing biz, here, BMC, is, necessarily, now,
only the *Broadsides* :

> we await Ashley's design
> Stay on
>   O

[Fontrousse, Aix-en-Provence]
Friday/ November 16th [1951]

Dear Charles

K/ *is* it, and all other damn mush best dumped. I
read, we both do, all about it with a hell of a lot of pleasure, and
do keep us on, all along. I never before had this perspective, shall
we ever so quietly say! Anyhow, it is great that it all goes ok.
Ann has a few messages, let me note same, and can then get on
with it:

1) Rubber pants, she thinks, and I guess she's right, don't do any
   harm, i.e., we didn't use them with Dave, we do with Tom —
   can't see that it has any ill effects, and it does save much
   washing;

2) she was, likewise, torn on the matter of the blanket, i.e., the
   same as Con, and said she wore it more often than she used it
   for what it was supposed to be used for. Like they say.

Voila, and will check with her, directly she gets back here & gives
me SOMETHING to eat, etc., and will add random jottings at that
time.

The thing—have finally got my hands on a copy of DHL's STUDIES; and spent yesterday afternoon reading them. Too much, simply damn, damn fine and I do get, altogether, your logic of calling him, so, American. It is a particularly *clear* biz; I have always damn well backed his way, but I love these instances.

Anyhow, once thru, and turn round to begin it over again; I have missed his damn books very much, we didn't manage, god knows why, to bring any with us.

The greatest: where he says, "Well, I have seen an albatross, too . . ."[74] How about that.

Re Cid—nothing I damn well suppose can now be got to, without his dirty presence, etc. Anyhow, I feel something of an ass-hole on the way I handled it all. In short, wish, now, I'd been a bit more sinuous. But what I do hate, in all of it, is this *constant* need for the figuring, it seems we are forced to spend more time on keeping his nose approximately clean than on any of our own concerns. His nose, that is, is not *finally* one of my own concerns, etc. Anyhow, anyhow. What the hell *to do*. My present status is, out, i.e., I did jump it, I couldn't damn well sit longer, but I expect this will bring some kind of note from him; what, then, to do. I damn well don't know; the continual drain of his asininity gets bitter. These poems to us all, etc.—not, as you suggest, the least of it. He tells me he's got another ready to put against the two stories, and it will be, I begin to think, over my dead body. If we can't get him to these least feelings of *some* sense of another—what is the damn use?

The way he does use either of us, and I get to feel it's yrself who will get the worst of it, having made, damnit, the real ground. This trading on Pro/ Verse doesn't seem to me sufficiently different from what Emerson had attempted; I wonder if one could suggest that to Cid C/ in any way that wouldn't annoy him; I don't damn well suppose so. But it *is* fact. I gave it the wrong title, there, i.e., Ars Poetica—the actual one is even more bitter, to me at least: Some Notes Toward a New Prosody. Haw, haw. But what is one supposed to put up with, or how damn far can we go with this biz? He tells me, very easily, "It doesn't really say much more, I mean: much newer, than O's PV, but I think most people will follow it more easily . . ."

Not, damnit, to trade on you the same old way, but this *is* damned irritating—the way he runs on. He hits me, the same, i.e., with that christly title . . . , "This essay, as you can sense by the title, goes along with yr study of fiction . . ." "Fiction. . . ." Ah, etc. *What the hell to do*???

It seems he won't send copies to either of us, I enclose the section, the last, saying all he seems willing to about it; which is, in brief, nothing. He tells me Fang liked, or something to that effect, what he was getting at; this doesn't cheer me too much. I don't figure Fang as, shall we say, an active American poet, etc.

The simple truth: I should like to stamp on him with both dirty feet, I can't see anything else to be done.

Certainly, get your hands on it; at any rate, do damn well ask for a copy. I did, back there, I got nothing, but it is part of the record at least. This *use* without having been given *any* chance to see what that *use* was. Democracy, like they say.

Blah, blah : sum & substance of these last three letters. I expect the next will be the wailer, if I still rate it with him. Those eulogies of GRACE (as per: "For me: VARIOUS SIZES, THE RAIN, MY FATHER, ROUND & CANON, prints, and yr GRACE constitute the most solid achievement today, anywhere in the world, by unknown creative people . . ."

blub, blub . . . I feel something like a very wee thing, etc.) do *not* sound like much more than mediocre adv'ts for a poor grade of beef. Beef.

"A blowing rain today run through by iciness . . ." I suppose I did ask for it.

But that makes no damn logic for hanging on, even to the magazine, *if* this is the damn last say; this trading, now clear, is not going to be a damn thing but messy, we save him as much grief by cutting, as we may, even, ourselves. The horse-laugh should be ringing by #6 to say the very least.

Fuck it. If we could hold on, would be the damn thing; will see what he says, to the thing I wrote, i.e., saying I was out, etc. It was quiet enough, put, mainly, on the assumptional use he tried to make of other people by means of myself. Also, this rushing me along to a 'novel' — this, after I just went down for the count. O, well, etc. I suppose I am credited with a remarkable resilience.

All of which gets damn tiring, all of it, and cheap, at that. Have batted it long enough; the end. Will get to the rest shortly, waste of damn time to bother, damnit, with the above.

Write soon, all

best love to all 3 of you (1 2 3)

Bob

[*Added at top of letter*:]
Still no issues of #3 here; and he knew I needed the material to finish up the Gerhardt job, or that was what I wrote him.

[Black Mountain, N.C.]
sunday november 18 51

RobT:

yr two, mit enclosure, on the SHID, in yesterday: figure, you had cause, you had cause, eh? That is, sure hold yr hand. And as for ORIGIN, it's a dead duck, just like that — that idiot,

christ, what the hell made that mag hissen but youen? when i
think . . .   or better if he'd think, & NEVER FORGET, for, such,
better remember, or, their fatuity . . .   in fact, memory of such
things clearly the mark of major men, that, they know, their
sources & their own unfoldings.

He's twisty, and so fucking coy, & so goddamned inarticulate.
                                                                    I
even don't weep over ORIGIN, feeling — which is a delight — that
publishing will go on. Certainly for you. I'm not so sure for
myself. But that never did equal the fact of the acts of recognition
such as your own, and the *subsequent* publication, in ORIGIN,
due to you.
              My hunch is, he'll be brought up sharp, and come to
his senses, by yr letter. I don't think he's had that much time to
get a false sufficiency. And if you feel any room at all in you for
the present act of ORIGIN, fine. Though of what matter how
long. . . .

     anyhow, to the news of what i am up against in similar
realm: MISTER KASPER. came in here yesterday, and is a most
troubled lad — that is, *this* is a mission *unknown* to his fellow
partners, MISTER Pound, & master Horton! Even unknown to
others Washington that might tattle & tell!
                                   What gets me, is, that,
the lad (& he's that, a green goose, & not at all mischievous, just,
rammed to the muzzle with the Old Man's attitudes, and those
imitative behaviors which they all get, the idiots — the quotes, etc.,
the up-&-at them at rising of the da-hawn
                                 (only, again, he knows,
that, the enormous tragedy of the dream in the peasant's bent
shoulders is the "softest" (his word) line in Pound[75] — that must be a
little the opening by which somehow I got in
                                  And it's that I can't
figure, haven't yet been able to dig out, is, how come the character
came on my work, and how come the same wants to publish
same — EVEN THO HE CLEARLY STANDS TO WRECK HIS
RELATION TO THE B S

For that's what it amounts to, that, the Master has sd NO (the quote is, "Keep away from Kikes, and Olson"—and apparently these are separate genera!)

Which ties with what you got, and also, does demonstrate that this whole Kasper business is NO OVERTURE

What the boy is here for, clearly, is to walk around me, particularly on what they call the great schism, apparently (the "break" between Ez and me! that unknown thing, which, still, bewilders me: Ann's doping of it still seems the only one, for it's all (the schism) over there, in Grandpa's yard—

how much it bulks is clear from the YARDBIRDS, this one & the rest

What he *hopes* for is some act on my part which will accomplish a rapprochement so that he, Kasper, can publish a selected O *without* jeopardizing his continuing relation to EP!

He is even a child abt it, saying (a couple of times) that "I cld do it, and not even tell him—and what could he do *after* the book was out?"

It is a comedy.

The nice thing is, the boy sees my own thing as "opposed" to Pound's—& seems to have come to this out of the work: that is, I get no evidence that anyone sold me myself but himself

My hunch is, that, he differs from the others simply because he wants to publish *writers*, not merely Del Mar, Blackstone, Agassiz, Confucius, and Mullins on the Federal Reserve![76]

Even his being convinced on MONEY, is (he put Ez on m thus: "Money lust versus the pleasures of the senses"

so

distinguished from Horton: for whom the fluorinating of water in Washington, DC, is his contribution to the "scholarship"

(the

Yardbird Fellowship)

Now I don't propose to just die away, and leave this area to
the Old Man, just so long as I remained convinced that the boy
came to read me straight, and wants to publish me for myself.

My
prediction is, that, right now, for a little time, he isn't going to be
able to take the risk with Ez: that is, (1) he ain't going to get out
of me some move toward Ez which (he came here hoping—why he
came without "permission"!) will take him off his own hook

and so
(2), for the present (he has only been involved with Ez since
August, so far as I can see—and he is in this difficulty, that
Horton, is two-three yrs in there, and on top of that, Ez sold
Horton to Kasper, arguing, "Kasper & Horton" sounds better, etc:
that is, the honeymoon was so attractive to this lad (kicked out of
Columbia graduate school last yr for using Pound guerilla tactics
in classes—got this whole story, & it is to his credit, that, he
fought that dirtiest of universities: Irwin Edman, Dorothy
Brewster, Mark Van Doren, Donald Clark (Milton), etc. And he
was defended by two men, one of whom I know: Raymond
Weaver's "wife" for twenty yrs, John Angus Burrell (the other was
a "Jew," Solomon, an existentialist teaching at both the New Schl
& Columbia)[77]

for the present, the thing means such fine eating off
Ez's table (as all such "friendships" with Ez do, that, like dreaming,
you meet a better class of people!

it's so heady, for a 20 yr old, to
be the publisher of, EP, that, he's going to hate to give it up,
eh?

think of whom he meets!

But here's this sign: that he is balky enuf, enuf of a maverick, to
get the idea to publish me, and further, to *dare*(!) to come see me,
even if surreptitiously (when he made his false start to come in
August, & told EP, EP sd NO, just that, flat; and so, this move,
is, an advance, for the lad

I wld guess that, the push for him comes from his whole reason
for having stumbled on the work of one Pound: it is verse which

is his original his gate: verse, plus a training in philosophy (the
latter is what gives him his satisfaction in Ez's thinking—Occam,
Duns Scotus, anti-Aristotle, etc

SO: I wld lead him on, & out, this way (with yr support, I hope,
in fact, I don't much care for any of it without you with me):

> on the assumption he wants, soon, to publish writing, verse &
> story, I propose to shore him by suggesting he do two things::

> > (1) face the fact that the "economic" act (even in Ez's terms)
> > is—and properly is, in the area of publishing now—
> > DISTRIBUTION: to cut thru the sleaziness of the
> > economics of publishing (not merely be a tool of Ez's
> > conspiracy, not merely be apparently "economic" by
> > publishing books on money, eh?)

> > & (2) that there are such other writers as Creeley and Duncan
> > who, the three of us together, represent a push which
> > needs just such swift publishing (as Kasper did on the
> > Fenollosa) and a distribution that De Boer,[78] or any of
> > the commercial idiots, don't know fr nothing abt—that
> > this whole biz is dead because no one is doing any more
> > than using New Directions already

Actually, what I also see ahead is the need for a publisher
who will publish the New Learning in a proper offset to the
limited NL of Ez:

> for ex., last night, Brooks Adams came up, and it turns out I
> can find out what none of them have been able to, who it is
> who now owns the rights to BA's Theory of the Labor
> Class[79]—or some such title I do not know of BA's which Kasper
> & Horton want now to add to their list

I think I have mentioned to you my own impression that THE
NEW EMPIRE of BA's is the most valuable of all BA's books (it is
the one in which I was interested to see that BA comprehended the
Near-East-Russian-Scandinavian corridor which led to Gothic

Europe—BA only understood it as a political & metal corridor, not
at all as the art and culture corridor it was, in contrast to what
history has only kept for us (the Mediterranean) and declaring, as
that other corridor does, a whole series of inheritances the
Americans have been for all their centuries the chief carrier of
(that is, the NE wooden house, etc—MOVE OVER . . .)[80]

Now, you will also remember my long exegesis to Corman abt the
sort of materials lying around unused & unknown
                                              in other words,
talking to this boy much of the night, it burst in on me that (now
that those studies of the past three-four yrs begin to come to their
head) I damn well have my own axe to ground, my own
CONSPIRACY!
              that culture morphology (given the twists, say, of
PRO VERSE, part II, and GATE & CENTER, and DHL (that fact,
that, he was 1st on to Frobenius, say—and that my interest in
Fenollosa is, as you have pointed out, to some clear degree at root
a different interest than Ez's) etc—
                        that such a drive—fast, such a
new learning—is something to push by getting the TEXTS issued
alongside the work you & Duncan & I keep pushing:

for ex., a book on the Maya, or on Herodotus, or Berard on
Homer, or Sauer, or Strzygowski on Church Art of Northern
Europe,[81] or translations of Frobenius, etc etc—the Sumer things,
especially
          all this (plus graphic devices such as I tried to lead
Corman towards—and I don't mean woodcuts, by god)—the
recovery of Barlow's work, say,
                        or AFRICA, with & without
reference to Frobenius
                        these are things which, it just may happen,
are the sort of push that this boy might just leap on as the
equivalent of what Horton & Dillam[82] & Ez are pushing at him:
                                                          I
have this feeling, that, Kasper is in their hands because they are
the only ones who have filled part of his need

HE IS DEFINITELY PULLED AWAY from much of their doings: anonymity, etc—for ex., without any provocation on my part, he beefed off abt that preface to the Bunting!

In fact his coming here is proof of his pulling against them on one conspicuous taboo

And

I have already sounded how far he is anti-semitic, by text

Well, just to let you know, and clear my own head on above heads directly. Damned shame you are not here, for the two of us to work this street as carefully as it needs to be worked:

that is, yr own careful research into this character has been immensely helpful: the fact is, I wld never have been able to appraise him without all the stuff you kept shooting to me, your figurings, plus Blackburn's info

(the latter I kept as confidential as you asked, but you will know I only use it for what it is worth, not thinking Blackburn's judgment is yet sufficient to be anything more than straws in what winds go along the Manhattan pueblo

(Dudek, only, so far, of that group, has got mentioned—and he only as "slow," fr Pound's eye, by comparison to this fast, hot lad, XASPER! (he is still, of course, gratis, there, because he did the Fenollosa in 14 days!)

Well. Will go out, now, and dig the boy up again for further conversation. As I say, I think it is too early to hope for much. But I think it'll be only a short time before the boy's craving to get other things in the Square Dollar Series besides Ez's kicks will lead to division

It is curious, that, suddenly, all publishing is in this uproar: (1) you whacking Corman; (2), this boy HERE!; (3) what you have done with Laubies, riding us both on Gallimard; (4), the Cahiers

du Sud move; etc etc (even, this, little biz here, the Broadside, wld
figure, to me, to be an advancing possibility:

> that is, the absence of student income (& a decrease
> coming soon, of five, maybe, or more, so that the place
> is getting close to collapse, maybe—unless I can get
> Williams,[83] in Boston, to warmup to my own idea to
> salvage this thing, and at the same time advance Chinese
> education in America by moving the operation abt half
> way between Washington & NY—thus enabling such as
> Litz and myself to visit, and have an income, at the same

time live in the imperial cities![84]

Yet, for the present, the cheapness of linotyping here in the South
(abt a third to a quarter cheaper than north)

> > > is something to push:

if i cld get a printer here who wld be as ready as Hatt was to go
by my editorship, we cld really make

> > (1) OUR OWN DAMNED ORIGIN

> > (2) OUR OWN DAMNED ORIGIN EDITIONS

> > & (3) SUCH OTHER PUBLISHING AS I SPEAK OF AS
> > proper learning to the now

(This bird did not bring back my Apollonius: it is in Jose Limon's[85]
hands, for possible production! Ha ha!)

> > > So, on Bottegha, it still is

yr copy is best, if you will rest assured that I shall see you have
my own, if there is any loss of same

> > > Sud I can get one of the

paper bound off to Laubies, to euchre Gallimard, etc. Will do that,
tomorrow.

OK? (Gallimard! It is now *five* yrs since they bought Ishmael!)
    And not a peep out of Mascolo in six months on the

announced intention to publish it in Dec or Jan coming up!)

    And will see you have cop[y]

[Olson]

[Fontrousse, Aix-en-Provence]
Monday/ 19th?
[19 November 1951]

Dear Chas/

    Bunch of books in here; namely, Williams' AUTOBIOGRAPHY, & EP: ABC & ANALECTS.[86]

    This last, what I'd liked, reading the first part of same, in HUDSON, etc. At least just that laconicness, etc. A tone.

Anyhow, confusion per usual; have a goddamn court gig tomorrow, on this place, & damn little to offset the bastard who pulls us in. But want to be moving anyhow—this is one way I guess.

This goddamn fractured item—was to have been, like they say, "much longer . . ." But this much worth the time perhaps? You say. I get hit with that whole hell, precisely, of IMAGE & NARRATIVE, and you shd register as oracle. Ok.

    Temptation, perpetual, to pull out on ANY suggestion of, relevance as visual, etc. Like: to say tree—gets me into particular tree, leaves, my first

having kissed anyone, so emphatically, under NO tree, etc.
WOW.)

THE DEAD

> You cannot succor me,
> you cannot change.
> Williams[87]

The unconversational. The pedantic & perhaps unwanted
(dead) — these mentors

The dead. The dead who are here, and otherwise —
and otherwise it is this, perhaps

Inconsolable. But unconceived, unbiased by no act
being not act, — the dead, etc. That she should die?

And I who loved her. What
of me

It comes back to prose, I wish to god I could get back to it — the
many damn occurrences, now to be used somehow. You feel the
whole works slip, going on without the vaguest tie-in.

Lines from same, longer cast:

Say that to them.

Complex of what was, or is, or (evermore), etc.
That was to be it all, and was no animation more (I finally READ
S/ ANTONY & CLEOPATRA !!!!)
than wanting.

Than wanting that, etc.
Say that to them.

Than wanting that . . .

Say that to them.

You, who, etc. Say that to them.

Etc. "The dead are passage. / Damn them."

All of which, not much. Thinking of that woman, the Princess,[88]
& she doesn't send back the copy of A/ ; did you ever hear
anything from her? Damn well suppose not, being, she must be,
such a christly dull woman.

("ABC" looks very cool, have never read it; only those references,
in other bks/ etc.
                    Damn nicely put together, at this first look.)

Hitting that, "O western wynd . . ." in an unwieldy collection of
"English Verse" (and *what* an intro/ — was Aldington, etc.)[89] : either
that, or that concision, to hump up so, SO damn much ON IT :
or what the hell is the excuse?
                    (Last night, Ann reading: poems,
etc. Faced with that fact, either you make it of such a fact, an
intensity, a displacement of the given (otherwise), 'this world . . . ,'
or no use whatsoever. She cd, did, put down so much, saying:
why does he say it so, etc. In such, shares with the common
reader — but they damn well have rights at that.)

Did the Gasp/ ever come back with any more ideas? I note
splurge, bk/ side of this pamphlet (Ez' list back last year).
                                        Hatt?
What goes there? That was damn exciting biz; also, past letter Cid
C/ sd he was hoping for a bk/ : No/ 8 of ORIGIN? Give me the
news!

So it goes, all quiet finally: life, etc. Is ok.

Write as soon as you
can make it. All our love to you — how does K/ look? (It wouldn't
really be DESCRIPTION!)

Bob

[Fontrousse, Aix-en-Provence]
Monday [19 November 1951]

Chas/

One in from you, and want to get this in with the
foregoing. Am flat on back at present; horrible wet weather &
finally got flu, & spending the day here, to see if that will
help.

Anyhow, rock-bottom. Don't really know now what to do;
france is so impossible a place for us — this house hell for all of us,
so damn wet & cramped, & no way to heat, etc. Nothing, after 4
months; not a single house open.

Wanted to ask you if the place
in Lerma was still open, perhaps? Have to do something soon;
simply dying here, in more damn ways than I like to think
of.

This whole place (europe) is *dead*, there is the war coming, so
surely you can *smell* it; death everywhere I have been.

It kills everything, every damn day; hopeless trying to lift out of
it; makes it all a greyness, and horrid for the kids who should
have none of this weight on them, or not like they have it here.

Well, enough. Is there any alternative. I damn well wonder; I get
so I can't believe it.

Thanks for the go on that thing for G/; I wish I knew what he was up to. He said he was to be here, mid-November; but I don't think he ever got out of Freiburg. Nothing but those 2 books, for over a month; they were mailed from there.

As for visitors: just B/ & MA, & that wasn't too good. This place kills everything, even one's damn friends.

Let me leave off; again, notes were very damn good. Have been too sick to get over to see Ashley, but once out of here, will do it immediately. Perhaps he will come since I don't show up; will hope so.

Terrific abt the bk *&* recordings; sounds tremendous. Re Bot/ Os/: if you have a spare copy, will send it on to her, certainly. I mean, this one I have: I wd honestly like to keep hold of. You say.

Tell what the Gasp/ does; or did. Ok. Yrs from the depths/

Bob

(To you, too!)
All love to Con, —I wish every damn thing were babies, etc. hell with it, but it *is* deadly here, at least at present

Have they done BULLFIGHT[90] already?

[*Added at top of letter*:]
No Kingfishers/ G wd never sent it on, damn him.

Tell Corman to go die, eh? I get to loathe him *altogether.*

[*At top of p. 2 of letter*:]
#2 [*of* Fragmente] not out yet as far, ie., as I know.

[*In margin*:]
Do send DUNCAN; that cuts down the others; Emerson was already out. Somehow, & I loathe the whole shitty biz, also at present.

[*A portion of a letter from Corman enclosed, speaking of an essay on poetics he has recently written ("Some Notes Toward a New Prosody"), described as "overlapping" Olson's "Projective Verse," with Creeley's comment:*]
This *does* it, I mean, what the hell to think? He will not see that demonstration is worth all this blather, that, having *one* formulation *in print* & a perfectly adequate one to boot, — to load on dilutions can *only* make it that much harder to get thru *to* the point, to make clear the necessary demonstration. I damn well will not eat this. It seems rationalization of a damn dangerous sort.

[Fontrousse, Aix-en-Provence]
Thursday November 22/ (?) [1951]

Dear Charles,

Yrs in, and gets me out of bed, being, finally, all that could; the fever still holds on a little, but damned if I can bother at this juncture. The Bold Spirit, etc.

What you say of Kasper: very damn fine. That he came, under those circumstances, knowing, certainly, the *reality* of Ez' dispositions on such matters, what counts. I don't honestly think it will take too much talk if he did that on his own hook.

What you say here, of what it could be: too much, it *is* all that seems to be worth the attention. I would take it just as you say, i.e., maintain the contact, keep these relevances & possibilities very *clear* in his mind, and let the yeast work of itself. What they all forget: it takes *new* men each time, — simple categories of age & energy. He couldn't do it for any of us now; not to keep up is not to care very much, I think.

Cid: copies of #3 just in, and they kill all further interest, or chance of it. I was damn well shocked; the colors, so dead, and all of it seeming to have gone papery, or something like that.

My god, are those two men an incredible *dull* pair: a shame, a damn shame for them, that they were given such space, in such a juxtaposition. No favor, certainly. I felt *sodden* after reading the first few; damn well loaded, lead-like, plodding shit, etc.

To hit yrs: well, it *was* another climate, or what the hell. A damn certain *air*. And I *did* love it *very, very much.*

The horrible continuum of 'moons' that I am the last of, there : phew. How about that. And Hatson's prose is stinking, not the slightest taste in having used it. Inept. He is. She is damn well unspeakable; whole thing obscene, damnit, simple filth.
The woodcuts I didn't like at all; but perhaps the dimensions noted wd improve them. The shrink seems final.

Harry S[mith]/s story: that beginning is cool; incidentally, have known sd man for a long time now, I don't think he'll ever make it much beyond. He gets this far, but farther: goes cute, gets pleased, etc. This is ok, even so, I thought. Seemed worth using.

But it is a *fearful* issue; literally, frightening. I think it is the sign of some damn slip, or to hell with it. It just seems over, goodby, etc.

Will get the copy of A/ off to B/O/ directly; sorry to have waited on this. Ok. And thanks for sending the copy on to Laubies, will write him too, and hope to have typed a copy of the Pro/ Verse, so he can have that in his hands, for whatever; I thought, perhaps Cahiers du Sud?

Laubies has the exhibition there now to occupy him (he sd, he got another one too) and as well, the Cantos to settle in; but I do think he'll be it on Fr/ outlets; he does move, etc. He got, for one thing, an invitation for Rainer to come in here, when no one else

could make it; I had asked every damn one I could think of.
Aldington was talking about the last war, etc. Incidentally,
Aldington never came; I don't think he now will. Ho.

Here's an item, will amaze & confound you, like they say: I got,
with yrs, a very polite & carefully labored 2 pages from the New
Mexico Quarterly, asking for prose, and signed by our old
friend:
      Kenneth Lash.[91]

The explanation: I have a friend there, Race Newton, also Bud
was, of course, and it's where they were living, the house, that
Lash now is in. Anyhow, he's editing said magazine at this point,
"I've been editor for all of two weeks, and one of my first concerns
is to get better stories." (He liked, however, The UH . . .)
                          He also
notes an odd-sound dep't: a 'Poet Signature' — "a group of 5-10
poems by one poet with a short introduction by Honig (character
who wrote the bk/ on Lorca, etc.)"[92]

All of which may add up to the proverbial, but will try it, in any
case; am most foot-loose, at this point. Also, will tell him to write
you for material, particularly for that apparent rubric (sounds
lovely, —   !) and anyhow. And anyhow. I mean, will try
anything, — once.

Will send him THE PARTY; first act of war, overt, re Mr.
Corman & Cie.

(Fuck you, Cid Corman, like they say.)

Probably an utter ass; I read the damn essay in WAKE — ah
. . . It was mostly flabby, but this letter is the same.
                           Rather odd
that he should want prose of mine, on the basis of that one thing
which seems to have pleased the New Critics, also. However.

Robert Creeley with sons David and Thomas, 1951.
Creeley papers, Washington University Libraries.

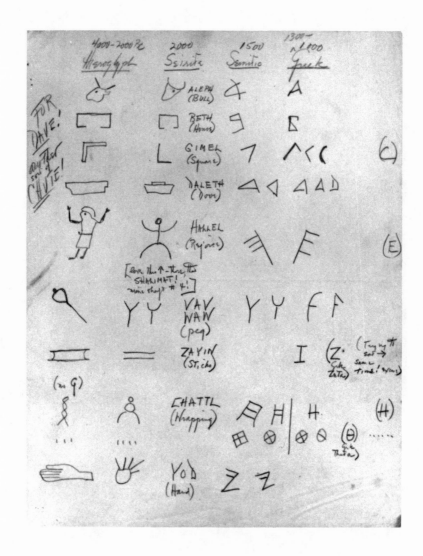

Alphabet chart drawn by Charles Olson (see p. 37).
(above and opposite) *Creeley papers, Washington University Libraries.*

		KAPH (Palm)	⊻ Ⴤ	K K
		LOYAH (Loop)	6 ⅃	∧L∧(N) LL
		MAIM (Water)	⅂ ⅄	⋀ ⋀
		MAHASH (Snake)	⅂ ⅄	N N
		SAMEKH (Fish)	⧧ ⧣ ⧧	⧧ (Ξ) Greek XI
		AYIN (Eye)	O	O O
		PEH (Mouth)	⁊ ⅃	⌈ ⌈ (Π) P P
		QAOW (Tape)	φ φ	φ φ θ Q Q
		RESH (Head)	⅂	P P (P) R R
		SHIN (Tooth)	W	⟨ ⟨ ⟨(Σ)⟩⟨
		TAV, TAW (Mark)	X T	T T

On pro-
sody. I probably wont send you the essay, simply because
I dont have the time to sit down & copy it.   Same reason
Charley wont see it, either.   Only Achilles has seen it &
it has his blessing, as apt and necessary. OK. My feel
is that just as mathematics achieved a new status when
Euclid was put aside, and advanced from new premisses, so,
I think, that prosody requires a new orientation, new premisses, less fixed in mode, than any set down now. And
certainly metrics all the way back to the Greeks, as formu-
lated, misses the boat of our current ways (& has actually
long been outmoded--as witness Shakespware & Donne, in particular).   It isnt a matter of saying that Pound & Williams,etc
are NOT poets, but realizing that prosodic formulations are at
fault when such writing is beyond piddling accommodations and
apologies.   My push is a larger accommodation, based on the
ear (time-space) as corollary) as center.   It overlaps with
PV, of course.   Any formulation, as I think you know,
is an approximation, a generalization, that must, to justify
its being, be capable of accommodating with reasonable exactitude
the specifics to which it is applied.   The ancient metrics,
which Ransom & Winters & Shapiro--our current agents--saddle
us with, are not adequate for contemporary writing. They havent
been adequate for centuries, but never so clearly before. If
you can think of any particulars that might go with such a push,
please send them on. Possibly a discussion of motion in your own
poems.   And if you think I'm off the beam anywheres, please explain. This is going to be one of the major thrusts in ORIGIN &
I'd just as soon face the fire of friends first.   Throw the
most difficult questions at me.   I MUST KNOW AS MUCH AS POSSIBLE.

I know I've only given you a rough sketch of my argument, but I
wd appreciate any thoughts that come to you, that seem essential.

Cid Corman's November 1951 letter to Robert Creeley, with
Creeley's November 19th note to Charles Olson (see p. 158).
Olson papers, University of Connecticut Library.

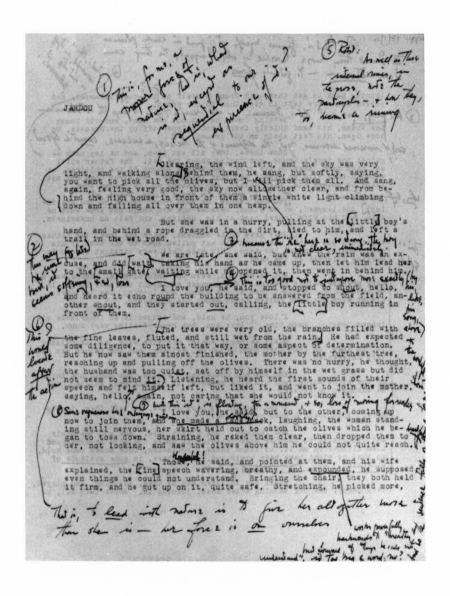

First paper of Robert Creeley's typescript of "Jardou" with handwritten comments by Charles Olson.
Creeley papers, Washington University Libraries.

Charles Olson, Sr. in the Worchester Continentals (standing far right). See note VIII. 109.
Charles Olson papers, University of Connecticut Library.

Shit, one wd damn well like it clean; but how, when & where.

Bud told me, Lash had left a lot of his bks/ there, in the house; they used to read them, all the DHL had little notes, "he should have, etc."

Really, a damn press : clean. I honestly wonder if we would be, either of us, capable in any sense of those pomposities of which Cid is? I mean, straight. If that's what it gets you to, such pretensions, easy leanings, I would keep out, I would say all of us, both, keep out. No damn good.

What you note re Hatt, etc. Something, jesus, something should break; it does, it always has, tho I hate that sense of it. I wd rather be breaking cleaner somehow than by such old saws, etc. But I do figure there is the means, and the pickup now to hand, of Kasper, of Hatt, I mean, simply the added weight gained this last yr, by the act of ORIGIN. Credit *just there* to Cid C/ — I will always wonder just why he did it in my own case.

So it is a fine damn day, at that, as my mother, god bless her, would say. She has that inevitable lean to the good, that, silver-lining biz which still brings tears to my fucking eyes, etc, faced with it.
      One time I knew a man, in Arlington, more or less of a drunk, but prided himself on how he could get into so many football games, baseball games, etc., without paying. He made a career of sorts out of it; working along, bumming etc., and this the main thing. He told me of divers times, etc., all more or less mechanical, I mean, simple disguises, or methods, etc. Not very interesting. But one night he told me about his mother, who lived up there in Arlington, off on one of those side streets, and I guess he didn't go home anymore, and hadn't for some time. He said she'd bought him a new suit, once, and after he'd pawned it, he couldn't go home, or so he said. But he did see her after Roosevelt had died, just after, and was surprised that she was so interested, i.e., she'd bought all kinds of newspapers, and had read every acc't of the death, and the disposition of the effects, like they say, and

so on. She herself saved stamps, and had a more or less usual collection, not having any money, etc. He couldn't figure out why the interest in Roosevelt, and so asked her, and she told him she wanted to know who got his stamps. Roosevelt not a collector of same, he wondered how the hell she had got that into her head, and found out, finally, that she was thinking of all the letters he must have got from foreign countries, and couldn't herself believe that he hadn't taken the stamps off the envelopes, and kept them.

The first time I ever knew, I suppose one says it so, any 'criminal' it was a man out on the Mass. State Reformatory Farm; we lived not so far from that, a friend's father supervised it.
                                    This man was
in for illicit entry—chronic. He was a trusty, about 27, or so. They had caught him in at the Boston Gardens. What happened: when the acrobats were on, all eyes upward, etc., they caught sight of this man sitting above same on the steel girders. He'd got in by scaling the wall, coming in thru an open skylight, and was sitting there, watching the show, on the girders that hold up the roof.

The old lady back of us, me sick, etc., loaned Ann some magazines, & I have been improving my french like they say, and fast. I.e., you try it:

"Non, jamais mon petite camarades ou les vieux amis de Papa, experts à me presser dans les coins, ne m'ont émue ainsi, etc., etc., etc."

Not very unusual, I suppose. Not too inspiring. However, life is singularly dull, or was, until yrs came. Odd that it should have woken me up so damn quick, and it did—anyhow, it was crazy to have it, and to get back some damn sense of purpose, even that piddling little 'purpose' they do drool so much about.

Old lady hasn't the slightest idea what she's given us, and they are pretty cool at that, because she doesn't read herself. Her son does, however, but he doesn't know about any of this, i.e., out all day working, and the mother feels it best if he should not know, etc. Another conspirator, in short.

I don't know, as said so damn many times—this country is, in most ways, as repellent as I expect they can get; but it is resistant, and damn that attractiveness, because it holds me like glue. I don't turn it off simply, or even away from it.

I wish I could move about a little more; Ann is just off to see the consul, i.e., our papers got all fucked up, and the local officials won't give us clearance, which means, as well, no car until we have same—so hope that may mean something. I.e., once we do have the car, now all payed for, it will be better. With kids, with the two of them, and our own habits, it is very hard to make any kind of sortie, or whatever, as things are.

Not much wish to know the people, I mean, the ones one gets somehow 'introduced' to—I never like it. I simply want some set into what ever is moving, or nothing. Either gratuitous, or simple current, —or why bother. The fatuousness of the fr/ intellectual, from what I've seen of him, in bks/ etc., doesn't need the physical fact to clinch it, etc.

Simply, —which is the road to

I do miss the New Hampshire biz; some nights, we'd got going on chickens, and wish you might have seen the letter Ira wrote me on the last Brockton show, i.e., too damn long, honestly, to quote, and not quoting all, not worth it. But it was crazy, —it's all crazy, that way some of them have there. Clearness. It is a special light.

But I want, or I don't want, but wish only to be more simple, I mean, simply moved—somehow to get as clean as can be, to move on the most minimum means. All directions, that tension. You get so set, so particular in the dulled sense, sitting too long in the one world. Not that this is the counter, etc. I want this mobility, not physical, in any case.

It sinks me very often, damn well into some kind of death, a feeling of simple chill & hate. Not at all good.

What other damn way to make, I wonder. The fucking world is
such a density, a damn idiot-squeezed place.

It was that hit me,
reading you on Shakespeare, and trying to feel how size, of that
precise sort you note, is lost in current examples. The dimensions
have done an odd twist, I think, and I mean it no more facilely
than you did yr same question (i.e., this is not the old bunkum re
universals, etc.).

All questions of tension, or the play allowable,
or the leadings. These seem all bound now, or wrapped too surely,
or tightly. One thing never leading to another in 99 out of 100
instances. Melville size, parts of Lawrence—a question of *play*, of
what is being aimed at, what is considered 'relevant,' what is the
taking of the word 'material.'

They damn well took off our skins
with that psychoanalysis, etc. Fools to let them do that. Now they
tell us all about it, but in so many goddamn segments, volumes,
etc.

Yr hit: how he *wd* (Shakespeare) say *something* on
everything, or simply: *whatever*.

23rd

Fever keeps on a little, or does, enough to bother, when I get up,
but to hell with it; so damn cold, raw, now, good one can sit in
bed, etc.

Ann got there, yesterday, to find it was damn well Thanksgiving,
and wdn't you damn well know it. The same damn thing
happened to her a wk earlier, i.e., she got there to find they were
closed on Sat/s—peculiar to the US, etc.

Anyhow, anyhow,
sometime: those damn papers. Whole thing absolutely screwed at
this point, we were issued a visa back in May, i.e., we applied,
like they say, & were notified, here, that we'd got one from the
Foreign Ministry in Paris; but. . . , the local officials won't believe

it, and won't check, and the letter is written in english, and the official translator moved to Nimes six months ago. Oh well, etc.

Thanksgiving: a little difficult, or it was, so thrust into same, to feel very much, yesterday. I loathe, I get to admit, etc., all such goddamn commercialisms, tho this one, well, it is damn hard to hit any not damn pawed, etc. Anyhow, I can live without them.

Am half-way thru, a little more, a copy of PRO/ VERSE, which, done, I'll send on to Laubies, but I sd this? Yes. Anyhow, will have that in his hands, by, wd say, Monday; can finish it tomorrow morning, and Ann can get it off in the noon, or afternoon. Etc. Ok.

Returning the magazines, just now, to the old lady, the son was also there, Ann says, and edged round to the pile, on the table, to see if they were ok, and shuffled thru to one particular picture of a yng lady with a fan, etc., his favorite apparently. Mine too, as it happened. The mother looked thru, a couple, seeing him do it, and hit on some horrors, and said, o, what a nice looking young lady, etc., to get: not *that* one, mother, you don't understand at all!

My wife, like they say — a minute ago she finally made me some lemonade, i.e., have been here a week now, and I think she got the lemons some two days ago, and the lemonade was brought to the bedside about 10 minutes before these words, etc. But it seems she needed the pitcher, so I have just drunk some four *quick* glasses of lemonade.

That wasn't the point, etc. They always say, but you *asked* for it . . . Four glasses.

Sometimes I think I don't hit her *enough.*

But she is very nice, *even so.* I think Lawrence was very acute on these matters — the fact one will never know, etc., or that should one hit anyone who tries, so, to know you : run.

(Sipping my fifth glass, here, etc. Wish it would mail, etc.)

Reading thru origin, again, etc. — I wonder if you wd honestly try
to pick, call it, 2 or 3 of my own poems, for possible issue in sd
Am/ gig? Do you think that wd be crowding? I can't, jesus I can't,
put more than a minimum of either of these men in — in fact I can't
see putting *any* in at this moment, having made that dreary,
dreary haul thru, etc. Perhaps Sam's THE HURT[93] — but the thing
is, think of some poor german, liking it, and spending the rest of
his life translating, or looking for, Sam — thinking, why he doesn't
get anything, is the fault of himself, that he can't read it well
enough, or the language has some ineffable *flavor*, some tone — I
couldn't face it. So? It would be inexcusable. Mean.

Tom now down here with me, Dave still asleep, his nap, etc. T/
has a real crazy face at this point; everything big, eyes, nose,
mouth, etc. And the biggest teeth I've ever seen on a baby in my
life. Too much. Has that old man's neck they all get; weird
combo, of the two ends sometimes, or so it looks.

And how goes it there with yr own? The notes have been a damn
great pleasure, hope that it all goes well. I had a letter from Helen
(my sister) two days back, and she said she'd continue to forward
whatever things of her kid's carries over, i.e., as the kid outgrows
them, she'll send them on, etc. Abt a 5 or so month start on you,
if I have my fucking dates straight, and I rarely do. Anyhow.
Damn good those got to you ok; often she means to, like they
say, but somehow doesn't. (I say that for my wife's benefit; a little
bitter on this score, I fear.)

With Bronk: I didn't get this impassable *heaviness*, until I read
them just now en bloc; *sullen* things, all of them. Petulant as all
hell. I think Sam gets beyond that, sometimes, but *such* an old
maid, so often.

I hate that continual : "we . . ." Speak for yrself, etc.

Anyhow, got to get thru this damn Am/ issue somehow. I'll tell you what did most attract me to Bronk, way back at the beginning: The Mind's Landscape, etc.[94] The way the rhythms make it there, the brokenness. As playful as he gets, I now see.

Somehow.

Jesus, *don't* forget the Duncan, or as K[enneth]/ Patchen used to say: Send in yr 2nd team, God . . .[95]

The biz of recording sounds too much; what is the whole layout on same, i.e., will there be just the I MAX, and then the bk, etc. Or will there be more recorded?

Goddamn, IF one cd get the wherewithal for a *real* damn GO, I mean, bks/ recordings, ALL of it. Well, anyhow . . .

It's a very *sane* thing, that idea to record, with bk/, damn well *fine.*

Sooner or later, and always more or less clear, I'd say: just as you say, got to get a direct means to issue, just as Ez wrote that: to publish the work of, blah, blah, blah, etc., and myself without idiotic and unnecessary delay . . .[96] Jesus, that *is* excellent advice.

Anyhow, anyhow.

Keep them coming; need them very much. Will leave the backside of this for further 'reflections,' etc. Perhaps a few odd recipes. Ok.

Write soon. All best love to you all,

Bob

Will get to that letter you noted directly, i.e., the one written just before the baby. Ok.

[*Added in margin:*]
24th: PV done, & goes off—also A to Bott/ Oscura. Ok.

[Black Mountain, N.C.]

Sat Nov 24 [1951]—and a damn shame i did take it worth while
to spend much time with the Gasp: he did not leave until
yesterday morning. But it was Tuesday night I gave him (actually
without planning any such thing) the mickey finn: i read him the
Gerhardt, & exactly what happened inside him I cannot say, only,
that, he was unable to speak, was obviously forcing back (it was
that sort of compression in a person which surely does prove that
the Old Man was right to say psychoses are substitutes for
character, this so resembled psychosis. And was simultaneously the
moment of decision for him, whether, then & there, he would or
would not deny me because of EP's warning. I could not peek over
his shoulder, so, i do not know to whom he then & there wrote a
penny post card, but I shld imagine it was to EP, saying,
announcing, he was here, and that was that.[97]

        I did not see him at
all Wed, being involved in a Board meeting in the afternoon, and
a faculty meeting until after midnight in the evening (it was time
well spent, for i opened up the issue of what pedagogy excuses
itself these days, except one which rests on ideas as only resident
in things & in actions, and so, where, otherwhere than, the guy in
front of yez)

    And when i saw him Thursday, and took him to his
2 AM bus, he was in recoil of a sorts, tho begging i give him the
book (selected O)

    (As I sd to Con last night after I had poured
out my final answer to Emerson—he sent me yesterday the END, a
letter fr him in [i.e. and] Eckman charging me with failure to
return the proofs!—this is some moment in yrs and my affairs! viz:

(1) you pulling out of Origin   (2) i having pulled out of
Praises   (3) me taking it altogether careful abt going ahead with
the Gasp!

> (What I did say was, that, any moment he feels able to act
> toward me as clearly & directly as his original interest in me
> stood for—that is, before Ez threw the roadblock, & saddled
> the guy with Horton—then, sez I, not only am I with you,
> Kasper, but I shall hope that Creeley will go with me, maybe
> Duncan, and that I and the others will stand ready to offer
> restoration of texts as well as Ez

> which was not a turning away fr the present reality: I also
> proposed that, if the slogan was, as it is, MAN STANDING
> BY HIS WORD,[98] then, it wld honor me, and make Ez make
> sense, if, at the head of the mast of the house of Kasper &
> Horton, it stood: EDITORS, Pound & Olson!
> > And to this
> bold play, by god, the boy rose up beautiful

My attack, thruout, was not on Ez, but on anonymity &
conspiracy—and that this sort of business I would not wish my
work, or the work of my friends, to be intricated

> > As I sd to you
Sunday last, my impression is, there is small chance, for the
present, the boy can spend his present excitement in EP—or feel he
can afford to lose the company it enables him to keep, eh?
> > But it
strikes me my job now is to keep open all roads thru to him. And
with that in mind I have sent him back to Washington to stay in
my house there and to call up Crosby, asking him to take over the
distribution (personal, not by way of his house) of *y & x*; also the
Broadsides, from here; also, hammering, yr work; also,
distribution, as a proper function for him to find out all there is to
find out
> So, if you have any further ideas, let me have em: he is
not, I think, what Blackburn sd: he is, rather, a green goose of

some intelligence whom Ez got the 1st crack at —

and surely Ez
never missed that sort of a trick, eh?

But what mattered was, yr own beautiful letters, even tho, for
you, the bottom they come out of must be a beaut: both Con and
I send you both the deepest love, & for god's sake ask anything
we have:

(1) i expected Crosby here for Thanksgiving, but no
word at all, even, that she is back in Washington:: do write her
instantly to c/o Morgan Co., Paris, on the chance she is there,
and knows a house, either, in yr parts, or, what I take is a much
better change for you now than to Lerma: ITALY

((((I advise
against Lerma, simply, that it is a big shift, and still, there, you
will have that isolation of language, and, to a greater extent, no
bizness of affairs — THOUGH, by god, I'd take those Indians as
friends of moment over any literary birds, olive farmers, or any
such, eh?

If you are set to go, then sail from Marseilles aboard the
Compagnie Generale Maritime, for Vera Cruz, and let me know,
and I'll guarantee you can get a house in Lerma: there are plenty,
and at a better price, I think, than the one we had ((this we found
out, at the end of our stay:

AND I'LL HITCHHIKE DOWN TO
SEE YOU! for I also know now how to get directly there: bum to
Key West, auto ferry to Havana, and fr H, bum a ride on lumber
& sugar boats to Progresso: from P it is only a four hr bus! I'll
come for Xmas — shipping Con to NE for same with her sisters!

Anyhow, take our sense of yr despair fr yr letter to tell you it is
beautiful, all you say there, abt the damnableness of these
things:

and that you confirm, on the spot, my own assumptions
Europe is dead, is damned helpful, god help you that you have to
suffer the proof!

Goddamn it, who do I know — nobody? — there,
to be of use?

Look, why not write Cagli — Rome — 24 via terme
deciane and say fer crissake this is an emergency, and, what has
he there? As you know, he is a real Joe but silent, two years: and
I figure if you write, saying I sd to, then, he is such a straight
guy, and of a heart, he'll, rise to it — ask him where you can land

Will figure more on this.

What I wanted to talk to you abt is
(crazy, in these presses of yr own things, and my own!),
ANTONY & CLEOPATRA

it is the very text of objectism — that,
& Homer's O, is all that I return to with lasting pleasure. And for
like reason, that, here, life is held in its own hand, without
intermissions of interpretations of same

It is, as any such thing has
to be, neither comedy nor tragedy: even these are divisions which
idiots & ironists only could be satisfied with.

I am so caught up I
propose to examine this verse, the linage & the image: for behind
the play is a measurement system of astonishing depth: a fly & an
eagle are both left of the same size, orbs. In fact, the orb is the
magic of everything: size, in space or in time, is metempsychosed
out of their deceptive formulative aspects. And I shld imagine that
it took the man six years of taking everything as a knot the size of
a fist to suddenly find the knot the size of a fist become an orb the
same size. It is wholly mysterious, in the same sense that the way
the Odyssey holds itself in its own hand is likewise.

In any case,
this is the vision I shld wish to offer an equivalence of: and do,
RobT, read it, and let me have yr sense of same: it moved me
again this week, as it moved me the two previous times I read it.
And I had forgot how imaginably consequent it is in my life: this
is physicality without materialism, morality without character,
intensity without spirit doctrines, time without eternity, and space
without horizontality, or, better, without science:

i am in love

[*broken off*]

[Black Mountain, N.C.]

Mon   ROBT   (Nov 24 [*i.e.* 26], 51)   I figure I got on to this
reading of Shks kick one way & am coming off it another, and
propose, if I can interest you, to figure it out. That is, as you'll
know, there been two questions about the man kept coming up
last yr & ½: (1) him on sex; (2) him, descriptive

The drop, just past, was: to get in on (1), juxtaposed to Herodotus
& Omer (that is, had noticed in Herodotus, a curious non-fix on
sex & all ancillary matters, a still unexamined tendence to move
without any apparent phallic root

                              on Homer, of course, i take it
he is as firm (Calypso, say, as sign) (or Nausiacaa, whom Joyce so
stupidly citifies)[99] as writer ever was — & that is somewhat
surprising, in that I wld assume that Homer is the isinglass who
cleared up the old clots in the wine which was the Cybele or
Prostitute Goddess all the way back behind him to the Venus of
Mentone, or whatever had been the fertility (& without any
particular humanist measure at all

    ((((hunch: that you square off against even the word luf, for
       strictest reason, that, what still stays humanistic is even
       here — that DHL is, patently, no, our father in his
       recognitions in this sphere

       with this difference, that, he fought the battle, and now, it is
       us who have the recognition without the necessity to argue
       the point

yet, the recognition, has not cleared any of us back to
ground, and until any one of us (you in BLUE, surely, most
noticeably, and in ITS, &, THE LOVER, close in to the
running wheels) keep making the substance without
humanistic reference (or trailings) then there is still this
jobtodo))))

anyhow (this is what I'm pushing on, I'd guess, & not yet there,
too twisted, myself, eh?)

     I picked up on S, with TROILUS & C, &
MEASURE, & last night was surprised to find myself reading
PERICLES, PRINCE OF TYRE ((which, *definitely*, is as little his as
anything credited to him, a crazy piece of pot-work for his
Company, if anything. Yet, the damn thing is exactly the crazy
sort of romance, & sheer tale, that, Herodotus is loaded with!

OK. But here's the jump: instead (once in him) of finding any
particular answer of (1), or (2), for that matter ((on (2), a
contrary)), I have come up with a complete revision *upward* of my
obligation & pleasure in him

     NUMBER 1: antony & C—

           (what i
was saying to you Sat PLUS—

  plus *composition*: my god, Rob't, how this man put his thought
       away *behind* the act of his story

            that is, his
   image & linage—there, how cool & clear he
   did his work

          & how definitely
he dealt with each thing under hand *in its terms*

         My confidence
abt A & C is, simply, that, this content I am most at home
with—this lighted world (I think I sd, this is Homer's, and I don't
know if anyone else's—and the act of composition is to hold what
holds itself as firmly & directly as though the maker was a hand
holding each thing in such a way each thing & all the things

together making a thing were free-wheeling, suspended as the earth
in space, moving

The play is the purest act of *motion & solidity* after the Odyssey

But even when he's off — as in T & C, and M for M — he is
working like mad to do the job therein
                                    & utmost flexibility: (T&C
        is carefully poised from a viewpoint inside the Greeks and
        outside the Trojans, making the Greeks the ones he's pissing
        on — and what a "squirting" (to use WCW's euphemism)
                                                            (in
        M for M, it is all one thing, life vs death — and exactly even
        in the using of the words: a straight direct confrontation of
        the Christian, actually Roman Catholic, position on DEATH
        versus the non-Christian (don't think a word will do except
        maybe "Elizabethan") hungry for life, for flesh,
        pleasures
                (what, in A & C is illuminated as what I wld, of
        course, tab OBJECTISM

(all the crap of pagan, as contrast to Christian, is undone by this
very man! one can see him working, through these six yrs of
puzzlement on sex (1601-1607: Hamlet to A & C), *against* — or at
least in question of, the sanction system of his society
(Christianity), and going toward himself to find out and state some
other sanctions

What rides me, is, how, each thing under hand is driven at, hard:
how thoroly he was attacking, every goddamned thing, never
coasting, so far as I can see, for a split second:
                                        it is very beautiful

And the issue, I'd hunch, is, A & C (Lear, granted, as, like — &
written, by god, just abt the same time — that is, like in the sense
of the thoroness, coming off, but, the "world" of it wholly different
from A & C:

that is, in A & C, multiples make the motion—there is no death at all in A & C (where, in Lear, death is the pain, the dying, 1st, of the Fool, from a cold, & then Cordelia, from a mischievous failure of a messenger to save her from Edmund's order she should be hung, & Lear, himself, of a broken heart

(the only death in A & C, is, just such a death, Enobarbus, & crying, like some thing in a desert, to the moon, talking to her as what's left him, having run out on Antony

IN

FACT, the moon in A & C is the hidden image of *change*—it is crazy, how the sun & nature are not allowed in to A & C, how the play is unbeaten by these violences, stands (actually) in their light (the day is what this play is, the *objects* of it stand clear, yet, the change or motion of it is all done by such waning permanents as moon, rivers, oceans: WATER

day & water, the whatever balance the play has (but there is no such symmetry—in fact, there is an asymmetry in the verse line & the image which annihilates balance, yet keeps motion, & exactly such "conservative" force as moon motion & water motion—christ, how beautiful it is

But back to this *multiples* biz; ((ex: as A dies, C cries: O the
               crown of the earth doth melt
or, better, *motion* of all *possibles*

((it even gets to a point of poising where it is possible for S to put the solid-melting as the metaphysic (if anyone likes such a word) in the image of CANDY!

he has Antony, I think,
use a wonderful verb "discandy"—yes, the lines are:

All come to this? The hearts
That spaniel'd me at heels, to whom I gave
Their wishes, do discandy, melt their sweets
On blossoming Caesar; and this pine is bark'd
That overtopp'd them all.

One conjunction gives me answer to Blackburn, whom, you will
recall, took IN COLD HELL as weakened by mixed
metaphors!

      Well, last Monday, I made a disc for Hatt — for the vol
(with recording) he plans under title I, MAXIMUS. In cutting I,
M, I decided to fill both sides, for the hell of it, and read I C H
(as well as the Round & Cannon, & the Tower).

                        Hearing it
afterwards, I C H was damned difficult to follow just because it
does push its metaphors, does thrust them on

                    but Christ, Rob't, it
is the only way a man of my order does know reality

                      and i'm
pissproud sure that Blackburn is giving me bad counsel, the
counsel of a milder nature, when he says, mixed

shit on such well-behaved meotions or mexpressions: I'm damned
sure one of the reasons Dante-Provence got so fucking much
attention from those elders, and now their younger followers,
regimen, areas & all, is, that, they have not known confusion!

Well, fuck em. Will dig my own field, wild furrowed or whatever.
For what I wanted also to toss up to you today, is, the second
thing (reversing what I sort of think I went in to Shks for) I have
taken away from this furious reading of this man:

                  that drama,
  done with his attention, has an advantage so far as time in
  narrative goes (Ann's statement, as tho it had never happened
  before the reader read it)

                just because the play is written with
the knowledge that, IT IS GOING TO HAPPEN RIGHT IN
FRONT OF YR EYES, GODDAMN EM

                    that this solidity of
present action in front of is something Mr S calculated on, &
yet, did not depend on, that is, that what I had earlier swiped
at him for — description — does not turn out to be accurate

                        that
the very advantage of his sort of theatre is, that, because it is

live peoples presently showing what is happening, any descriptive act is as you & i might, in talk, tell, and with no loss of force simply that it is us telling, and present, & so, the problem of fiction is hugely set aside?

that is, it struck me, thinking abt the effect of Enobarbus' description of Cleo on barge meeting Antony at Cydnus, that, just because Cleo & A have just left the stage (Alexandria) and Eno is talking Rome the fact that this incident precedes the action of the play makes its telling tremendously *past* (& so, in the context, tremendously dimensionally present, in the sense that, any active present is *also* past, — exactly that point you have been so alert to, and have, say, in the context you put the two of I T S (the beer table) in, allowed for the remembering to live as act of the present

And so far as SEQUENCE goes, of course here, drama, again as live action by solid people in front of curious eyes, jumps

Well, now that it's sd, wonder if it makes any point worth making

but it does for me in this sense that, i am

quite clarified by the discovery of how very "active" the VERSE of

these plays is in disclosing *not* character, not plot, not that

damned cliche apothegmic wisdom of the bourgeois genius, but

rather, the inner laws of the subject under hand, how these metrics

shift & how the verse itself is not mere skin & voice but is, rather,

the energy & the action, the PRESENT

(and i may make this importance clearer by suggesting how
verse outside drama or since him is only lyric in the sense
that it sings the man as writer rather than the subject under
hand

is that a distinction worth making? it sounds a little
as tho i am saying the dramatic is dramatic! but i don't
think that is all of it: it seems to me that this distinction
flows in so much of our continuing exchanges

on prose & verse, & on narrative now:

ex., for me, yr prose, in
BLUE, is, as rhythmic mastery, as much a management of the
presentness of that tent-show & the instant of his scream & the
throw-back to "she" in the store the day before & the consequence
of itself forward on you, the narrator, as the scrupulous care with
which the "telling" is managed

and i am also suggesting, i think, that — so far at least as verse
goes — my increasing interest in drama as such is due to like
causes, that, presentness & sequence in verse demand
narrative

and i'd also guess drama, maybe because verse, by its
heightened (the pushing of metaphor, goddamn Blackburn) requires
an acting present to deliver itself of its maker's person?

that is, i
shld not, myself, think that Bill's Dream of Love (however
beautiful i take the language achievement there) to be the answer
to what can be done with verse:

that is, I'd wager Bill's play is
like a one-novel, that, it is the only play he could write. And he
wrote it. That, the instrumentation is not at all capable of those
repeated and differing attacks that S made on each problem —
simply because verse was his instrument, not prose

(that all
contemporary drama loses by attempting to write in the people's
speech — don't believe, for a second, that blank verse was the
Elizabethan's speech! — witness Pericles as Shks' most popular play,

the one on whom his reputation was made the equal of Sophocles
(poem by Sheppard, contemporary, says so!)[100]

Christ, Rob't, give me the advantage of yr feeling on these
matters: don't feel sharp & clear. merely tossing it up for you.
puzzled, look it over, & tell me what, if any, light it throws, will
ya?

All's well. Kate now 8½ lbs—Con holloweyed from attention she
gives her, and that pleases me, that, this child under her eyes, on
her breast, seems such a damned wonder she can't read a book
while feeding her (as some others i have noticed!)

And in two
weeks plans are to try to hitch rides by stages to NE to get the
hell away from here for a month at least.

Love to you all,

Charles

[Black Mountain, N.C.]

tuesday   ROB'T   (Nov 27   51):

still obsessed by this play. do
hope you can lay yr hands on it, there. am most anxious to have
yr thoughts on its manner. feel now i knew nothing abt it when
getting it in to ISHMAEL: that is, did not know anything abt
magnification, properly; in Pro Verse came closer, & wld now add
A & C to such as Trojan Women, Hagoromo, & Odyssey. Yet this
sort of thing is not what pays off, for me: it is rather this
extraordinary verse, and i stay inside it, seeking to measure it
more.

Came on this exercise of mixed metaphor last night, after
getting last go off to you: it is Cleo, in answer to Antony's (who is

burned, she trafficks with Caesar) question, "Cold-hearted toward
me?":

Cleo.   Ah, dear, if I be so,
          From my cold heart let heaven engender hail,
          And poison it in the source; and the first stone
          Drop in my neck: as it determines, so   ((deter-
          Dissolve my life! The next Caesarion smite!   mines? mis
          Till by degrees the memory of my womb,   take?))
          Together with my brave Egyptians all,
          By the discandying of this pelleted storm,
          Lie graveless, till the flies and gnats of Nile
          Have buried them for prey!

or look, just below, the rip & tear of this thing, which all idiots
have suppressed, as tragedy of sensuality or whatever!
                                             Ant:
          I will be treble-sinew'd, hearted, breathed,
          And fight maliciously: for when mine hours
          Were nice and lucky, men did ransom lives
          Of me for jests; but now I'll set my teeth
          And send to darkness all that stop me. Come,
          Let's have one other gaudy night: call to me
          All my sad captains; fill our bowls once more;
          Let's mock the midnight bell

          Tonight I'll force
     The wine peep through their scars. Come on, my queen;
     There's sap in't yet. The next time I do fight
     I'll make death love me; for I will contend
     Even with his pestilent scythe

& Enobarbus, following, alone:
                    Now he'll outstare the lightning. To be furious
                    Is to be frighted out of fear, and in that mood
                    The dove will peck the estridge, and I see still
                    A diminution in our captain's brain

Restores his heart: when valour preys on reason,
It eats the sword it fights with, I will seek
Some way to leave him

No need for me to run on like this. Just, to give you a sense of
what a levy is made on natural phenomenon. For that, too, is a
sign of what is going on here, that the imagery is mixed because it
is all objects pressing in, as the gauges of the battle of
feeling.

And on way to mark how this in no way interrupts the
intensity of conclusion – the conjecture – is this crazy continuance
of melting (even death is only a dissolving into darkness: no
abstraction or extra-informing of death here, any more than any
forcing of meaning on to life:

the whole play is the exact opposite
of even a tendence to leave emotion unattached to cause and so
immediately to lead emotion to become abstract

au contraire:
marking the process, i take it the play can, by a conceit quite
opposite to its own, be seen to be, to rest on a prefix, DIS (as in
discandy, & several more):

for DIS- has three usages, the first two as verb:

(1) separation, or parting from
     (which is Antony's problem thruout)
& (2) reversal, undoing (uncandy), depriving,
     negation (which is the motion of reality
     therein)

& (3), (as noun) opposite of, or absence of, something![101]

Final quote: This common body   (meaning, the pippul)
Like to a vagabond flag upon the stream
Goes to & back, lackeying the varying tide
To rot itself with motion

Deeply involved with this thing. Puzzled at issue. But seems most to hand, powerfully, what was wanted!

Cleo: (skin)   tawny front; gypsy

Ant: (eyes)   glowed like Mars' plate
     (heart)   burst the buckles on his breast
               & now the bellows & the fan to cool a gypsy's lust
     (size)   the triple pillar of the world transformed
               into a strumpet's Fool

their love: (to measure it) find out new heaven, new earth
               (Ant) Kingdoms are clay: our dungy earth alike
               Feeds beast as man: the nobleness of life
               Is to do thus: when such a mutual pair
               And such a twain can do it, in which I bind
               On pain of punishment the world to wit
               We stand up peerless

nature: In nature's infinite book of secrecy

SHIT, to hell with this sort of thing. Forget it. ok

    what i wanted to do today was to start to catch up on affairs, & to get off to you Duncan's poems copied — & to start by reading em & acknowledging his Song of the Borderguard for the BROADSIDES

    am abt ready to copy for you — have written him — puzzling lad, he is so damned fine, yet, the posture, is still somebody else's — or so, for the likes of me
                              ("No sparkle," the lady says, abt me, these days, and of course she is patently right, goddamn her. goddamn her. goddamn her.

toofuckingclose everything is

know it, goddamnwell, myself, that i
don't ride. and am fucking troubled, thereby. out. out.   out.

but then, where, is out?

Will cover my discouragement by copying
d. herewith for you. shit. shit. shit.

before i do, just, to say, we both hope the flu has flown, that the
fucking worst of there is over for you — christ, why don't you just
throw — get aboard a train (if you can pay the passage) and land in
Rome, the four of you, without any more adamn: trust that
bastard cagli to take care of you:
        he is a man of heart, surely
                and
is my lad
   (and if not he, there is MIRKO[102] — same address, a real
   guy, from all i ever heard — never saw him
             but more
   broad based humanwise than cagli
         or carlo levi[103] — he
         cld be sought, if the
         others not there

              or
a guy from here, Willie Joseph[104] (queer duck, but rich, and worth
putting the bite on — shld be reachable by way of American
Express. Will try to get more exact address. Seems to me Italy's
the best jump
      But do jump. No sense you putting up with a day
longer. And if anything shld go wrong, cable me, and I'll fucking
well get some bitch or son of same to dig up money to keep you
there until something happens. PLEASE
          what good am i here,
except, to see you four who mean more to me than anyone where
you can swing yr cat?
        PLEASE, robt, call on me. i have only

emergency powers. but those i have—or have always had. am a
crisis man. or grandstand. hate peace. and drag. die. am dead.
call. call. call.

go. lad, don't waste another day dragging faggots
home: the picture of you in bed and Ann & Dave fetching bundles
in that dreary worn out Yurrup is too much. go to the sun of
winter. get to rome. goose cagli. anybody. who the hell are they?
don't wait on gerhardt: make him motor to rome if he ever does
get in the saddle. and take bryant with you, go to rome. go.

&

for christ sake, DEMAND OF ME: will be headed north around
Dec 8, and will be in Washington where Crosby may be, or Suzy
Hare[105] (who has idiot friends the world around—or at least
Rome!—and who else?

And then slowly to Boston—and why not
pit [*i.e.* put] the bee on ES? for YOU? I am sick that you shld for
a moment be sick—or discouraged. Goddamn wrong, for, of
allofus, you are moving, and certainly moving, and i cannot stand
that you shld have any drop—any of the thing i am most master
of, fucking gloomy swede

(Tells me, the Gasp, that, EP's crack
now is, it ain't Jews I hate, it's Swedes![106]

and in such mood of
eating off my arse, i agree

in fact did never disagree, that
homogeneity of nationality (to be more accurate than he with his
nonsense of blood & race)

is more than I have   !

goddamn her.
goddamn her.

very congested, that's what—no flow—no rhein[107]—no wildness

(as i sit here, snow
starting down
SNOW,
that shifty gd thing used

to give me ease — as much did, and don't
anything any more

        or not ease, wildness

              am bared to what i never

knew
    the goin-on
    beyond me

        this i do not know how to grab hold of

          and so, excuse, this babble, only

YOU PULL UP & OUT

        if you were clear, i cld endure my own
        failures

          ok. ok. forget it. only,

          PLEASE,

             olson

[*Added in pencil:*]
The point, on Duncan, finally is that the Third Sex deal is just too
goddamned EASY,
        WEH,
for a diehard, axehead, Puritan as me — but where MY structures
are (out of the sun) just now has me on the hook

P.S. #2: hours later having finished copy of Africa — is it my envy,
or 2nd sight, but much of this comes out tricky — & ending bad,
miserable.

[Black Mountain, N.C.]

Wed   RBT   Nov 28   51

(I, again burned—as was, with Gerhardt—over this
Duncan's Afrika R
                    (& just sittin, gabbin with Con over coffee,
tryin to wear the burn off—not talkin, of course, abt duncan at
all!
    (instead, our dreams, of last night, her turning Mildred Adams
here (wife of the anthropologist)[108] into a fat twotoothout frizzled
blonde like a dame i was humping just before Con & I met, and
whom she knew, &, of course, hated—and Con saying,
"humanizing her," that is MA, & saying to herself in the dream,
how much nicer she is this other way, crude & fat, how much
better
            & i, a great biz during the night, that, my eye as fast as an
airplane, and running swiftly up river beds (Red River of North,
say),[109] 1st ships plowing through shoal water, and I puzzled they
were out of the blue channels, and then the water thinning, finally
drying, and only arroyos in which cattle are running, not from
fear of the plane but merely making their way fast & slow up
these river beds
                    (& the other, Louisburg Sq! and the time of the
Revolution, and the great thing that it was at once the event & a
rehearsal or pageant of the event, a battle, the Battle of Louisburg
Sq, and I late and moving along the right side of the sq adjusting
my Continental uniform having just rode up furiously, and
dismounted—thinking afterwards, it was my father's uniform he
wore as a member of the Worcester Continentals![110]

Crazy. But from there we were off into cause & effect (1st,
dreams, Freud etc., and I attacking Con's waving figure, crying,
cause only yrself can know, & anyhow, one huge modern fallacy
is, that there is any mathematics of proportion between cause &
effect, that *effect* only matters
                        (that the smallest thing for me is the
eye on a dollar bill!)

((or, by inversal, that, the fist image as orb as all the things in A & C is a more correct spatial proportion to that particular world (A & C) and is exactly parallel to observable sensations of proportion, differing, as proportions do, in our experience, every instant

ANYWAY (leaving aside for the moment that it is when men, Gerhardt or Duncan, take up continents as their subjects—Rimbaud, too—that I am curiously provoked[111]

also, that, this *act* (now often made) suggests to me that, anthropology, archeology, geography *are* allowing enlargements ((see below, but, just here, think of how carefully DHL had put such behind him—if you do not know Fantasia of the Unconscious, see if you can pick that up the same place you got Studies: that is, I happened to be reading all the crazy stuff on Atlantis & Mu (Ignatius Donnelly, etc)[112] at the time I stumbled on DHL's F, and I assure you his shots—even in the Intro—are beyond compare

WELL: Con, then (she has been reading Bill's autobee) quoted his slam at Shakespeare on the doctrine of hold the mirror up to nature[113]—and we were off, and back again, to my speculations on this wondrous bird.

My argument was this: that Bill & Ez basically don't read S, or read him as tho he were such as the poets & novelists *since* him ((I take it EP's ironic mockery of *drahma* is another of those backhanded recognitions of his: you can't cut that guy's light off anywhere, no matter what he did with it))

that they were cutting the way thru the shit of mirror-nature *since* S. but that there is something else in their biting & let me have it fast, that, they are biting at their own inability to make the particular yield a like dimensionality as he did—that their gripe is, that, somehow, they can't do any more than see themselves in the mirror!

now it is DHL who shows them up. Surely he was as scrupulous
to keep his eye on any particular as they were. Yet, by god, DHL
did manage to illuminate what you call the density, the damn
idiot-squeezed place, eh? And give his illumination the very
increase of refraction that Ez and Bill both (for my small change)
don't manage, usually, or dominantly

that is, what they were seeking to cut away was a rot which called
for their knives: the only fucking illusion of size that our language
offered *after* S was, ABSTRACTION. And so the literature was
descriptive, entirely so, either, of the individual (lyricism) or of the
society (sociology)

and god bless em, eh? that they did cry, no idea except in a thing,
no idea except as action. Ok.

My fatuity, thereon (to Con), was, that, these two lads give us
two lads the job we are pissing at: to force the particular to yield
dimension

& on my present kick I'd argue two things. The first I am more
certain of, that, it lies in the act of the imagination as that act is
only ultimately expressed in the rhythm & texture of the language
(the present chaw on Shks sent you the last two days, but more,
yr BLUE, & anything i might have done which has raised you,
say
      that is, Lawrence, for my nickles & dimes (there is a
noticeable particularism & inflation in this image) — except in
COCK & LCL — always leaves me short of the very thing EZ,
particularly, and Bill, sometimes, have: language
                                        yet, DHL,
because, I'd guess, he was confident of another dimension neither
Bill nor Ez (as pure born Americans?) never were confident of: the
phallic: DHL d d bust through to the sort of "drama" that Mr S
was led to — (& led to, I'd swear, by his *language*)
                                        ((that is, I see
no signs that S was anywhere in confidence on the phallic as root
as DHL was — as, say, Homer too was (Calypso passages, ex., of

the most cool presentation in this area imaginable)

in any case,

DHL, in COCK, I, was farther ahead than any of us *yet*: & here, by god, his language, for my taste, is *perfect* (thinking fast, I don't know of a single syllable, there, out of place, eh?) ((by contrast, the bastard, fucking up Kangaroo, three-quarters of the way thru, breaking in, "So you don't like a novel, eh? Well, why don't you do something else? Go fuck, or something. Why read me? etc etc (straight smart guy, like EP, eh?)

which gets me to this, that, my confidence is, that mr S was just as pissed on, squeezed, as any of us by that idiot density you speak of: that, days, he had his boom lowered as thee & me (these days, eh?)

but that the act of his language & — I am now on guess #2, and it is one i am still damned chary of — *the act of a play*

In yr own

beautiful passage in this letter in last night (which I hauled off to Peeks, alone, in a grabbed car, to read over beer, and a chicken dinner — 2 beers & the dinner & the letter all eaten between

11:45 — and 12:10

you have it, there, ... look, let me quote the whole thing back to you as I just now read it to Con:

It sinks me very often, damn well into some kind of death, a feeling of simple chill & hate. Not at all good. What other damn way to make, I wonder. The fucking world is such a density, a damn idiot-squeezed place.

It was that hit me, reading you on S, and trying to feel how size, of that precised sort you note, is lost in current examples. The dimensions have done an odd twist, I think, and I mean it no more facilely than you did yr same question (i.e., this is not the old bunkum re universals, etc.).

All questions of
tension, or the play allowable, or the leadings. These seem all
bound now, or wrapped too surely, or tightly. One thing never
leading to another in 99 out of 100 instances
          (((O: except by a whole series of petty & phoney devices,
               like culture references, politics, etc—in EP;
          this unfair, but you will know against what admiration it is
          put
                         or, what is really dirty, the present usages of
                         DHL—blood, fuck, & all the filthy realism and/or
                         romanticism of anarchists (Rexroth, & the English
                         crew) or the Millerites
Melville size (you continue), parts of Lawrence—a question of
play, of what is being aimed at, what is considered 'relevant,'
what is the taking of the word 'material.'
                                   They damn well took
off our skins with that psychoanalysis, etc. Fools to let them do
that. Now they tell us all about it, but in so many goddamn
segments, volumes, etc.

                              Yr hit: how he *wd* (S) say
something or *everything*, or simply: *whatever*.

OK. That's *it*. How did he do differently—or DHL? I'd take it
DHL's is one damned wonderful way, and that beyond COCK he
wld have gone like a house on fire
                         Tell you what: found, in
writing A, that, I was quite aware of being led—and then, often,
putting in, my self! That is, that thing was a damned queer feeling
of being *out* there, of being in an area where it was *required* to
say *whatever*
          the occasion called for it
                                   and that i felt immensely
nervous at *departing from* my own particulars!
                                   How abt that?

In other words, I imagine the heave called for is a damned difficult
one—that to write verse (even as EP) is, in a sense, a sort of
ducking! a sort of coming back to home when, the movement, the
motion, is just where *other* dimensions *take over*

It comes to me
this way this morning: that we are born in a time which makes it
necessary that we do both jobs (or *all*, whatever is how you put
it

in the present context it comes out both, in this sense, that we
are demanded to use the language *and* invent a vehicle which will
be as dimensional as (I take it, with my gold dollar, by this
point!) ((or by my three one-dollar pinned on the wall Origin
Series

not square at all, not at all!

The fucking thing—as usual—
comes out too pat, and that you will, of course, throw away—
which proves again, how right the two papas are, were, that, it is
the thing & the act only

Yet, I—maybe because prose is not the
side of language i can make supple (not that i fucking well make
verse, either, supple enuf for my goddamned dreams

O shit,
Olson, only, what you have sd there, is so beautiful, and raises
me

& as far as I am at this moment, it is still the
huge thing, *what vehicle, how the language*

and i am no nearer a
solution everytime i go for a ride!

still improvisatory, & only
gone
perhaps why, any discriminations, come out so dry

Feel as tho i lost the clincher—& for good cause: we just gave
Kate her first water bath. Just goddamned *charmed* by this little

thing. Obviously too early to be bothered at all by her cries, or whatever. Makes sense. Enjoy sitting her on olson' chest: we must look like some Byzantine mosaic, the "size" & proportions, eh? (Con gets her in the mornings, when i am, of course, asleep, and says, that, then, she is ravissant—was her word, this morning, when they woke me, and i looked over, and there the two of them were, staring at each other! But too dead to move, or even put on the eyes to see ((had a fucking hell of a night, going over, what i am and have not done, wholly pissed off, & sore, sour, even plotting to jump & go anywhere, so wild to break present stale: thot, to jump a boat and come see you, just to unburden myself! Imagine, Olson, that open!

(And it is just such a point beats me—as witness that awful thing to you, at the break of our WCW crisis: can't lick this feeling of *unexpressed* life—tears at me, beats me, that, I am barricaded, cut off, have been, as long as i have lived: murderous oppression. Don't imagine you know such a thing? Say that, in a sense of defeat, no arrogation to myself of any special business, merely, that, I am flawed. It bites me. Gnaw. And remember—can count on two hands—the times, was otherwise: and always, think of sun, & sex! How abt that, Mr Fraud!

Or, in that conversation with Con—she arguing, i was dreaming of rivers because she happened to tell me that she read a review of a new book on "The Salt Rivers of NE,"[114] and I saying, horseshit, just fucking freud shit. And she reminding us of a thing (the very 1st po-em) done Gloucester, on Annisquam River, in which I had used as image which, as I tried to locate the thing (knew she did not mean "tidal rivers rushing," that dream) it came out, this day, thus (Mr Fraud!):

French but chias

(the original, and as of herself, Miss Wilcock, as, once, I saw her, & just jumped her, in a French job, brown, cut on the bias[115]

wow,

what's, on my mind!

OK. And that's all, I bet my final five dollars! (Which I wldn't pay
for it, never, finding any pleasure in same, eh?

Love, the full thing,

to you: Olson

PS: ya. the point seems to have been, that, that squeeze, as you
had it, can only be licked by devices of dimension — & simply
because the density *is* dimension

that DHL had the best,

maybe, in, the root

but that S, without it (I'd swear) managed
the best he cld with verse in drama, that *play* being his — &
my own best chance?

Ok

[*In pencil:*]

PS#2: Don't, please, misunderstand omissions of several answers to
things asked — am whipped on, these days, trying to hold
together, hold — something. Will be straighter, shortly,
figure. Will now try make copies more Duncan for ending.

[Fontrousse, Aix-en-Provence]
November 29, 1951

Dear Charles,

So very great to have yours, and this afternoon I
went into Aix, to see Ashley, and to see about having him go
down to Marseille with me on Monday, to see about getting to
Yucatan. I can't honestly stop it now; I am so deeply *sick* with
this place, that even this sane kind of rising you do here, with
your reasonable objections, can't hold any of it. I, at least, am
gone.

Which may be stupid, I don't know. The thing is, I know nothing whatsoever at this point, and that's the exact total of these past six months, a damn final sweep of any surety or authority I had got to in New Hampshire. One speaks so gingerly of these things; by 'authority' I mean that kind of intention that will *not* be put off with the detail or ornament. It isn't got easily; it's lost damn bitterly.

Anyhow, we have to do something, none of us, or at least Ann and myself, none of us can look to anything in this *place* with much excitement now. Asking her, for the 20th time, etc., do you think we should, I am so querelous, so eaten at this point, she says, why not. Or why not get out of here at least, and I still don't know.

I don't want to put the slightest weight on you; obviously, I am thinking, and what else, of those first letters you wrote me from there, from Lerma. I have them here with me; it's difficult to mistrust their excitement, even granting one man's meat, etc. I am thinking of simple *things*, not *one* of which can be got here, not a single damn *one*.

Getting off the bus, walking, then, up the street with him, simply said, I think we're going to Yucatan. It made absolute sense to him, it does, it does more and more, to me. He has been here some two years, and said, I just get now, finally, what you seem to have hit much more quickly, but I have the feelers of some 3 people, out. I.e., Dave and Ann, all three of us, are in some sense being hit here. Even with Dave's happiness at having got in with the kids.

But let me ask you, again, the questions: 1) how about kids for Dave?

        2) how about food for Tom & all of us?

        3) do the houses give you room, i.e., with the two kids, it takes about 4 or so to make space?

        4) is cooking a headache, i.e., can you get that bottled gas?

        5) are there any things, in particular, we should either try to get, or avoid?

Well, the 'list.' You must know it well enough; but best put now, etc. Ann has been all but dead with this place, icy dark hole, etc. Not room enough to turn around, and trying to cook in an actual dark for us all, with us all all pressed round her, etc. That, I don't know, or I don't think we could make it, again. Kills the work when the house is too crowded, or simply doesn't give space for the divers members inhabiting same.

Simply to think of that boat, it is *hard*, damn *hard*, to think of these matters with any coolness. I don't see that that kind of 'coolness' is, even so, worth it. I am very excited, ok.

As for loneliness, and all: the past 6 months, and before that, the five years, have certainly had that aspect. It's worse talking to someone you can't damn well talk to, than to no one at all. Sometimes in NH I would go three months without saying anything to anyone but Ann; I know enough about that side of things. I would rather not talk at all, honestly, than talk to those who are hardly listening, etc.

And have done it, i.e., have put up with that alternative. Here, the space given me, or any of us, is very small; and shifts. I don't have, as said earlier, any place for this typewriter, etc. Simply signs, etc. A week goes by when all the time I take out of this room is to go to the john, etc. I never say anything more than hello, to anyone, because I don't speak the language, like they say, and even if I did, I don't think I would to most of those that go by us here.

The one man who counts: Ashley. Other than him, and we don't, finally, see much of him (some half dozen times in 6 months), there was only Mitch and it was hell talking to him when he was here, he was so damn much under his own web. The letters have been a great deal more pleasure to me than were the conversations, because of that.

Two days ago I spent a whole damn afternoon, just looking out the window, just damn well looking out the window. It is a hellish damn thing to get caught with, this willfulness, this deadness of the attentions, so very dead, i.e., that they can be so lulled, so completely suspended. I spent most of the six or so hours in an amazement, that I could be doing what I was, just so, doing. I felt dirty, even sick with it. But wanting to lift, I got that whole hellish weight again, or what jumps in, anytime you open your eyes, or ears — this death.

Anyhow, that's how it is. I want the cleanness, the bareness, minus all these dead encrustations, minus all this doom-sense that seems impossibly stuck on them here. A/ said: the two people, the only two who were capable of articulating *any* of the circumjacent reality were incapable of *speech* with their own people; the man now works as a civil servant somewhere around Toulon, and that's it, that's all they will give *in* to him. Trying to make pottery, they used to stick around the place, there in Aix, after the others, and got, at last, beaten for it, I mean, spit on, shit on, etc. That's the goddamn ground-tone, that's the fucking feel of the whole fucking place. MOVE, and they shoot; that's all. They were living on 10,000 francs a month, in a room with no heat, some 5 miles from the school; the wife was pregnant. How long can you hold out against it? They give you not a damn inch; any of them. If they are nice (as Laubies certainly was to me), that niceness is a distance more damn dulling than even the hate; it follows you like a skin, it mocks you with agreement. I want out. But that's damn clear, anyhow. One wishes he could pull those that *matter* with him. Fuck it.

So, Lerma. Tell me if I'm wrong.

Kasper sounds ok; I'm in, or altogether willing to do *anything* I can. I mean simply, when the time comes, let me know. He sounds ok. I figure Blackburn may have had his own axe, there, at that. B/ is probably apt to want the too comprehensive comment. The mark of the dispassionate observer, etc. Anyhow, would figure you know better; that simple. Ok.

So, to get this off. Will report, what happens Monday. Will check on the boat, etc. Can't get off, probably, until mid-December, or later. No money, or not anything we can move on, until then.

Damn, damn waiting, but anyhow. Tell us about the Halazone
tablets, where can you get them and so on; feel like an explorer.
How abt New Yr/s? We cd get abysmally drunk!

Anyhow, SO
GREAT. CLEANS THE WORKS. All dearest love to you all,

Bob

Two items I forgot:

1) that Ashley is sitting down to that thing
for the broadsheet; up till now he hadn't had a room, etc., no
place to get at his materials. He wants to do it, and will, I think,
do it ok; I didn't want to push him on it, at any point, because it
was this favor, of sorts, and as well, can't see getting much if
you're leaning over the shoulder, etc. I hope that will be done,
then, within the next three weeks, at the latest. He moves into his
place this week, should start on it, he said, directly. Again, very
damn sorry there's been this delay on it (my ideas, like they
say) — hope to god the product makes it worth it, and do,
honestly, think it will. He is a careful man, and a clear one; and
has the other ingredient that makes for the good things. Ok.

2)
Was that Emerson, like they say. I got a contract for the booklet,
today, and have signed same for better or for worse, and I
suppose it will be, worse. Such a damn mixed biz in any case. He
is feeling very sorry for himself on the shoddy thing with you, and
whines, still, about it; he always puts it with that vague
obliqueness, i.e., some people are nice people, etc. I can't honestly
hold his hand, I don't know just what he does want from me.
Certain enough that he knows, at this point, he won't be the
publisher of your poems, etc. You are, still, be it said, a 'fine poet'
in his opinion; he always was so very considered in his opinions!
Nothing swerves the noble E/, etc.

Anyhow, I figure this can be,
to see, if he can do it again. Fuck it, it doesn't matter, not on this
stuff anyhow.

How he could so *muff*, I mean, drop, fumble,

fubdub, etc., the thing with you . . . , I don't know. It was in his hands, in his hands, in his hands, and still, somehow, some damn way or other, he did. Or he didn't, hold on to it.

You see, I still believe he wanted to publish that book, odd as that may damn well sound. I can't figure it, damnit, or can't see any more light than you can; it is a fog, to put it so, etc. But that he did issue the poems in GG#3 with the notice, and that he did make that obvious move—what else? He could have got out, certainly, earlier, if he had been figuring to.

Even now he sound fattily concerned, or in it all, some under conviction, perhaps, that he's dropped something good.

Etc., etc. I wish I could get my hands on the A&C tonight, I could use it. Otherwise, I saw a copy in the room of the man with whom A/ will be sharing a house there in Aix; I figure I can get it away from him long enough. Ok, and will write you directly I can get the book. Everybody seems to have brought the Complete Plays of Shakespeare but me; I always was the slow one. Ok, and write soon; will be back directly.

[*Typed upside-down at bottom of page:*] Ann is worried abt scorpions; can you get washing done? She is sick of the stone here; how abt that . . .

_____

[Black Mountain, N.C.]

FRIDAY   ROBT   Nov 29   51 :

Just crazy today, wild, crazy, excited by a whole series of sights, breaking:

ex.,

walked out (to get away from Con—it is a spring day, today—&

got sp[l]ashing around abt Shahn's "line" as against the "Italian"—&
what Klee's is. And so, to the Gothic: as Shahn or you or
Twombly or self are, more Gothic than, Renaissance, granting that
these two distinctions are only late, end points of something much
more interesting, which is neither, which, way back to each, is,
how expresion is best wrought:
                    that is, Beardsley, having it,
Beauty, is difficult, is making the proposition which undid the
Renaissance[116]

Anyhow, the pleasure, of talking to a boy as open & sure as this
Twombly, abt *line*, just the goddamned wonderful pleasure of
form, when one can talk to another who has the feeling for it—
and christ, who has?

I so like this lad, and Motherwell (who has pushed him, arranged
a NY show opening for him next week) has just made a blurb for
him (for a Chicago show the summer produced for Twombly—
what a winner!) which is such nonsense that Twombly himself (he
is a cool one) when I sd I didn't believe M wrote it, knew instantly
what I was talking abt it[117]

(By the way, am to do a note on T for a show of his at
Washington & Lee:[118] & look forward to it, for the lad is a
conservative, as i begin to think any archaist is (eh? DHL?
RC?)—that is, "radicalism" in art (I mean, of course, solely
positional) looks as thin as avant guard, as bourgeois, as, realism.

But what got me up, has me tossing—in the blanket—is again Mr
Shaxpeer

And last night i was excited to write that, at the moment, I think I
got a breakthrough into his system. At least this: that, all that has
been he for 300 yar is arsey-versey or, backwards. That his verse
is where his plays arose, not the verse as, the result of, his play—
(which, like all i am seeing these days, sounds said, but i go on
batting away that it contains some further perception than the
statement appears to contain ((tho here i await yr responses, for, i
need your response on this fiercely))

Proposition: that his image system is the clue (not the metric, say—that is, blank verse was the machine, & he was so prepared to accept it (like a new car bought in '92, and satisfactory until '08, got him around, and ran like one of those old electric jobs old ladies still enjoy, and how smoothly and graciously they do get 'em around, the lovely noiselessness, the—how did he have it as the mark of verse: limpidity, of same?[119]

OK. ((Or this, to mark, how, blank verse was, satisfactory: Grant
     White keeps putting in these wonderful footnotes on S's
     tags—this one is on the last 8 lines of LEAR, which,
     palpably, are interpolations: "Were it not that S. always
     falls into feebleness with rhyme. . . ."[120] I love it, love it!)

Anyhow, this: that by 1601, he had this system:

     (1) the play arose from ONE METAPHOR—the candy of
               A & C, say[,] the eye of LEAR
     ((that is, Homer, if Berard is right—and he makes more sense
        than anyone—raised any *character* from the physical
        characteristic of *the place* (Circe comes from the fact that the
          headland where the action takes play [*i.e.* place] was a sky-
          hawk's rendezvous: Cyclops emerges from the pock-holes of
          old volcanic fissures—as tho Yellowstone had been come on
          by you & me, instead of by Jim Bridger!; etc.
     (& all this from Phoenician sailors' directions. . . . .[121]

but Mr S is another sort of poet, that, he takes his images where
he finds 'em (& not necessarily in himself: that is, I figure now it
               wld be most illuminating for me to look at Cinthio,
               say—where he got the Othello tale; or Holinshed
               (where Lear); or Plutarch (A & C), and see *if* any
               clues to these dominant
AND SINGLE metaphors
                         (root, base, buried—and not at all
                         buried—crazy things, which, can be
                         shown to be OPERATIVE
fr start to finish

And (2), then, a whole rash of multiples, eh? the MIXED
METAPHORS (made possible, goddamned it, *by* the SINGLE,
UNMIXED, CONTAINING intelligence

For you see, how, this is no more than what we had found afore,
eh? the SINGLE CENTER, or GATE

gate, most, here, in the act
of, the imagination, that by this SINGLE ACT he enters

plot, character, & the other characteristic of the
cloth of it, the verse, the MM

Anyhow, has me wild, to find, how goddamn PARTICULAR such
a perception forces each play (at least fr 1601 on) to be & to stay:
you can't get out of it — you have to stay in — it is all like a hoop,
a fine steel band, so porous, flexible, yet firm — conservative — that,
one can at last talk abt the formal force of this man, can start to
examine it, can speak of him COMPOSITIONALLY

instead of the
exterior measurements it strikes me he has, fr him to now, been
altogether measured by:

dramaturgy — characterization — plot — big scenes — soliloquies —
etc   etc   ALL THIS SHIT, leading like, the biggest turd of
all: universe-all

VERSE, ALL, & ONLY: my god, wild: look, LEAR:

eyes as sight versus other sight: Gloucester, blind: "I see
feelingly" or *the heart* as Tom-a-fool, Tom-a'cold,
Coxcomb, in stocks, not in the mouth (Cordelia),
hanged (Cordelia)

eyes out: bleeding rings — ZERO — round O — WHEEL (of fire, of
fortune, of rack)

so, NOTHING as original condition (dominant word of 1st
scene) issuing (after all the disfigurement & disguise) as NEVER,
NEVER, NEVER, NEVER

((death is here also darkness—as in A & C—only, not, the
darkness of rot or dissolvement, but, of the closing of the
EYES

& is strictly played against the *act of darkness*: so much so,
that, the womb (which is constantly in LEAR & in
EDMUND—the other huge figure) comes out a wheel, a
hole, a round O too!

  Listen ((((Edmund's brother Edgar to him just after he has
put a hell of a mortal hole into him with his sword:

   Edgar: . . . .
      The gods are just, and of our pleasantest vices
      Make instruments to plague us:
      The dark and vicious place where thee he got
      Cost him his eyes

   Edm: Thou has spoken right, 't is true;
      The wheel is come full circle: I am here.

& NATURE—jesus, here, what a Druidical thing Nature "dear
goddess" is

 (it is fantastic, Robt, how, here nature is conceived: as against,
 say, A & C where, it is all solidity, all OBJECT—and here, it is
 all MOTION, phallic (female phallic), literally THE
 MOVEMENT OF THE ACT OF DARKNESS!

and gives the place a motion—the play itself—the world of it
rocks

—does not spin, as A & C, as earth—in plunging in & out or back
& forth—is horse, or stern of ship—is up & down, out &
round—is

god, jesus, is something so known we know nothing, is what it is,
& no goddamned interpretation, is, the thing
          and gets that way

by, is, the VERSE

> (I get giddy, that i can't say this, that, these
> outlines will destroy *where they came from* —
> for I got them in in IN the play, in IN, the
> verse, no where else — and am confident you
> wld find em there too! WILD

And so many other things happen *as consequences* of this
dominant image of eye & womb, of man as a thing which
HOWLS first, before it has sight, and HOWLS last, because, eyes
are finally no good, eyes have to be lost to have proper sight, and
proper sight only leads to the darkness of which he came, because,
those who see feelingly are too slow for those (Edmund) who
say — not by blindness, but by choice against blindness:
    "men
Are as the time is"

> For there is another thing happens here, that

ECHO, too, is a law of this metaphorical system: Lear constantly
repeats nouns and verbs, usually five or six times, the same word,
as tho it was returning from the concave walls of a stiff, steel
space:

. . . Howl, howl, ... is picked up by Kill, kill, . . .

Never, never. . . . nothing, nothing. . . .

> god, these words,

RETURNING

I'm telling you, I never guessed what *composition* this man was
exerting: and it is something to avoid all musical images for — it is
not music (however much Bach, say, might be the only man one
could talk of in say such a play as this — for it is COLD, as Bach
is, not of the crap usually sd abt this PAIN: the pain here is
darkness & *right* (cap R) That's another paradox here, that, pain is
so buried (as nature, as womb, as wrong: why Edmund is so big,
is no devil, no iago, no demon-monger —

IS, actually, LEAR'S *SON*

> (this is the craziest thing of all, that,
> the intrication is so exact — and the
> play's plotting as a result so careful
> and clear — that I can put my finger on
> exactly the moment where Gloucester
> who bred this bastard (Edmund)
> actually hands him over — tho, it is
> only, of course, in the image that this
> happens — to Lear

& here's the wild thing: that at that moment Gloucester goes
poof, like smoke, out of the play (as earlier the Fool also

> withers away fr the play, the but[t] of
> the storm, catches a cold, is (the
> Coxscomb) is the weakest of all before
> storm — is like a blown ear, of Lear
> himself, which merely *breaks off*

oh, god, i am either crazy, or in the presence of, something very
fine, RC:

for Edmund is the thing Lear is only the previous generation of, in
this sense that they are the only two creatures in the play who
understand that they issue from nature — that anything else (stars,
fate, or self-reliance) is as secondrate as is the sort of conclusions
that Edgar and Gloucester come to *after* as intense suffering as

> Lear, say, or, the Fool (this is a lovely side discrimination of
> S's, that, these two E & G are just not of a texture sufficient
> to be any different, after their pain, than they were before: it
> is not a moral position that they emerge with, but a passive
> humanistic one, that, suffering is only always worse than
> what you can call "the worst," and that ripeness (merely
> taking it) is all men can do

But not Lear and Edmund, the two antagonists: not they: they
both know NATURE is more than gods, is other than themselves,

and that the act of to howl or the act of to kill is the action—the
only action—men can oppose, and oppose even in the awareness
that the wheel will come down, will turn and crush, will bring
darkness to darkness, and there it is. *But* in between, they have
acted, wildly as Lear acts—hugely & imaginatively—or coldly, as
Edmund

> (christ, which all puts an end to the shit of Nature's
> increase—of Contra Naturam[122]

> by god, Robt: here, right before my eyes, is the answer i
> sd i was after to the Old Man: there is a cheap half-truth
> behind that proposition which this S enables me to
> expose, no?

For the other is a form of moral choice (again, why, Confucius is
sterile) and is so restricting—denies men their realities in the face
of a social system of control—a substitution for Nature by appeal
to her—a cheap trick, this deal—for the hidden term which wrecks
it is hogger of harvest[123]

it is economic, & not accurate naturalism whatsoever: (((at this
point we shld examine most carefully Remy de Gourmont's
Natural History of Love, that vol Ez translated,

> for, I wld guess,
it is here that this bad science of EP's was picked up: a biological
mechanistic romanticism abt how nature behaves, how beavers
replace beavers—a natural selection nonsense which is Darwin, i
goddamn well bet

> behind EZ intelligent opposition of evolution i'll
> wager there is a hidden, unadmitted use of same!

(Jesus, sure: sure: sure

> that is, Edmund is a Kike, an Olson, sure
> as hell, eh?

By god: look this over. It looks straight.

> (And the point ultimately
is, VERSE: eh?

[*In pencil*:]
Have to go keep a C O out of 5 yrs in Pen[124] — will
get this off, & be back on

                              All love,
                                 O

_____

                              [Fontrousse, Aix-en-Provence]

November 30, 1951

To add a bit. I had got hung up with the biz of the poems, or not
too much that, or so much, as interested. The series is odd, damn
odd, i.e., to read them so, as a bunch, they have a damn odd
singleness. I have tried to throw out anything that didn't seem to
set, or was sententious, or wasn't simply any good. It leaves me
with 11 poems, but that's ok; I don't honestly care much about
length, etc. In fact, I feel somewhat to the opposite.
                                            The final
contents are like this:

Still Life Or   (and have copied it, other side)
Hart Crane (1)
Le Fou   (which is title poem)
Littleton, N.H.
Helas
Hart Crane (2)
The Epic Expands
Guido
A Song
Canzone
Love   (the last one)

I wish I had your say on that A SONG; I like it ok, but feel, as
usual, no assurance. But, at that, I do like its movement, or how
they say it. I like the way some of the things are got to, etc.
Juxtapositions, etc. And the point, also like they say, about the
sense of perpetuity is my own, and like it or not, that's it. I hope,
in any case, that it isn't hit too dully there. Ann has always
objected, I think, to the 'gross,' but I don't know any other word,
and, too, she does forget that it isn't simply a fat man, etc. To be
snide, etc.

Anyhow, that's it; I am very scared on all of it, because, with the
poems, I feel very remote and far away from them, and they are,
finally, the only things I can ever get to read, as, say, someone
else might. And I don't much like that distance, to be honest.

                                                                Ann
says, and she likes it ok, i.e., this way of them, the set, etc., they
are each so single, each one seems a different man.

                                                    That could
either be Williams' 'unformed' or your, a poem has its own things,
each time, and a man has to come up, each time, with the
language and syntax demanded by that fact. I hope it is the latter,
but that's slapping the back, etc. I don't have any of that
confidence.

                    But I do like some of them very much. HART CRANE
(1) I like, in parts, as much as anything I have written; I also like
the 'Shine on' in the LITTLETON one very much. I like the feel
and ending of LE FOU, and it is the only way I've ever seen
things, like they say. I like HELAS, the language very much at
times, and I like THE EPIC EXPANDS and always have. I felt it
was one, for once, on that thing that was into me that I didn't bug
with sententiousness; I have thrown away THE LETTER, for
example. GUIDO, for the move, and rhythms, the lying into the
move there. STILL LIFE OR for parts, again; it is the earliest of
the bunch, and one of the first times I ever took it I made
anything. Before that is almost all black.

                                        Such a damn lonely act
of aggression, anyhow. Jesus, it *is* spitting damn well out into
nothing. I wish to god they were all like stones, or trees, etc. Just

to have that authority. Being what they hate, these damn readers,
any man's making his work 'unconditional.' And would say, at
that, the only similarity I have ever taken to exist between
yourself and the old man is this same thing, authority. Not only
to say what you mean, but to mean what you say, etc. They don't
eat it very happily.

        Etc., etc. I don't know. Very wheezy about all
of it, very cautious and stupid. I hope to god he makes it, or don't
really care, at that, thinking, one way or the other, it will be ok
with me.

STILL LIFE OR

mobiles:
      that the wind can catch at,
against itself,
        a leaf or a contrivance of wires
in the stairwell,
to be looked at from below.

We have arranged the form of a formula here,
have taken the heart out
           & the wind
is vague emotion.

To count on these aspirants
these contenders for the to-be-looked-at part
of these actions
        these most hopeful movements
needs
a strong & constant wind.

            That will not rise above the speed
which we have calculated:
        that the leaf
remain
     that the wires
be not too much shaken.

Still thinking of Lerma, what else. Can't get rid of this damn excitement, and hardly want to. Cold as hell here tonight, cold coming up out of the floor, and both kids sick with colds. Too much, and can't make it any more and damn well no need to. Back to the Indians, like they say, they can give me back to the Indians. Much too nice here for me, much too good, etc. I can't believe any of it.

Write soon. Your letters so great to have. I will keep on, will try to keep this dullness out, etc., but anyhow. No damn matter, but that you write. All our love to Con & Kate; tell us how it goes now. We're waiting.

[*Unsigned*]

[Fontrousse, Aix-en-Provence]
November 31, 1951

Chas/ yrs here, the two, and very great to have them; many thanks for the Duncan. Reading it, of two minds, to put it that dully. I didn't make the content, at all, I didn't go with, I think, what he was sounding off from, the 'nature' even, or this too simply, I think, characterization, I mean, of the deep thing vs. the undeep thing, etc., etc., etc. I have your own feeling, or some of it, about the 2nd section, but that, too, is not my own taking, and I am not, by him, brought to his.

Perhaps just too dead to read it. I like his verse, the way of some of it, very much; I don't like very much, almost nothing honestly, of what's up. Simply a question, for me, of what can interest me, and this can't now, I have the sense of repetitions, and I can't afford them, now.

I wonder that he can; I don't like that ending at all, I don't, I think, even see its line in the whole poem, i.e., how, just how, it is supposed to follow, or to follow with strength. And not understanding, perhaps I don't like it, but anyhow, no, I don't like it, this poem, and silly not to say so. I have been able to read it twice, but quick at that, and with all the damn hell of present headaches. It's hardly fair to him; I will go over the whole thing, again, and more intently, when things are just a little better. They are godawful today.

And, again, I don't see, finally, going to Italy, or to anywhere in Europe. Nothing I can imagine myself, or any of us, as now being able to hook on to. I don't want to meet anyone, or to talk even one damn word more to anyone here; a damn waste of wind, and time, and to hell with it.

Will just get to Marseille, on Monday; just see that goddamn consul, & likewise check on that Boat Co/ you note, and see when the hell we can get out, after the 14th or so, of December, which is when we'll have loot to make it with.

I had a letter from the Dr, this noon with yr two, saying pleasant things, etc., about holding on, etc. Fuck it. He should talk. This is no place for yr lad, and I can't see acting as tho it was any damn longer.

I will try & get that copy of the S/ on Monday, too; then can read A&C, which, by your comment, and these quotes, is already into me. Once read, will write you on same, and damn anxious to get it. Am damn well ripe, will be coming from L/s STUDIES, at that.

To clear, somehow. Jesus, I feel for you, too. It is a dull grey damn world, at this point, and I can't *allow* it, I can't damn see that it *is*. Or why, or what is any more, than it always is, the damn human fuckup. Damn them, damn them, damn them. But all that damn well has to be handled, anyhow.

Hope it gets better there. Will miss you, there in Lerma, but you will be by, I'm betting, sooner or later; and we will be there—what I sing to myself, etc. Ok. And write soon again, and keep on; only lift I get.

Will the house
be a headache, i.e., getting one there? It would be great to have
something set, what with the kids & our knowing none of the
language. But don't let us bug you too. Any ideas — the greatest.

[*Added in margin*:]
What abt D/s SONG OF THE BORDERGUARD (or early stuff, in
HEAVENLY CITY, etc., I think it was): I get scared abt G/s Am/
issue. Damn bug.

[*Added in margin of first page, re Duncan*:]
He's good, damnit, I know that from reading the early stuff, and
this too, for that matter; but I don't make the material, here, at
all — it puts me very much down.

[Fontrousse, Aix-en-Provence]
Sunday/ Dec 1st [1951]

Dear Charles,

     I very much hate to jump like this, particularly
since it gets to involve you. But anyhow, get to feel that Lermas
isn't the out we first figured; simply scared that it would be
something like this present fix, for Ann, and so for all of us. Hard
as hell to figure, & being so dead, now, haven't any of the means
to.

     But I damn well hate to drag you in, and won't; not, for god's
sake, to put you down on any of these kindnesses you offer. I
don't forget them; no one else, or no one but Ashley there in Aix,
or Mitch, or Bud, would even see what it is now like for us. To
be able to pile it on you, spill over, is immense help.

     But I don't
see bothering Mrs. Crosby, or the others, frankly; or not with

something like this. If I can put it without maliciousness, & I am damn full of that, it's that they wouldn't see it, all of it, & not getting it, what it is, can't believe that it would make a damn thing to ask anything of them. I always felt off, writing to Mrs. Crosby this past summer; nothing ever warmed up, I suppose. I hated her for whizzing thru Aix like that, and I hated her for sending me a note, on the stories, saying she would read them, etc., and then never saying anything more. I am so damn full of spleen, anyhow, at this point I can hardly say anything but I don't want to bother her, damnit, or anyone who can't see what it is like. Fuck it; we will get out anyhow.

What I figure: simply to hold on (we have for four months, and can keep it up) and see what can be finally found around here. Ashley is on the lookout, and I count on him to come thru with something. He knows we're leaning, etc., and it doesn't put him down.

Anyhow, anyhow. I do wish we could see you all; these times the distance is hopeless, a damn killer. I felt, then, those two days ago, and even till this afternoon, it would be that boat, to Lerma, and all of this washed out. But there are the damn fears—or what it would be for Ann, and the kids. And so for me too.

Well, this to get off to you—hope to god you hadn't begun anything. Feel horribly that you have. You are the only damn one we could let all of this out on—small damn pay.

Goddamn it, it is a christly mess, but some damn way or other, there must be a fucking out. If we could get our hands on that damn car—we have it, have the damn paper, and possession, but we can't get thru the fucking red-tape, on residence, that keeps us from driving it (i.e., you need all these damn papers to get the necessary licenses, etc., etc., etc.) Good lord but it is a dull, dull business. But now figure to hold on, simply to get thru it here, and not move, and have it all over again somewhere else. Jesus, we are horribly bad at it; I can't imagine that others do it all this miserably hard way. Anyhow. It could not be worse, I damn well think; must, must, must get better. Write soon & get me out of this—the letters damn well do.

"As an honorable man who abhors exaggeration, etc."[125] I damn well see what he meant.

All dearest love, even this blast is pressure *off*, and feels *damn good.*:

Bob

[Black Mountain, N.C.]

Sat D 1 51

Robt:

I am struck by the body & importance of contemporary learning as against a continuing hidden assumption that ancient learning (I mean of course what they mean — Greek, 500 BC on) is somehow more, & more important than, contemporary learning

It is probably not simply Ez's old saw of the culture drag-arse: "30 yrs behind the time," even that itself arising from a too solid weighting of cause — efficient cause.[126] That is, contemporary learning *does* follow so patently from ancient work (as, the grounds, of Medieval & Western learning were Aristotle, say, Avicenna, etc.).

But here's the ungranted thing — that at a certain point there was a profound departure, & though the "vocabulary" of learning as it had been may have seemed to be maintained (mathematics, e.g.), yet, sometime in the last centuries (conspicuously, for my attentions, in the Non-Euclidean departure of Lubachevsky, Riemann, Bolyai Farkas: around 1830, say) a different vision of reality, and of learning as a tool fit to find out anything about reality, set in.

I wld imagine that it will soon be more apparent that the divergent
body of knowledge now in man's hands is strikingly different, & of
such a different order, by comparison to what had been, generally,
for 2400 years, that a whole series of effects are now to be dealt
with as a result and with a whole series of new tools.

((It interests me, to recognize, now, that I underlined
Arab learning in the G & C piece correctly, as, a
"sport" — so far as the general story goes — and as
probably the grafting which produced, eventually, the
new learning: from the beginning warred against the
Greek, and eventually, the war of the two produced the
New.

Also, that, still, no one will gauge this who
remains unwilling to go out the back door of those
altogether too magnificent Greeks, eh?))

I say this by way of preface to the tenacity with which biology
governs still so much thought, especially in politics. And I am not
simply picking at — or picking up on — the go yesterday which
ended with that (breakthrough?) on the Old Man's mischief. For it
also involves an incident last night with the new protozoologist
here whom I like very much, a guy named Sprague,[127] definitely
their best addition academically, simply that he is a superb
research man (in parasites which immobilize crawfish & shrimp)
and the sort of sincere man who suffers, thereby, a proper naivete,
both in his own incapacity to see particulars except in such careful
small orderings as science is capable of & in the usual failing of
such, that, as human beings, they are involved in systems of
orderings & action (the human systems) which do not order them
self as science can. The result is, that peculiar oscillation (Einstein
the most conspicuous example) between their own precisions in
their own business and their ridiculous optimisms in regard to
men's affairs. Sprague was looping from corn whiskey by dinner
time, and also had been dragged down, suddenly, from the rear by
the death of a friend, a man named Carl Behre (Bare-ey), owner of
the Pelican Coal & Ice Company of N.O., and brother — this seems
to be where Sprague came to know him — of Elmer Behre,
zoologist, at LSU.[128] Ok. Now Behre's widow had written Sprague

offering her husband's library to BMC—a library of Marxist economics, plus a good deal on China & India. What Sprague wanted to know was, could he, in good conscience, accept the gift, in the light of the fact that Behre seems to have spent all of his life he could keep from his business on promoting human welfare) was Sprague's words (child guidance, against discrimination, etc.—and seems to have had to pay for it, in NO, all his life: a Harvard man, etc.!

What Sprague broke out with, was, "It all hinges on you. I've lost a lot of sleep over you. I'm not convinced you believe in the many . . ." It was beautiful, the thing I like this guy for, the seriousness, given the stupidity, with which he keeps inside of his resistances, however essentially wrong & merely torpid his resistance is. Yet, his intelligence, & its sharpening in its own areas due to the care & completeness of his work, won't let him turn away from me—any more than he was able, finally, to turn away from education, even though, last year, he had left, and had—as he put it—stared a mule in his ass farming his wife's patch down in North Georgia.

The incident, coming fast on my letter to you, forced me further into this dichotomy I here deal with—the invalidity of the biological for analogies or for ultimate gauge of human nature & human action.

((The thing also has considerable immediate publishing urgency due to the fact that one of EP's pushes on Kasper is the planned issuance of Agassiz in the Paper Dollar Series.[129] I heaved off on this one, & was surprised to find I hit Kasper where it hurt. And now he is sending me postcards of correction! Saying, read Agassiz on the Ice, etc.))

That is, rather than such, or de Gourmont, I'd say, republish Pliny's Natural History! Or Herodotus, who is full of crazy science, non-science, of course.

And this leads me to think what's involved here is, actually, METEMPSYCHOSIS—and the restoration of

METAPHOR as the human "science" proper to human affairs &
actions —

and yet without loss of PARTICULARISM: this is
maybe the battleground, the push: *how* to stay as precise as New
Learning has made us, & at the same time discover orderings more
precise to *man's* peculiar life-system than all these apparent truths
about him as species (that word is where I wld attack) allow —
however persuasive they are, however accurate they are — & they
are — they are not finally usable.

OK. Which puts us to it, eh? And I figure it is again a matter of
paradox — that, such sciences of space, the earth, & of man like
geometry, geology, & anthropology are as massive as they right
now are *for cause*: that man is finally only measurable by sciences
specific to his froward necessities rather than any such generalized
sciences as those of matter, or organic life, or — such as
mathematics — of abstraction, the languages of abstraction which,
no matter their worth, ultimately (because they are not speech or
the language of human motion) do man in — & do him in simply
because they are removed, by one step, from his own tragedy,
that, it is his action that he blunders in, forever.

For species thinking has two human lies in it: perfection, &
progress. Or, put another way, necessity, & chance. (This is
evolution's dirty stick — the stars can still be looked at, without
teasing a man to commit suicide in space & eternity, but the
microscope, like the telescope extends man's sensory system
beyond his fingertips & eyes, & so, betrays him, stretches him too
thin for his organism & function. Such knowledges of nature only
give man false frames of [re]ference for himself — essentially
abstract, & so generalizing frames. They do not — I'd have it, a
dictum, CANNOT — teach him relevance.

In any case, my
impression, by way of Sprague, say, and Pound, is, that these
truths as analogies lead men into false action — politics, e.g., as
imagined either as hope (Sprague) or rule (EP)

For here again
Confucius sticks in my craw. That word "government" anyhow

(((the parliament of nations, the government, of the world!
eh?)))

even WCW letter to RC.[130]

There is something exterior in that word which won't get beaten.
The idea that what any of us has to do by *ordering* is extendible
to *government* seems to me to be a phoney based upon some
notion that nature—because she continues, goes on, is
"successful"—is something for man to look to for clues

— as tho there was a single one except as each single one
of *us*—and not as a creature of a species, but as a
goddamned living *human* thing—cells, tissues, health,
etc. beside the point as finally shit—species shit—as
each of us by ourself figure out an ordering which is no
more than our own—and if it has value to others, is
only, because it is a single human person's act

—i have
not yet known any example where any other
imaginative act than one inside the particular person
making the act has moved me sufficiently to change me

finally, one has to make this distinction as the only one
which excuses learning—that, otherwise, one is fooled

I come to this another way: the old kick, objectism. That is,
space, say, or earth, or other men, is a determinable, can be
decisively seen as separate. Can be known, & pegged
— and of course here is where i'd claim learning & all
knowledge—biology, politics, Marxianism, Freud—are
nothing to be scared of, are, TO BE KNOWN FOR
WHAT USE IS IN THEM.

But that that USE, has, limits—& so value—just exactly as that
knowledge stays in its place—is seen to be the finest aid to get
objectness very sharp and clear—the outlines, the facts, the
difference.

But the rhythmic & action notions which
evolution & all such things as Marx and Freud spawn — that the
rhythm of things — spirochetes, say: or the rubber band of the
universe, or the rubber face of same[131] — has anything to do with
human rhythm or human action except as possibly on some planes
& at some times is, to me, demonstrably one of the DANGERS —
the fallacies — the best men of our recent time have been suckers
of, for.

Environment, for example — our oft kicked place. Or
habitat. Or food. Or sex. Or that yr pineal gland was also once
the eye of an electric eel! That men kill & eat each other is of
more moment to me than any of these "facts":

that Roosevelt
forgot he cld die, screwing, some portrait painter, eh?[132]

Or that
anyone of us — no matter how far we push what we have — get no
strength whatsoever from the act — we can be broke, as a feather,
no matter how much structure the act of ordering may give us,
eh?

That men are not iron or, amoeboid, that they are anything &
still nothing more than this species no one has sufficient tools to
make any different than his ultimate capacity

Ok. No need to
labor this. Better, if I counter what I was on, at the end, yesterday

Man is not unknown, he is only inextricable from the
governing fact that he is man.

Why — I sd — I am Edmund
& cld be Lear

Or I am Callisto, and could as bear have
fathered Ulysses, eh?[133]

Or notice my skin is
heliotropic

And that I prefer ceruellas[134] to mangos

— that i shit & generate, or can run a society does not
stop the necessity to formulate, and to continue to push
on to the next back wall

Or Orion—who is beautiful—is less beautiful because i
know it is false that his pattern is observabelt [*i.e.,*
observable, *but with possible pun on Orion's belt*] as such
to anything but a pair of my eyes

or beavers, that, there
is any more value than a lesson, that, the guy with the
best teeth & the most will to work will live to produce
more of his same another day—and the poor damned
toothless willess sap will go and die for lack of food, eh?

All this observation is no more good to me than, that the
phoenix took such care with his father after his father dies
that he carefully made a ball of frankincense in which he
wrapped his father in order to fly with this lovely fragrant
corpse across the dryness of Arabia to drop the body in the
Nile waters so that it could be carried into the Mediterranean
and not be carrion of flies, or human beings, or anything but
fish[135]

As, by the way, Seth, the bad brother of Osiris, carefully
strew[ed] the 14 pieces he cut Osiris up into, into the same
waters, and fish ate Osiris's tool—as tho, it were, the way
the story goes, a tender part![136]

So these are crazy facts?

They tell me more about myself
than anything i ever got out of the general dissection of a foetal
pig as a dissection in place of a human cadaver. YET, exactly that
day, the extrication of the pituitary of that pig gave me more of a
sense of how we are kinged by this gland than I could have got
from Pliny, eh?

In other words, all & anything is of use. But that
there is any principle for action other than the use of yrself as a
blundering idiot is a breeder of false action, false conclusion, and
basic imposition on the most wonderful thing of all—our
differences.

OK. Will shut up, let me only have yr valuing of
anything sd, to force me further, eh?

                              All's well: the baby—Con
says—started to talk sounds last night, when I was out! And we
had the funny business of taking her into the village yesterday
afternoon and having everybody look, coo, talk—crazy, how
much, her existence invites their attention

                                        —ok

                    WRITE EVERY DAY!   olson

                                        [Black Mountain, N.C.]
                                        tuesday dec 5 [*i.e.* 4]   51

robt:
        Item #1: will get out of here, & be gone a month, come the
weekend: so, write, thereafter, for a while, to the old address—217
Randolph Place, NE, Wash 2, eh?
                              Am stir crazy, to go—god
knows how: figure to give Con the Dec salary, and hitchhike
myself. Which I shall enjoy: to be on the road, & on my own, ok.
ok.
        Shall probably go NE to join Con & baby & her two sisters &
their five kids (oldest, 5!) for the holiday. Tho don't crave that.
Rather, wld lose myself, somewhere, eh?
                              No letters in fr you, in a
hell of a time, & miss same.

        OK. Thing still is Edmund. Tremendously caught, this run, by
the cut of his figure
                      (o, yeah, What-I-am-Thought-Of Dept:
Nation, this week, says—a propos a Melville review—Olson
indefensibly wild, "Freudian," & intellectual—quote. How abt that
for posy, eh?)[137]

And last night saw, 1st time, Goose #3 — you, & Olson anthology. Only thing bothers me ((have altogether dismissed myself therein!)) is, that, there, he has *our* Guido! Didn't know that, or remember. And wanted our BROADSIDES — so far as possible — all to be fresh, new businesses. So, ROBT CREELEY, please sit right down and write me a NEW ONE — sit there, Fontrousse, & write me IRA & LITTLETON.

                                 ((Still, Goose, or here, or anywhere, publishing smells: i find no quietness, firmness, & dignity in the act of print in any of these endeavors

                                                 — will say

for Ed [*i.e.,* El] Cid he did do decently his derring-do
     (((how dirtily In Cold Hell is spread in that issue! i figure i am well out of such hands — such vulgarism))

Ok. Beside Edmund, finding out more abt this man's verse, and figure next few years will see a Shakespeare text will look as though contemporary poets edited the punctuation, the way those stupid capitals, semi-colons, exclamation points, & all the First Folio crap will be done away with: in fact, wld, myself, like to restore texts of A & C, Lear, and the romances. For I feel sure the scholars will not dare to take the step of applying their own new knowledge of punctuation as they have it from the fact that the 2nd Quarto Hamlet can be shown to be printed direct from S's mss. It is crazy, how, the punctuation does make the verse limpid — sure, we'd know that, yet, to see it in action in his lines is SOME NEW THING there:

     look at this short one (if you have a Shks handy, just check it against this wholly different reading:

here is the Quarto 2:
                             "What a peece of worke is a man, how noble in reason, how infinit in faculties, in form and moving, how expresse and admirable in action, how like an Angel in apprehension, how like a God: the beautie of the world; the paragon of Animales; and yet to me, what is this Quintessence of dust:

Oh, let me copy off for you the 1st soliloquy :

O that this too too sullied flesh would melt,
Thaw and resolve it selfe into a dewe,
Or that the everlasting had not fixt
His cannon gainst selfe slaughter, o God, God,
How weary, stale, flat, and unprofitable
Seeme to me all the uses of this world!
Fie on't, ah fie, tis an unweeded garden
That growes to seede, things rancke and grose in nature
Possesse it meerely that it should come to this
But two months dead, nay not so much, not two,
So excellent a King, that was to this
Hiperion to a satire, so loving to my mother
That he might not beteeme the winds of heaven
Visite her face too roughly, heaven and earth
Must I remember, why she should hang on him
As if increase of appetite had growne
By what it fed on, and yet within a month,
Let me not thinke on't; frailty thy name is woman
A little month or ere those shoes were old
With which she followed my poore fathers bodie
Like Niobe all teares, why she even she,
O God, a beast that wants discourse of reason
Would have mourn'd longer, married with my Uncle,
My fathers brother, but no more like my father
Than I to Hercules, within a month,
Ere yet the salt of most unrighteous teares
Had left the flushing in her gauled eyes
She married, o most wicked speed; to post
With such dexteritie to incestious sheets,
It is not, nor it cannot come to good,
But breake my hart, for I must hold my tongue.

So far as I now know, just to get it down for any future use you
might care to put it to, the only text now in print from which to
start to see this sort of way of looking at all the plays is:

THE NEW SHAKESPEARE—Hamlet—Cambridge Univ Press—
ed., Dover Wilson

Also, in this same series, The New S., Wilson has edited *Measure
for Measure* among the comedies there edited (maybe some of the
others, don't know)

And Faber & Faber issued his edition of ANTONY & CLEO (tho
this—unless he has done the xtraordinary—is suspicious, as it is a
Folio Facsimile)

S's address, how straight he attacks any given statement under
hand! This one can learn from, without regard to the differences of
the problems of statement, eh?
                                 And such new punctuation takes
off so much of the rhetoric and declamation which the 1st Folio
(the base of all texts since) put on—and apparently these
deformations were put on the moment S delivered his mss to the
Company—apparently even Burbage[138] acted these things according
to the miserableness of the Folio punctuation, etc.
                                 —Wilson argues
that Shks—after 1600—was no longer in any position with the
Company to direct or dictate the use of his material!
                                 And I tend
to go along with him. The picture that emerges is damned
interesting—that, at the very moment that he made his major push

Hamlet   1601
  Troilus   1602
    (All's Well   1603)

        Measure for Measure   1604
        Othello   1605

        Lear   1606
        Macbeth   1606

        Antony & Cleopatra   1607

Coriolanus & Timon   1608

then, romances, 1609 Cymbeline
                1610 Winter's Tale
                1611 Tempest

The point is, maybe, when he
started to push out — to push
drama as he had himself wrote
it — way the hell beyond what it
had been (starting Hamlet), he
may well have left his Company
(at least their sympathy) behind
him, eh? That they couldn't help
but use his plays — he had long
been their chief supplier — but
what he was now up to (3500
line plays!) was not what they
asked for! (Evidence, that,
Pericles (1608-09) — which I damn
well don't think he did any more
than fuss with some one else's
work — was what his "name" was
most praised for!

((((Well. Just one of those days,
when, it is merely the facts
which my mind is capable of
recording, eh))))

(((& this strange one, that, the
year he was all done — & 49
yrs old — 1613 — the King
James Version published
                        (in
which he had hand — at least,
brushing up, the Psalms)

                        by
his act there, the Bible (& by
the influence of his verse
previous to its translation on
that translation?), he moved
down into the "folk" use of
language straight through for
250 years, until Melville
bemoans the loss (to himself)
of people's knowledge of the
images & rhythms of that
testament
            ((M was aware of
the loss to himself abt the
Civil War, & punctuates it in
Billy Budd, 1891))

Have, over the weekend, been running down that hare I
scared writing to you Friday: de Gourmont, & the "Nature"
old P may have been working with
                    De Gourmont is too
smart a character to leave himself open — but the
POSTSCRIPT! by EP, is something! (EP trying to pull a
Lawrence, a Fantasia of Paleontology [Biology *crossed out*]!)

The proposition is, that the BRAIN, is a clot of semen! That here is man's galvanic offset to the OTHER TOOL — and by god if he doesn't talk abt himself & head attacking the vulva of London![139]

WOW, This, you must read!

Just these random things on Edmund, to close off, & get something to you for yr grist, eh?

another way of posing E as "son of" L, is, that both of em appeal for sanction to Nature as Procreative Goddess (& are alone in this), with this huge difference, that E does it *as generated* (as bastard, & so, with only Her rights & no legal ones, to Her as his necessary Law)

and L *as*

generator

and i suspect the reason for the dimension of this play is, that, what Lear is proposing — asking Nature — is TO CEASE PRODUCING, dry up in her the organs of increase, break the molds and spill all seeds germane to man

It is his wild demand. And only the restoration to him of Cordelia causes him to cease that demand — and then, it turns out, the alternative is, his heart must break

It is a huge argument of the heart as a thing of light against the eyes (which open in the womb & close in death: these are the two darknesses which make the wheel which turns between them)

— and

each are broken, one way or another. And ultimately only the ceasing of Nature's act — her, the female, and definitely that — not at all man as male as a part of same

in fact, the male (again edmund is the poser of this) is the day man, has one business: to be alert to leap on the back of the day

(okay, to kill or to howl

Lear has the latter competence

And the two of them — at the end — are broken, Edmund by the
eyes, and Lear by the heart

    (the Fool catches a cold, Cordelia is hung — these two,
    anyway, from start to finish, are Lear's only objects of
    affection

        what changes — for Lear — is that his attention to
    these objects shifts — he is brought up against the necessity
    of enlarging his heart: that is all:: he finds Nature cannot
    diminish herself!

Edmund makes no discovery: he merely loses. But what is clear &
clean abt Edmund is that he never invokes Nature by complaint —
or even to demand anything of her. He merely figures to run
parallel to her. And this he does:

                The wheel comes full circle: I
am here. A cool one.

If he is the son of Lear (he is that also in the sense that he is
successfully what Lear's daughters ain't, a manipulator of his
father's goods & lands (Gloucester) — he wants what Goneril &
Regan also want. But they are mere termagants, bitches, literally
witches, hags, monsters — not of bastardry of nature but of
themselves.

        (((((((((I can't, at this latter day, take this play by
a handle of evil or innate depravity whatsoever. In its different
way, from A & C, it comes out to me an objectist's act likewise: a
posing, not on a huge hand of the day's business, of the round
earth & love, but on a wholly other geometry — of *the inside* of a
round thing (as against that outside) — of the hollows & huts,
hovels, hearts — "I cannot heave my heart into my mouth" — the
echoes — "death is the earth," says Lear

                (its physiology is
internal — the organs — and its geography is the earth & the vault of
heaven, with Nature as procreative thing the huge rear, "the
mystery of things"

[*In pencil:*]
OK. Let me have yr thoughts. What do you think — any use, to

em to do a job on A & C & L as, these things? Well, no—it's done, now, to you. I can no longer much believe in "essays"!

Crazy, tho—the way the two plays came to me by their imagery! Beautiful worker, that man.

PS #2: One thing comes clear—how S *points* Edmund by opening his play on him—& giving him 2 of the only 3 soliloquies in the whole show (the other is Lear's)

& *PS #3*: The movement *away fr* soliloquy (in A & C, & L) is *clear*

Wld figure S as catching on—just in these years between H & Lear—that the lyric & psychological both dead, as straight on. So he killed what he bred, the soliloquy. Think, now, all after him was retrogression, because these very advances of his were not seen as *undone* by his very self.

PS # 4: The Romances, then, became a wholly *new* attack—the return of the "lyric," the folding in of the psyche, the birth of an *art of decoration* or *masque*—where drama, now, again I'd argue—must move off. *Not*, fr his tragedies, etc

———————————————

[Black Mountain, N.C.
5 December 1951]

Robt: wed.—wanted to add this: that the idea that, just now, a man cld damn well come close to restoring Shk's verse as it got itself writ, excites me, as an act of restoration as important as a translation—& more.

As a matter of fact I am interested in trying it on, say, A & C, &
Lear (tho it is probably one of those things a man might do but
doesn't because he ain't more than one, eh?). My argument for the
gain of it wld be that—in neither of these two cases is there any
likelihood any of the scholars will do it out of piousness: for my
memory is, there is no good *quarto*, of either of these (as there is,
the 2nd Q, on Hamlet). In fact, there is *no* quarto of A & C, only
the Folio text. And the two Qs of Lear are both bad, as I
remember. (Will be checking both these facts in Wash., at the Lib
of Cong.)

But the A & C as we have it is based upon a good mss and this
may explain why its verse is so conspicuously limpid.

Anyhow, I'd figure that, very soon, on the basis of new texts by
these "bibliographical" scholars—Wilson, Pollard, Greg[140]—one cld
put one's hand to these plays (even with no more info than the
"correct" punctuation of the Q2 Hamlet) and turn out a lively text,
eh?

What it comes down to is, that a man, to do this job right, wld
have to be (1) himself a poet, and, I'd guess, a contemporary one;
(2), somewhat knowing in how the language was *pronounced* in
Shk's time; and (3), acquaint himself with what these scholars have
to offer about S's graphology

(Crazy thot: why not, myself, do a *preface* to these two plays—
AND A CAREFUL "FREE" TEXT of both, and get somebody
interested in publishing them: it wld be a way of issuing S that
wld be fresh—that is, putting two plays into such juxtaposition
one to the other in the same book, thus making the point I have
been making to you, that, each play arises from the verse common
to itself, by way of the controlling image—and in these two
cases—THE OBJECTIST SHAKESPEARE, eh?—being a
counterpoise of IN & OUT
        what abt that   what abt that   what abt that   (by god,
        maybe i cld float myself an advance, on such a proposition, fr
        a commercial house! & heave out of here—get this done this

spring, as, a going over to, my proper business? Let me have yr response to this at Washington, and maybe i cld stick up one of the houses in NY passing thru there this month? Giroux, say, at Harcourt? (tho he has been singularly cold to all my suggestions)[141]   Or Viking? tho i do not like those people   Maybe i ought to hit such a "literary" character as Erskine at Random (who bought Ishmael for Reynal — he might take to such a concept[142]   (And i might have the advantage that, Olivier, is storming NY again, just now, with, his & his wife's A & C,[143] the children here tell me: on the instant I wrote Motherwell sticking him up for a ticket to see that show — scalper biz, like all theatre, and one of the reasons i gave the fucking thing up — too gd necessary to "plan" to go

In any case, the whole idea is a cheap substitute for a better one i haven't yet had the guts to tackle — an idea i have had for some time: to do a GLOSS of any play which catches me at the time — that is, to let his verse be the provocation for passages of my own alongside, you might say ((it came to me 1st three years ago abt this time when i happened to read Tempest))

The pronunciation biz, is, actually, one which i imagine only a poet wld be likely to dig (none of the textual scholars seem to think of it, & as a result, leave themselves one-armed: e.g., in that soliloquy herein, note sullied where "solid" wld seem to me to make more sense

    & my guess is, that, solid, then, was sollide, & was
    pronounced damn close to sallide or sullide & so got falsely
    heard & transcribed.   OK. Anyhow, IDEAS!

[Fontrousse, Aix-en-Provence]
December 7, 1951

Dear Chas/

Holding on, even if dead with the dullness here. Still trying to pick up the S/ and hope to, tomorrow. Phew. Anyhow, all this coming thru very clear, very damn fine.

This last: A/ said, or had, with his usual clarity, there is no 'progress' in art. Why I have hated this sense of 'evolution'; it compells that immediate falseness.

The differences, say, between Ez in that SERIOUS ARTIST, and later qualifications, might be of the point; note that he had it, we get our only usuable data re where medicine (science) leaves off with a man, from the artists.[144]

In any case, all this has a fineness, a precise damn sight. 'The thing is to be perfect . . . ,' but they don't get it. One wants to have the exactness of his *own* abilities, at least a consciousness of them; but this predicates *no* 'end.' Even the Doctor's 'there is no end to desire . . .' kills that sense of it. Not that one simply wants, etc. Or so simply, tho it is almost so, at that.

And not only 'abilities' — too fast there, being too dull. I mean, I think, that with this same predication of means as ends, with that emphasis (and doesn't that stem from this same false patterning?), one is over-rushing the particulars, and odd that it should be these men (such as the one you tell me of) who have this tendency to do so. I expect it is, perhaps, the wish to have relevance, or to have an impressive relevance. Too damn bad.

Anyhow, I think you are very, very clear. I think those two positions noted in CMI, i.e., of the staking, or riding, would also throw the same thing, i.e., put it there.[145] It is a question, damnit, of a position, and of the use of that position, somehow. And no 'place.' Etc. Well, that has been killed anyhow, or at least between us. The 'positions' you'd got from those physicists, even that immediate thing in ICH, — But a field is not a choice . . .[146] Ok.

Isn't it the same damn 'comparison' here, that lean to equivalents that doesn't see how equivalents are possible? Damnit, the base sense, there, in the Fenollosa. That thing of, 'sentence.'

Klee: that one will *use* anything that falls to hand, but not by that use, be less the *thing* he is. Or vitiate. Or subtract, etc. Or finally nullify.[147]

There are no truths as analogies. I can't believe it, anyhow. Not in this instance. Likewise, no progress, not in their dead sense of it, nor in, I think, any sense but the horizontal. (Force is, & therefore stays: what one has to do with.)

I don't say much. This to get back, and will be on again soon I hope. Feel somewhat better; a few things clear, or we have the car just about set — likewise headaches with the divers officials. I had a letter from Laubies; had got yr PRO/ VERSE & liked same very much. Will try to figure something for it. Ok. Keep us on. Will do my damndest to do likewise.

All best love to you all/

Bob

[*Verso envelope:*]
I just got a letter from Kitasono, and he says he's translated The Grace into Jap/. He had the 2 — Party & same, and seems to like them. I'm confused by this apparent lean on G/ — both him & Gerhardt now — but damnit KNOW my own damn headaches.

Black Mt (still!   100 things
Monday, December 10 [1951]

Robt:

    1st, it has just dawned on me, the fact that fucker-upper
Emerson has issued GUIDO, is nothing for us to fuss with, thus—
that, as you say, Bryant wld prefer to do design for story. OK ok!
Suddenly, it dawns on me, who ever sd (if I didn't) that these
BROADSIDES need be verse! Just now, for ex., PARTY—jesus,
this broadside form is perfect for such as, no?

                              And it wld be
wonderful for me to get out one of yr stories here, eh?

Look: if you like PARTY itself, fine (figuring either, you'd give it
me over the New Mex X, or, just write me anudder, eh? Whatever
you say. BUT in any case, i think this is THE solution, no?

                                   For I
am most anxious to make this series all unpublished stuff—
otherwise, it ain't the fun it can be to any of us, that, here, we
have a place where all new stuff can move.

                           #1 is out, and I am
mailing you a copy straight mail today—as many as i can steal
from cernovich. (I am not satisfied by it—that is, the lad's too
fancy for my taste—and the 18 pt Garamond distends that
particular piece (the bullfight), makes it carry more expression
than—precisely that piece—is meant to ((that is, the point of it,
right?, was exactly its flatness, on, such a subject, eh?))

                                   but i did
not want to get myself into the publishing end of this business, or
i'd be ragged & nothing wld get done except if i put my own hand
to it:

    and i figure this is a sort of dream, anyway: to get out
single pieces, with some handsomeness ((in fact, the dream dates
back exactly to fall, 1940))

((((& it now enlightens me further, in this respect, that, I am
forced further along my own logic of what is proper publishing
for a verse-maker like myself:

> not books, but, such single
> sheets—and executed, immediately thereon the writing,
> worked out, while the thing is in hand, to its finish, issued,
> as such, sitting by itself, as *quietly* & handsomely as paper,
> press, design can make it

((Already—here—I have come to crave a deep return   —in such
publishing—   to the quietness & dignity of type & of paper

> yet

the solution (that is, somewhere up from Spiral Press
conservatism—quietism—& these loud Black Mt creatures, who
think color—COLORS—will do everything!

jesus: BLACKLETTER, blackletter eh?

> ((& one further thing, or

two:
(1) i imagine i told you my desire to design a new type, last fall: a
type based on half-uncial ((the alphabet which followed the
first, or Roman, eh?—neither upper or lower case, but, a type
in between, and I'd guess magnificently correct for the sort of
emphases i am interested in—without the shouts CAPS put
on—

> well, this desire is even stronger, now, that i see how 18
pt (I was willing to go along with Nick, to see) is merely
billboard

& (2) that, in calligraphy as it now being practiced again, there is
something the revival does not get its sight on: that is, that, it
is not a return to a medieval script which is called for, but a
formalization of our own handwritings—that is, just as in the
half-uncial, the job would be, to declare a type apt to our eye
for type now, merely taking the principle of no minuscule or
whatever the big is—the job wld be to work out a
formalization of stroke which could take any of our natural
hands and by formalizing it only to the degree any one can
read it (that is, so that natural runnings of minims, e.g., the
n's we all crush, etc. would be restored

                                        —o, fuck it, just
figuring some of these things out

We are buggered as to how to move north. To cart a baby
presents problems new to us. It's 12 hrs to Wash.—14 by bus—
overnight by train. And money! Yet, we both want out. Want to
jump this place: sick of it. And even without a baby we have
never been able at the get-away! So here we are dawdling precious
days away. Well, not actually: much had to be done. And still I
have not one pair of shoes to appear in a city in: & no cobbler, in
this paradise of the practical arts, eh. Ho Ho.

Your wondrous push of letter on Lerma, then, the killer, all came
in one mail, and we were like as tho it was at a serial! Will he get
to Marseilles—will he make the Sieur de la Salle—& get the girl,
get Lerma! It was too much, lad, just too much—for we wanted
you to do it, we both were hanging happily on that outcome,
figuring, by god, we'll up stakes and *bum* our way—baby & all—
to visit you, there, our people, our home, that sun, sea &
yrselves!

> You never did get to tell us what swung you off. Figure it
> must have been *another* move—plus Ann's natural concern
> for two young kids, thar, eh?
>   And figure (as we told you fr
> there) it wld present its problems. Yet, so far as health goes,
> both Con & I—after yr ride in those letters—were allowing
> to each other that neither of us had had such damn fine
> "health" as there, & so, I think we would now follow (as of
> Kate, say) a rule of thumb—that if *we* were healthy, why
> not she, too—finally, any other figuring becomes a drag,
> no?

That is, dysentery seems to be the major problem with children,
no? I don't know. Christ, we had not a touch. But there—kids
pick up, suck, eat random stuff, eh? Well, just don't know. Can't
say. Just can't say.

In any case, you don't ask anything of us anytime which is anything but a pleasure—more than that—a damn big chunk of wonder—to do, see? And wherever you want to go, dig this citizen. I'd ask anyone anywhere for anything you want, you people. So, don't say, you put any weight on me. On contrary: you lighten my goddamned days.

And so keep me on all moves, or hungers to move: just whistle, lad, and if there is a gd thing i got to give, it's wonderful.

And above all don't be embarrassed by any shift: as a professional of same myself, I am experienced!

And

if the Lerma thing still feels like the end of the rainbow, take these things as sure:

(1) that a house will be waiting for you
   (2) that for you & Ann the health ought to be the best
      (3) on the boys, i just don't know—except that Licia,
          Mariano, Ignacio Novello (in fact ma & pa
             Novello are friends such as are rare, &
                KNOW things, their

environment
   on point (4)—i do figure you'd rise—as you say, i rose—to
   those people more than to the Yurrupeens: simply, that, they
   are ahead (even tho the American thing is giving them its
   worst foot)

Yet i go back & back to the sense that, those people, there—those Yucatecans—once the white will is off their lorn[?]—will MOVE:

& it is what you or I are able to see *because* (I take it) we is amurrikans;

that there are us to be counted on the fingers who are *different* from our fellow countrymen YET are of this country:

I surprised myself, Thursday night—last spiel here before the break—by pouncing on Melville again in a running jump from Homer to Shakespeare to ourselves, & coming up with a

perception of him that the writing of the Ode[148] may have
knocked out of my head. But let me try to catch it back:

                                                        i sd i

was sick of any citizen who has to go to Asia to seek an
animism fit to offset the spiritual or internal principle which
Judeo-Christian civilization has rested itself on

                                        Yes, it was this
        sudden pairing of *animism* as the recognizable *outside*
        going-on ((the rage of phenomenon)) with the more
        familiar "soul" gig (& without loss of that gig, merely, a
        straightening of it, a clearing, from, J-C c!

I don't suppose it sounds anyway fresh, but, for me it war — and
came out of that pairing: Antony & Cleopatra AND Lear. For
what has moved me, there, is, that this man S *was* (as i now take
it Homer & Melville also were — at least those two, and I'm not so
sure who else) right and left handed, that the damned wondrous
thing is, that, these two plays are, together, a demonstration of
the necessary end to all dualities —

                        that spirit & flesh are no more
divisible than individual & society are (the latter, the latest — 19th
century shit — of same easy, discourse definitions — words)

& that Melville damn well made clear what americans still can't
get to (because of the colonialism stretching back to that fucking
Moses): that the American outrage on nature — on all outside
things — is as proof of their animism (at least of his, yrs, mine,
say — again, not wanting to count more fingers than i have on *one*
hand!) as our failure to buy the Judeo-Christian package (seasonal
stuff) is no proof we don't have "souls."

That is, the struggle still is also to be clear our doctrine of
pragmatism — that easy screed against objectism — in blindness of
animism as, validly, the way to put what makes all things as live
as any of us might seek to be

        that is, the coldness of S in these two plays *is* the cleanness I
        had not previously been able to figure, there — had it, in
        Homer, but, there, the lack of his language stops final

surance; & in M was sure, as, the world well knows, eh? that, that man, had the grasp even if he—like Ben Jonson had it, of S—"wanted art":[149]

those two plays reduce to the damndest loveliest bald propositions: that, A & C, all things, including that gypsy or the rule of the world, are as perfect as candy, and, put in the mouth, candy— melts

in Lear, it is the heart which is not easily heaved into the mouth; yet, only when one eats his heart, can he be full of what wretches, too, are full of—and of the pain of it, he dies, of a broken heart

Either way, the end is—the end. What matters is, what goes on between the beginning and the end, what "success" men manage—& surely, what is the act of truth is, simply, that each manages what he can—I still take it that Mr S's distinction is his clarity that there is no hierarchy, that there is only differences of capability

(that one can throw the scales between Edmund & Lear, yet, that, so throwing the scales you don't do any more than disclose that Edmund is one man and Lear is such another

& that the gauge of this difference is not to be sought alone between them, but in such surrounding distinctions as, that Edgar & Gloucester (despite as maximal suffering as any of the people of the play endure) come out of it all with nothing more than G's flat:
  "I see feelingly"
          & E's:
              "The ripeness, is all" (or the
              "readiness"—Hamlet sez this, or vice verse)

that S—or any man—has the necessary clarity (the sense of reality here is the only use of the phrase i cld allow) when he can dispose his people with their differences without weighting those differences by some act of choice other than the degree of dignity involved in the suffering & its issue:

that is, Enobarbus also dies of a broken heart, yet, Lear's
heart (& not necessarily because he was a king, though, by
god, these worldly distinctions do have efficient cause, eh?
and are well used by same S as by above Homer ((i take it
Calypso is a measure of a difference in women between one
who can enjoy herself straight out by the very best fucking
and Circe, who, has to spice the thing up with certain
nastinesses))

   his heart's breaking is *other than*, is *more*

And let it be left at that, eh?

       that there is *no balance* any more
than there is any *ladder*
  ('an thou canst not smile as the wind
  sits, thou'll catch cold, shortly')

if a man is true, then, in him there is truth; if he is driven to
justice, then there you can observe justice; if he is as Edmund is,
then, you are in the presence of a man who wants to take what
birth, he figures, didn't allow him, is, a grabber, but a cool
enough one to grant that, licked, he is licked, and no crap called
for. And that there are human creatures who are none of these
things — not even ambitious — but are like something from another
genera of the same species, are literally witches: Goneril, Regan —
as their husbands — Albany & Cornwall — are something else again,
the living dead: the sort of things (& I have known some) whom
one forgets to buy a ticket for at the box-office, even when they
are standing right beside you!

This is the sort of disposing of living things which I dub human
phenomenology — and which same only makes any ultimate sense
to me: no plugging, not a damned thing added to the facts than
the most wonderful thing of all, the motion of same facts & things
in their relevances to each other

       and with such motion (I only
think it can happen when the out & the in are both seen as one)
  image only can serve: why, I press on, now, again, metaphor
  as a means of living — of *moving* — is called back into business

(which ought to be a firmer
way to get at what the act of "imagination" might have once
meant—that word, too, has got to be seen as emptied of content,
& so: of formal use—that logic, like soul, are parts of the same
half-truth, that Judeo-Christian system exists by: that man is the
wonder, that thing I never saw, something which lives without
reference to things—and so, by the rigor of its own logic, without
any other human being

> (thus, the one-one *relation*: man to God is, the only
> flower of same: a flowere which, now, like the flag,
> rots itself with motion in the stream

This, also, came into my mouth, last week: that by the soul logic
(the animation of any other thing than a human being disallowed)
there can be no motion or participation which another human
being, simply, than, the soul of me is such an exclusive thing I
cannot possibly make a passage over to an act of identification
with your soul

> thus, increasingly, others become indistinguishable
from all other things. They have to, simply, because, the soul seen
as personal and human cannot do any more than say, you are a
thing, ultimately, an object. And I? am different: I, know my soul!
I cannot know, yours.

Or come at a way which I take it is the only allowable one,
the correction: the act of life is not local, is distributed, and the
human distinction is what RC put when he had it: conjecture. On
such grounds, life is anyone's or anything's just exactly to the
degree that they move us:

((I have a fancy for that verb, simply because, it is ultimately
the only refuge that even the J-C's have:

> God moves in. . . . &

I am moved . . eh?

That is, that the *ordering of motion* is the only morality. There is
no other, and act is that ordering, even on the most rudimentary
levels of action (I am assuming a distinction between mere activity
& action). And for me the act of metaphor (or however one cares

to be specific about the act of art) is the most illuminating simply
because (1) it can't exist without actions
   which are not illuminated—in the sense that we all fail
                       and (2) that it depends upon
the maximum use of that which i take to be the human distinction:
conjecture.

Whence follows something which cuts across all immediate shit abt
art's act in society ((the problem is a phoney anyhow, simply,
because, society is a divisive word the 18th & 19th centuries
appear to me to have invented—or at least gave false circulation
to, in lieu of any comprehension of an individual's multiple
takings, eh?)):
               if the act is conjecture for order, and its content is
the imperfection of any one of us, then, the act of art is an act of
restoration, in this sense that, its proportions are—when the act is
good—restored to where they came from
                           that the act of
recognition (which is now I take it understood to be a function of
art which, for some time, was forgotten, or, neglected::: the whole
present drift toward a science or practice of mythology, & the
parallel movement to drama, & specifically, verse-drama has made
"recognition" now almost the newest cliche) in any case, for me,
now coming on two yrs since G & C—where I think I myself thot
it worth saying—this is already inadequate

and i wld push on to this proposition: that the act of restoration
(that anything—color, line, sound, a word, whatever—has to be
returned to where we found it ((this strikes me as the same
principle as, (1), above, that, there ain't no "material" except in
human actions—that a man's own actions are not very interesting
except as he forces them to conclusion—that merely that he acts
has been grossly "dramatized" by most all the Cellinis of art,
writing allowed as one of same!

recognition by conjecture & restoration by the order of image

Well, all such statements only leave me more buried in my own gall, that, I fail. Shit.

Yet, something here rings right, the moment i think again of S, and the sight he raises for me on Homer & Melville: that suddenly S too seems to me to be presenting a reality as firm & lucid as the Odyssey (I am never wholly content that Moby-Dick is that good—it is just that the existence of that man, 100 yrs ago, is a leg up, eh?

> in any case, M had that dignity which comes from a like measure to those other two—or, to put it the way the experience was, I find it possible to move around in his world as in theirs with a sense that that world makes sense to me as the way my own world is—even though i am able to participate in own world only by fits & starts, that—most of the time—I am fucked up by my own stupidities

There was something else I wanted to tell you, but I am afraid it was the baby went out with the bath.

It was in this area of consideration.

Can't get it back.

Anyway, damned glad all things went to hell over night (the baby was off, Con got fussed by fucking visitors last night, & I was kept awake until 8 AM by a dirty little "saint" working in the photo lab down under us here). For Con & I came to our senses, and have simply forgot trying to get out of here today, or tomorrow maybe even—just, have squatted. And so, I have seized this afternoon to get back on with you:

> ok; please keep after me this "vacation," eh?
>
> & shall keep on with you as i move
>
> love
> charles

[Fontrousse, Aix-en-Provence]
December 13, 1951

Dear Charles,

Some damn temptation simply to keep quiet,
because it is not too good still; mainly this cold, and a usual
dreariness. The thing would be, I think, to get off, a space of
sorts, but now impossible, and we all hang on here in the one
room.

Your letters coming thru. Don't get nervous on that, i.e., I
am making them, and they are very clear. Not to put it so dully.
But I want to get the book, read it, and make it myself; all of it,
anyhow, seems, or damnit, is, straight. I can't see anything off.

Reading what I can get hold of. Melville's TYPEE; and the
PIAZZA TALES. These a week ago. Hit, again, by that language,
and, this time, the commas. Something.

Likewise, some of James'
short stories; at least one part, in A BUNDLE OF LETTERS, the
girl there faced with the other's 'haughtiness.' I liked that. I like
him very, very much at times. Or at least I believe in the
consciousness, etc.

Otherwise, Coleridge. More to the point at the
moment, and have, this morning, read more of his poems than I
ever had before. DEJECTION: I liked very much. A clean &
beautiful thing; very free I thought. And even bits & pieces from
the others, certain movement, here & there, in something like the
CHRISTABEL: She kneels beneath the huge oak tree, / And in
silence prayeth she . . .   Just the last, etc. Little things like that he
gets often: I know 'tis but a dream, yet feel more anguish / Than
if 'twere truth. It has been often so . . .   The last again. Etc. I am

not able to do more than read it, etc. I have that Portable thing;[150] and the collection looks fair enough. The letters were what I was looking for; or, perhaps better, things like the Biographia Literaria. Who knows.

Anyhow, not much in hand. The other afternoon, looking thru some books at a friend's place, that Yeats' selection, THE OXFORD BOOK OF MODERN VERSE. I read that part on Pound; never got clearly that distance, even substance, of 'time.'[151] He couldn't get, I think, even the possibility; was that simply a man's own character, etc. I don't think so.

Also, Jack Hawkes sent me his new novel, THE BEETLE LEG. It has a good deal, mainly the means to coherence he hits on — that he lets it out, the things, then stops short. In that sense, or use, very good. I feel him, though, a sort of Blackburn; there is the immaculate technique, though not B/s often coldness, etc. H/ makes the expansion, and with, oddly, his sense of detail. There are many, many similes, but most I don't choke on. Best, in any case, his sense of how a coherence can be addressed, etc. Or got to. I mean it hits at the falseness of a 'logic,' etc.

Too dull, in any case. I can't get to much. I had a dream about you both last night; an apartment house where the elevators opened directly into the rooms. Many lights. A kind of shaded, or pleasant affair. You were both on your way off for somewhere; children, not ours or yours, in it, cousins, or something of that kind. Party, and hurried drinking, even a band at one point, but all pretty intimate, like they say. I was in love with your wife; she was very damn kind, then, I mean, a very crazy softness & feel to all she was saying. I think I said it all, there, to you, or that I did love her, and we talked it over, though hastily, because the plane you were to go on was almost ready to start. But, talking, we were too distracted, or I felt myself expecting your anger, and you were more or less incredulous. Sic transit, etc. Phew.

I wish I could get back to work, I feel a hell of a lot pulling these days in spite of my own sluggishness. I always get some impetus from reading other stuff, a kind of use at that. Or one, etc. But can't get much at the moment; too cramped here, and it's the problem of literal space. Though writing this, etc. I suppose, etc. No, but it isn't so simple. Place too much what I would be talking about directly, or something of that sort, I suppose.

I was worried about the GUIDO, reading your last letter. I mean, in this present place, etc., so dead and no hope I can see of making any alternatives. Also, that Ashley is into it now. But I saw him and certainly there is no objection, etc. The wish to have each thing new is altogether clear, and have it myself. Well, say what you think; I like the poem, but if you figure that prior issue would kill it, for the series, I can see it and fair enough.

(All so much a fugg anyhow, such damn things; would to god we could both sit clean of them. Though I have hellish aches about Cid & all; I feel pretty much an idiot, now feeling the pinch, etc. But I can't see it was wrong; I couldn't take his interference, etc., especially being so very well intentioned, etc. Fuck it. Ann says, *when* will you get famous so we can get *out* of here???) [*A line added under* will, *with arrow drawn to it from the line under* when (*changing emphasis*), *and with question mark and* I guess so! *added below.*]

Not much like Christmas. My mother used to say, so damn often, your father was such a Christmas man, etc. So loved it, like she said. I don't seem, or at present, to have taken over that aspect. Dull, dull here. Pinched, etc. I was thinking of even that—to watch his woods fill up with snow[152]—with tears. How about that. I am pretty maudlin at this point. And what I used to kick at I would, most usually, now wish to hell I had hold of. But these are the earlier memories anyhow. We made those damn bird things, lumps of suet, etc., and I can think of the jays driving off the smaller. Those names, etc., I can't damn well now think of. But you know the thing. Clear, damn clear, and space. Not a trace of it here. I used to go trapping, as a kid, or thought I did; I

had about 2 or 3 old rusty traps and went down by a small
brook, where I saw tracks, and put the traps by the water, breaks
in the ice, etc. I never got anything, but later, about 2 years ago
in NH, when some coons were eating our corn, I set two traps
and nailed them, both, the first night, and had the hell of seeing
one dead there, in the trap, because I hadn't even thought it would
catch them, and didn't get down to look until late afternoon.

It is
all a fucking accumulation anyhow, I wish I could hang on to that
clearly.

Hence, viper thoughts, that coil around my mind : it says here.
Ok. I turn to you, it says, etc., or rather, I turn *from* you, and
listen to the wind / Which long has raved unnoticed.[153] What a
scream . . .

Fuck it. Do write, and say what goes. Feel so
damn far off, now, altogether a distance. Hope it's cooler; I felt so
hellishly restless after either of the kids were born—damn well
room's what's needed. To get clear, to come back, etc. How it all
was them, I thought.

Ok. Damn dull, and forgive me for that.
Sometime do you think you could make a recording (old style,
i.e., not long-playing) of anything you want, of yours, and send
it? I will gladly reimburse you for sd costs, like they say. The
things I had there in NH were very damn well useful. I wish I had
them here. Say what you think. Write soon, ok. Will do same. All
love to you all/
      Bob

To add this: all the stuff in, and many, many thanks. So great to
have the photo, because I didn't part with that other very simply.
Ok. The poem is very, very good;[154] variations here accomplished
damn well excellent. Think that the positions made are damn firm;
I had an earlier one, in my head, the one which made somewhat a
similar use, say, of the 'past' content, that one this past summer,
and figure you to have got all such in here, hard. It is all in the
damn hand, anyhow.

Not to make the usual 'comparison' but
because they were both here, so, etc., it's hard not to make use of
your ODE to show certain things I don't like in Duncan's SONG;
mainly, I think, his own use of recurrence, I mean, of the things
so coming back, words & their substance, with the effected
change. There is a touch, I think, of complacence in his use of
such; that it is not an actual touch, each time, but too much the
blackboard & pointer, say. I don't know. I can't yet read him as I
want to; there is some distance, anyhow, between what I would be
after & what I take him to be.

In any event, the recurrence, in
your ODE, is so crazy, is so goddamn much the beauty of it. All
of it, I mean the literal writing, that progression, is very firm,
doesn't allow any looseness. I like it very damn much.

The idea
for THE PARTY is damn well it! I saw A/ yesterday, and he can
make it, and is, at that, much more pleased than he was with the
poem. To get it moving quicker:

1) can you get us a type-face book, —nothing here we can get hold
   of, and it would make the work much easier to be able to
   specify, and to be thinking of, a literal type;

2) also, would you say which type-faces will be available for the
   printing;

3) also, would you suggest any possible limits, or ideas, re how
   you might want it to look—mainly, that I suppose the necessity
   for it to be some manner of 'pamphlet,' granted we are not in
   the Public Health Service, etc. What I mean: the length will
   mean it comes to perhaps four pages inset, or stapled, perhaps
   'cover'? Can we figure free on this aspect? What I am worried
   about, or thinking of at this point.

(Does Cernovich want any
kind of uniformity in the divers things is what it all comes to;
is there any particular objection to such a 'pamphlet'? Granted
it won't be a trite thing, etc. I want a good big page, plenty of
air, etc. Ok.)

Anyhow, it is terrific to be thinking about. Much, much greater, honestly, than the poem; I have just written Lash, and will end that here & now, like they say. He had time enough to say, if he wanted it.

Ok, and will try to have this go faster; if you can, get the type-book here soon, say, and that should push the works. If it will be bother, A/ can write some friend there & get it ok. So don't bother with it, if it's trouble. I'll try to see that the whole thing is set, i.e., type, character of paper, everything. That way it will break it all down to the literal printing, will take away all the ambiguities.

All the S/ biz I'm holding for the book, I haven't been able to get it to date, but will. But more matter what all this is coming to; I think it's very much on the works. Has held me more than you can be thinking.

I get on a little, in any case. Things somewhat cooler, though still the headache of room. But to hell with it. Hope you make, or made, Washington without too much mess. Inevitable that there should be some; phew. You should have seen us making the haul from Paris to Marseille — was something. Two 'lovers' opposite in the compartment, a little bluish light that kept on all night, and I sat there, with Dave across my legs, all night, awake, listening to their bullshit. Agh, etc.

We figured Lerma was the damn last card, and that, as much as anything, why we didn't take off. I mean, after that, I can't see quite what would be next. Otherwise, Ann had some fear that it would be a headache for the kids, and also, I think, that the isolation might be a problem. In any case, I hold on to it, I don't know just how much of this present place one can take — it is easier, having the car, and also A/ & the one or two others there in Aix — but I don't feel easy. And I think this season, dull as it is, would be what I should be pulling from. Summer, much too nice, etc. Anyhow, will see. Anytime you all make it there, or can, to Lerma, let us know; will hope to be right behind you because it just isn't it, here.

A card from Paige,[155]
acknowledging the issue sent; I get a list, in it, of all his
occupations. They are many, i.e., a novel, another collection of
Pound letters, etc., a volume of short stories, and three books he
is translating. I laughed, at least a little. But envy him even so; so
dull as it's been, etc. That was about it anyhow; he says he'll write
soon, etc. I don't expect much, but he might be a way into
England, etc. I don't know. I tend to the grandiose.

I haven't
heard anything from G/ for too damn long; I always get so damn
nervous. The thing, that it might be time, now, to think of a
press, here, or in Europe, because Laubies is also interested, I
think, & has the energy & position, etc. It would be cool, I wish
G/ was less sunk but know how it must be there for them now.
Cold & all. Not good.

I never heard anything more from Cid, after the letter; I can see
why. I have not felt very happy about any of it, but can't see that
there was any good alternative. What do you do when they begin
to push, anyone, for that matter? Too close, it was, to say, take it
easy; and otherwise, much too much of a lean, granted the present
fix. Well, I don't know. I've felt the pinch, god knows, even in this
short time; but I take that more simply than any question of
having him riding on me, etc. Etc. To hell with it.

Enclose picture
from Dave; some of them are too much.
All well again, and that
much to the good. Weather, also, not so bad, or at least some
sun. They say spring comes about March. Ok.
Write soon, and
keep us on; will do likewise.

All dearest love to you all,
Bob

[*Drawing by David Creeley enclosed:*]

[Fontrousse, Aix-en-Provence]
December 24, 1951

Dear Charles,

        Waiting for the gun, etc., and though we're still in
this house, not too bad at that. Yesterday we got the tree up,
stolen, and is ok; all we could find that was like spruce was
something loaded with prickers, but anyhow. It looks real cool &
find myself slipping into the complacent smiles, etc. But I don't feel
very easy, I can't, or never do much, at this time of year, or,
better, with this kind of thing, i.e., Xmas.

        So many kids
hereabouts will have such a dead thing, no money, etc., and what
to do. It's not a sentimentality, I can't think it is, and can't ride
over that sense of it, or why they get it so desperately for what
they have no way out of.

        What do you do. I have such a mistrust
of anyone who can't see this, or who does, and makes it 'the

people' or some such thing. It never has that generalness; it's always specific. Tonight some of the kids who were here this summer will be coming back, i.e., their grandmother lives back of us, on the hill, and her heart isn't good & she is feeling poorly this morning. Nothing for them that I know of more than one or two little things.

Fuck it for now anyhow; it doesn't leave. I was going to say I got the BROADSHEET ok, and like the poem very much.[156] It sets very well and though I feel some of that size-problem you'd noted, I don't think it bothers.

My main feeling, well beyond the poem, is that C[ernovich]/s design, or sense of design, is a false direction. I see what you mean, or meant, by 'colors' (how they think that can do anything, etc.) and *wish* they could see it as: how best to set the text for maximum effectiveness. Not even as 'unit' if such a concept comes to mean, that which will alienate the text.

Here, I felt some of that problem, that the design was random (and why shouldn't one criticize such a thing, i.e., as design, in the same manner he wd a poem, to wit, is it capable of substitution, or, better, is any element of it, either as whole or as part, allowing for *another* word, or color, or line — which one must believe could exist, in it, with an equal effect, etc.).

It is pleasant, Ann put it so, etc., but I don't at all like it. Such things as the crease, breaking the poem so, take on an odd importance, or obtrusiveness, if not handled so very carefully. The crease, there, seemed almost an impertinence; I can't think the poem was being thought of enough. (The type, alone, seems justification for that feeling.)

Anyhow, I am so damn crotchety today, though there's little enough to be bugged with. Ashley will be doing the drawings for THE PARTY over these few days, I think, and hope they come all right.

(He told me he was going to do them so, i.e., he's going several places, etc., and one is a dinner tonight, a small one, friends, etc., and the night before last I met, not with him, the woman who is going to give it (married to a painter here who had been sick with tuberculosis for some yrs, and who had found all his friends leaving him, etc.). Talking, I found myself feeling her very very familiar, until, just now, I saw who it was, and/or, it's my woman. But I don't want to suggest that literalness, i.e., we'd both agreed that the drawings, or anything of that kind, had better escape from any literalness, i.e., of attempt to be the 'same,' etc., or too much so, etc. I wish you might see some of the work he did in Spain; it is very damn fine. But at least these will, I hope, be around, and you'll have the Party ones anyhow. He is a most subtle man; I get to see that.)

All of which—I don't know. The whole idea has got such closeness, i.e., is so close to what I had been hoping for, ever since you had suggested the idea of single story editions. Really, it is a terrific break, and thanks, all thanks, for it.

Well, enough of same for now at least. Will keep on it, and hope that it goes ok. Again, if there are any particular limits, you want us to count in, tell me & will see that they are held to. Ok.

I had a letter from Cid about 2 or 3 days back. He was fair enough, i.e., he made no mention of my own letter, and rambled on as though nothing had happened. I felt somewhat that I was being given the 'rational' treatment, but to hell with that. In any event, it didn't help very much; I keep on feeling that it's a dead thing, at least my own part in it. I haven't yet answered him, but will soon; I don't think I'll send him anything more until it is much clearer, all of it, than it now is. The only objection to his letter was that, even with the lovers, say, 'nothing had happened . . .' I can't allow that feeling, but because, very obviously, something did. As well, I have little belief that he'll now see any more of it than he ever did, and I don't feel, literally, strong enough to buck his encroachments at this point. Let it all slide, etc., is about what I can do now.

Otherwise, I do feel better, much better, and hope to get moving soon. At least I can think of it, and I couldn't even a week or so back. The whole act, of writing, had taken on such a weight, or deadness. But there's nothing else I can do, I think, or can get what I want from doing.

Anyhow, I can think of the divers 'lines,' call them. Seeing this or that, I can, sometimes, feel the variations possible, and if A/ or B/ or C/ wd say, that's how they felt about it, perhaps I could make it something the same, and yet from some other position. It is so damn tenuous anyhow; the little excursions into company, like they say, even seeing a few people now & again makes me so nervous I fumble everything, and found myself dropping a whole box of matches after being introduced to an attractive woman.

Trying to get back anyhow. Hope that the next few wks will get to something.

One item: A/ and this other man, Hellman,[157] were telling me abt Music Appreciation in the NYC public schools, i.e., how they used to do it when they were there. They had chants by which the pupil was supposed to remember the divers things, etc. For everything, I take it, or they sang me some dozen of them, and seemed capable of continuing for god knows how long. But, a sample:

This is
the symphony
that Schubert wrote & never finished . . .

Try it for yrself. Ann has been singing it for two days. Phew.

Ok. All love to all three of you, and hope that Xmas was the greatest. Anyhow, this may make it for New Year's; have a ball. And write whenever you can get the time.

All best love,

Bob

[Weymouth, Mass.]
Dec 26 [1951]

Robt—

Both of us damned worried about you—no word from you in two weeks has us scared the flu may have turned worse

—anyhow, this, to ask you to have Ann get us word if anything ever holds you up on word—one gets concerned, eh?

Not that I have been any shakes (spear) myself: arr. last night here in one swell fr Washington—8½ hrs Wash. to Wellesley Hills! Crazy (possible, now, New Jersey Turnpike, go 90 for 120 miles—fr New Bridge across where lovely old ferry was (did it 4 hrs Wash—NY! Crazy—& wonderful sense of flight, eh?

Almost dreaded coming New England & chiefly that wld seem necessary see Corman, eh?

But have taken bull by the bag, & will see him today—drive right there, ring his bell, surprise him in lair—& see.

Only way. But scared of issue!

OK.

Idled a week Wash. after idling three-four days B.M.—vacation shrinking, & no sight yet of New York, the Beloved!

Look—write, or have Ann get us off a note Washington address. Do hope nothing seriously wrong (got off to you last, I think, a photo & an ode in peculiar mailing hope did not go askew.

OK.

Kate fine (still her own damned self, & so no drooling babe!) Con fine

Love to you all

O

[Fontrousse, Aix-en-Provence]
December 28, 1951

Dear Charles,

Yours here today, and very, very ashamed that I
had made this worry for you—nothing the matter at this end, but
the usual, and that isn't enough to excuse the silence.

I don't
know; I get so cautious of the letters, my own, that I am saying
nothing that I mean to, and only confusing things by allowing
them to go out in that character.

Anyhow, the one enclosed was
supposed to have been mailed back then, and wasn't; things so
much a mess what with Xmas. It was very pleasant; kids & all a
very great joy.

Now, I have a heater up here, in the bedroom,
and I figure to get back on. At least will try to; I have made some
distance from that feeling back a month now, and just the space,
here, is a good deal.

Ok, and I won't let the silence get in again;
do keep writing yourself, it means a great deal.

I had a very decent letter from K/ Lash, in answer to my own
asking him for release on that story—not that he had taken it, etc.
But he was very kind; he even returned that copy saying he
thought might have need for another, i.e., simply to be that
pleasant, and at his own expense, etc. I did respect it. The tone of
all the letter was very honest, and careful with a care I have some
respect for. At least he does not propose to know everything, etc.
As that earlier article seemed pretty hopefully to suggest.

He says
that he'll write you as soon as the holidays are over; hope there's a
letter there at BMC when you get back. Would be great to have
this new outlet, and they do pay a little which also helps. (At least
he didn't jump back from the story; I sent him a copy of
ORIGINS #2 & #3, not having any of #1 left. Hope that he doesn't
shy off. Do figure him worth trying, just on the basis of this one

letter. So many would have been shitty about it, etc.)

I think A/
is well along now, and once you can give us that information
about types (i.e., what he might plan to use, etc., or what
selection he can count on), I hope it can go fast. It will be pretty
quiet, and will feel best having it so. I didn't mean to jump on
Cernovich, but the colors were a little wild for me, and the lean
on them, on that way, I thought too much. Anyhow, let's hope it
works out; it is a terrific thing to look to, honesty.

I had a letter from Cid, quite astute, or he didn't make any
mention of my own. I wonder, now, how you found him. But to
hell with that, or I suppose I should be staying off such as that. I
just stick, still, at his way, it isn't my own, I think it's wrong to
allow any joining. I really don't know anything, at this point, and
best to keep that clear in my own head. I did write him back,
mainly about the #3, and wish I had not in some ways. But fuck
it. It is dull to think of, in any case.

Will write soon again; again, damn sorry about this bother. Tell
me if this gets in ok; I was afraid an earlier one (about ODE &
all) may not have got there.

All best love from us all, hope you
had a fine Xmas,

Bob

Notes

[References to pages and notes in previous volumes begin with Roman numerals designating the volume number, e.g., I. 110, II. 53, etc.]

1 Possibly in *The Ladybird* (London, 1923), pp. 80–81: "she had suddenly collapsed away from her old self into this darkness, this peace, this quiescence that was like a full dark river flowing eternally in her soul . . . this love of hers for the Count: this dark, everlasting love that was like a full river flowing for ever inside her."

2 See the passages from *Kangaroo* quoted in note II. 80.

3 "*Je est un autre*" ("*I* is an other"), probably – Rimbaud's famous declaration, in letters to Georges Izambard, 13 May 1871, and to Paul Demeny, 15 May 1871.

4 In his "Preface" to *Monsieur Teste*, p. 6, Valéry promises a hero who is a "monster," "the very demon of possibility."

5 See not only Olson's "The Law" (VII. 240–41), but also his 19 July 1951 letter (VI. 164) and note VI. 175.

6 *The Chinese Written Character as a Medium for Poetry*, p. 19: "There is in reality no such verb as a pure copula, no such original conception; our very word *exist* means 'to stand forth,' to show ourself by a definite act."

7 Both passages are from Stendhal's reply to Balzac, in the Scott-Moncrieff translation of *The Charterhouse of Parma*, pp. lxxvi and lxxx-lxxxi.

8 Stendhal (also from the letter to Balzac) as quoted by Pound (and here translated by Creeley) in "The Serious Artist," *Pavannes and Divisions* (New York, 1918), pp. 237–38.

9 In response to Creeley's initial letter to Pound in 1950, the latter writes: "Am not quite clear as to what you mean by 'at 23' in connection with something you referred to as having been doing for 40 years? Not that E[zra] cares whether you are 63 or 23 . . . only one might as well know, to avoid confusion . . ." (*Agenda*, no. 4, 1965, p. 13).

¹⁰ See *Compton's Pictured Encyclopedia and Fact-Index* (Chicago, 1950), I, 176–79, under "alphabet," containing all the information following in the letter. Olson would later consult Sprengling's *The Alphabet, Its Rise and Development from the Sinai Inscriptions* (Chicago, 1931) directly, and invite Sprengling to teach at Black Mountain. (He wrote John A. Rice, founder of Black Mountain, 21 March 1956 [photocopy of letter courtesy William Rice]: "Sprengling is one of the men who busted the Sinai inscriptions and, from his knowledge of Arabic, was able to identify the Seirite miners who caused our alphabet to spring up between them and their Egyptian bosses in a turquoise mine there — wasn't it about 1750 BC? And the first known sentence in our alphabet, 'I, Shalimath, boss of mine shaft #4, to Baal-at, greetings'!")

Olson's set of *Everybody's Cyclopedia* (New York, [1912]) in five volumes had been stored in a Worcester attic after his father's death and has now been added to his papers at the University of Connecticut Library.

¹¹ See *Did Homer Live?*, pp. 61–67; identified in the *Compton's* article as being a ninth-century B.C. basalt slab.

¹² Cf. his father's injunction, "Put a tackle on it," in "Morning News" (*Archaeologist of Morning*, p. [112]).

¹³ Herodotus, IV. 147 and V. 58; but see *Compton's Pictured Encyclopedia*, I, 179.

¹⁴ Leo Frobenius, *Erythräa: Länder und Zeiten des heiligen Königsmordes* (Berlin, 1931).

¹⁵ "Jackson Pollock: Is he the greatest living painter in the United States?," *Life*, 27, 8 August 1949, pp. 42–45.

¹⁶ See Pound, *Guide to Kulchur*, pp. 105–06: "By genius I mean an inevitable swiftness and rightness in a given field. The trouvaille. The direct simplicity in seizing the effective means." In *ABC of Reading*, p. 84, Pound attributes part of the definition to Aristotle: "Aristotle had something of this sort [the limited value of analogy] in mind when he wrote 'apt use of metaphor indicating a swift perception of relations.' "

[17] *Make It New*, pp. 3–19.

[18] *Polite Essays*, p. 25.

[19] Harry Levin (b. 1912), professor of comparative literature at Harvard (and former classmate of Olson's); author of *Toward Stendhal* (Murray, Utah, 1945) and *James Joyce, A Critical Introduction* (Norfolk, Conn., 1941), as well as editor of *The Portable James Joyce* (New York, 1947).

[20] "La Chute," apparently enclosed with Olson's October 4th letter.

[21] See Olson's 5 October 1951 letter to Corman on "The Soldiers," *Letters for Origin*, pp. 81–85; also the one "on general strategy" from 11 October, in *Letters for Origin*, p. 86 (or complete in Glover dissertation, pp. 138–41).

[22] Max Raphael, *Prehistoric Cave Paintings*, trans. Norbert Guterman (New York, 1945), pp. 22, 25, 30, 31 and 37 — a study of Franco-Cantabrian paleolithic art (from sites in southwestern France and the Cantabrian Mountains in northern Spain).

[23] See Olson's 8 August 1951 letter to Louis Martz (VII. 77) and note VII. 57.

[24] From William Carlos Williams's acceptance speech upon receiving the National Book Award for *Paterson (Book Three)*, March 1950. Creeley had written Williams, 7 April 1950, for a copy (letter at Beinecke Library, Yale University).

[25] First appearing in Williams's "A Sort of a Song" (*Selected Poems*, p. 108; *Collected Later Poems*, p. 7): "Compose. (No ideas / but in things) Invent!"; later, part of the epigraph to *Paterson*.

[26] Wallace Stevens, in "The State of American Writing, 1948" symposium, p. 885 (see note VI. 170).

[27] See note I. 83.

[28] Probably Paul Goodman's *The Copernican Revolution* (Saugatuck, Conn., 1947). His three novels preferred by Creeley would be *The Grand Piano* (1942), *The State of Nature* (1946), and *The Dead of Spring* (1950).

[29] John Hawkes, *The Cannibal* (Norfolk, Conn., 1949).

[30] The cave at Lascaux, outside Montignac in south-central France, discovered in 1940. See the photographs in "Cave Paintings," *Life*, 22, 24 February 1947, pp. 64–69.

[31] Richard Aldington's *D. H. Lawrence: Portrait of a Genius But . . .* (see II. 110 and note II. 87).

[32] Alexander Schneider (b. 1908), Russian-born violinist. In 1950 he established, with cellist Pablo Casals, annual summer music festivals at Prades, France.

[33] "How the Alphabet Was Made," a comic fable, in Rudyard Kipling's *Just So Stories*, first published in 1902.

[34] Olson's "The Ring of," written October 1951.

[35] Pound's "signature" (and no doubt Pound's spelling) from St. Elizabeths during this time (see also I. 56), reflecting his legal status and his psychological state (see, e.g., his 1953 letter to Louis Dudek, quoted in E. Fuller Torrey, *The Roots of Treason*, New York, 1984, p. 248: "You are NOT supposed to receive ANY letters from E.P. They are UNSIGNED and if one cannot trust one's friends to keep quiet RE the supposed source whom can one trust . . .").

[36] See Olson's 27 July 1950 letter (II. 82) and note II. 53; also his 1 October 1950 letter (III. 62) and note III. 17.

[37] Larry Eigner (see VI. 208 and note VI. 206).

[38] Pound writes in *ABC of Reading*, p. 198, that "Rhythm is a form cut into TIME, as a design is determined SPACE."

[39] French painter (b. 1924) and translator of Pound.

[40] Léon-Gabriel Gros, French poet, writing articles and reviews for *Cahiers du Sud* at the time.

[41] *Les Cahiers du Sud* was begun in Marseille in 1915.

[42] See note VI. 88.

[43] See Creeley's 14 August 1951 letter (VII. 98) and note VII. 72.

[44] Palaeolithic soapstone statuette. See e.g. fig. 1B in Erich Neumann, *The Great Mother*, trans. Ralph Manheim (New York, 1955).

[45] An early version of "Jardou" (see pp. 111–16 below).

[46] From Olson's "La Torre" (see also Creeley's 3 August 1951 letter — VII. 47).

[47] See Olson's 24 August 1950 and ca. November 1950 letters (I. 112; III. 152), with puns on the Poundian group calling itself the Cleaners; also note I. 23. See also perhaps Olson's "ABCs (3 — for Rimbaud)" (*Archaeologist of Morning*, p. [52]): "We call it / trillings, cleanings, / we who want scourings . . ."

[48] See Creeley's 3 October 1950 letter (III. 73) and note III. 22; also his 22/23 September 1950 letter (III. 19) and note III. 2.

[49] Pound's concluding sentence of "Date Line" (*Make It New*, p. 19): "It is quite obvious that we do not all of us inhabit the same time."

[50] *Liberty* magazine, a mass-market weekly from 1924 to 1950. It listed reading times at the beginnings of many of its articles; e.g., a book condensation might be "Reading time one evening," or for a piece of short fiction, "Reading time 7 minutes."

[51] See Galpin, *The Music of the Sumerians*, pp. 13ff.

[52] Bernard of Clairvaux (1090–1153). The popular legend of Bernard and the Virgin is recounted, e.g., by Marina Werner, *Alone of All Her Sex: The Myth and Cult of the Virgin Mary* (New York, 1976), pp. 197–98: "Bernard was reciting the *Ave Maria Stella* before a statue of the Virgin in the church of St. Vorles at Châtillon-sur-Seine, and when he came to the words *Monstra esse matrem* (Show thyself a mother), the Virgin appeared before him and, pressing her breast, let three drops of milk fall onto his lips . . . The legend, which was painted by Perugino (d. 1523) in a graceful, lyrical altarpiece now in Munich and frescoed by Filippino Lippi (d. 1504) in the Badia church in Florence, was in wide circulation in the Renaissance, and was recorded in Manrique's *Annals of the Cistercian Order*, published in 1642, which inspired Murillo's enraptured version of the vision."

[53] See Bernard of Clairvaux's sermons on the Song of Songs, *On the Song of Songs (Sermones in Cantica Canticorum)* (London, 1952), pp. 24ff., or *On the Song of Songs I*, trans. Kilian Walsh (Shannon, Ire., 1971), pp. 8ff. (although there is no mention in any of the texts or translations of "the tongue, going, in" as part of the kiss).

[54] French, the "disposables," the "disengaged."

[55] Terence Burns, former Black Mountain student, mentions in a letter to the editor, 6 January 1976, how "with photos Charles showed us Young Mao   Papa Mao   then Mama Mao   and told us Mao was an androgyne." See Olson's sense of "androgyne," however, in his letter to Corman, 10 February 1951 (Glover, p. 35): ". . . that combination I would see as just as much prime to creative work now as the androgyne is to politics (Mao, say) . . . that of documentarian & the selectivity of the creative taste & mind." And cf. the figure of John Smith in *The Maximus Poems*, p. 127.

"Autres" is French "others."

[56] Olson had written of "the body, its / 38 doors!" in the unpublished poem, "A Shadow, Two," from 29 May 1950.

[57] Corman's "Some Notes Toward a New Prosody," which would be published in *Origin*, no. 4 (Winter 1951-52); and see Creeley's 16 November letter (p. 143 below).

[58] A series of block prints, woodcuts, under the general title "The Rhone," by Richard Boyce (b. 1920), teaching at the time at the Museum School in Boston.

[59.] Olson's "A Round & A Canon," appearing in *Origin*, no. 3 (Fall 1951), along with Creeley's story "The Grace" and poem "Love," and Richard Wilbur's "Speech for the Repeal of the McCarran Act."

[60] The epigraph of the first series of *Origin*:

> "O my son, arise from thy bed . . .
>   work
>   what is wise."

(It might be noted that the root of "origin" is Latin *orior* "I rise.") See also Olson's 31 March 1951 letter (V. 114) and note V. 12.

[61] See also Olson's 18 February 1951 letter (V. 22) and note V. 12.

[62] Olson adds in ink on a retained carbon copy of his letter the translation, "and on the reed the dark flutes of autumn wind softly," for the line from Trakl's "Grodek" (see p. 116 below). The previous phrase from Gerhardt's "Brief an Creeley und Olson" may be translated as "the end of our weakness."

[63] The chief crops of man's earliest agricultural age. See especially Henri Frankfort, *The Birth of Civilization in the Near East* (Bloomington, Ind., 1951), p. 35: "The outstanding new feature of the neolithic age is agriculture, with emmer wheat (*Triticum dicoccum*) and six-rowed barley (*Hordeum hexastichum*) as the main crops."

[64] Corman's letter of 5 November 1951 to Creeley (among Olson's papers), in which he requests enough Ashley Bryant cover-art be sent by Christmas to encompass "any discrepancies of mind" regarding the cover, and questions the wisdom of Gerhardt's plan to use two of Creeley's stories in *Fragmente* rather than "Jardou" alone.

[65] Columbia Master Works M-MM-554 (New York, 1945), a seventeen-record set (78 r.p.m.) issued in three volumes, with Paul Robeson as Othello, Jose Ferrer as Iago, and Uta Hagen as Desdemona.

[66] Sonnet 129 (see Olson's 30 September 1951 letter — VII. 216 — and note VII. 144.).

[67] For a full account of Edward de Vere, Lord of Oxford's relationship with the Queen's Maid of Honor, Anne Vavasour, see e.g. Charles Wisner Barrell, "Verifying the Secret History of Shakespeare's Sonnets," *Tomorrow*, 5 (February 1946), 49–55, and (March 1946), 54–60 (Barrell coincidentally identifies Vavasour as Shakespeare's Dark Lady). In Olson's copy — which he had apparently loaned to Ezra Pound in St. Elizabeths — there is a note by Pound: "1st intelligent article on the Sonnets I have ever seen."

[68] *Pleasure Dome*, "an audible anthology of modern poetry read by its creators and edited by Lloyd Frankenberg," Columbia MM877

(78 r.p.m.) and ML4259 (33⅓ r.p.m.) (New York, 1949), on which Williams reads "El Hombre" (*Complete Collected Poems*, p. 42; *Selected Poems*, p. 3).

[69] *The Melville Log: A Documentary Life of Herman Melville, 1819–1891*, 2 vols. (New York, 1951).

[70] Deduced from a letter discovered at the Massachusetts Historical Society by Olson.

[71] See note VIII. 43 above.

[72] Just east of Aix-en-Provence. Subject of a series of paintings by Paul Cezanne.

[73] The chapter of *In the American Grain* on Sam Houston (pp. 212–215), rather than the section of Williams' *Paterson* Book II, beginning "The descent beckons . . ." (New York, 1948, pp. 96–97) and later published separately as "The Descent."

[74] D. H. Lawrence, *Studies in Classic American Literature* (London, 1933), p. 151.

[75] See also Olson's 28 June 1951 letter (VI. 90) and note VI. 105.

[76] Authors chosen by Pound for publication in the Square $ series. Eustace Clarence Mullins's *A Study of the Federal Reserve* would be published under the Kasper and Horton imprint the following year.

[77] Edman et al. all taught the humanities at Columbia; Donald Lemen Clark (1888–1966), e.g., was a Milton scholar. John Angus Burrell (1889–1957), an associate professor of English, had edited several fiction anthologies, and Raymond Weaver (1888–1948), who also taught at Columbia and whom Olson had visited in the 1930s, was the pioneer Melville scholar and biographer. Albert Salomon (1891–1966) was one of the original émigré teachers at the New School (since 1935).

[78] Bernhard De Boer of Hoboken, N.J., the chief distributor of literary periodicals (including *Origin*) at the time.

[79] Probably Adams' *The Theory of Social Revolutions* (New York, 1913).

[80] See Olson's poem "Move Over":

> . . . north and east
> the carpenter obeyed
> topography
>
> As a hand addresses itself to the care of plants
> and a sense of proportion, the house
> is put to the earth

[81] See note I. 131.

[82] I.e., Dallam Simpson (see I. 27 and note I. 11, etc.).

[83] Paul Williams, former Black Mountain student and occasional benefactor of the college.

[84] See also Olson's 16 May 1950 letter (I. 28).

[85] (1908–1972), Mexican-born dancer and choreographer.

[86] Pound's *ABC of Reading* (Norfolk, Conn., 1951) and his *Confucian Analects* (New York, 1951), which first appeared in the *Hudson Review*, 3:1 (Spring 1950).

[87] From Williams' "Three Sonnets" (*Collected Later Poems*, p. 30).

[88] Marguerite Caetani (see Creeley's 23 September 1951 letter — VII. 183 — and note VII. 123).

[89] *The Viking Book of Poetry of the English-Speaking World*, ed. Richard Aldington (New York, 1941).

[90] I.e., Olson's "This."

[91] See Olson's 22 June 1951 letter (VI. 66) and note VI. 69.

[92] Edwin Honig (b. 1919), Harvard professor, poet, and author of *Garcia Lorca* (Norfolk, Conn., 1944).

[93] Samuel French Morse's poem, "The Hurt," *Origin*, no. 1, p. 22.

[94] William Bronk, "The Mind's Landscape on an Early Winter Day," *Origin*, no. 3, p. 129.

[95] Patchen writes, e.g., in *Sleepers Awake* (New York, 1946), p. 16: "SEND IN YOUR FIRST TEAM, GOD!"

[96] *Make It New*, p. 12: ". . . and the foreign editorship of the *Little Review* was undertaken 'in order that the work of Joyce, Lewis, Eliot and myself might appear promptly and regularly and in one place, without inane and idiotic delay.' "

[97] Kasper's postcard may not have been to Pound (or it may not have been mailed); it is not among Pound's papers from the St. Elizabeths period at Lilly Library, Indiana University.

[98] The Chinese ideogram used as epigraph to Pound's *Confucian Analects* (reprinted by Kasper and Horton in their Square $ Series, p. 3). Pound identifies it as "Fidelity to the given word" in his translation of Confucius, *The Unwobbling Pivot & The Great Digest*, p. 35.

[99] Through the character of Gerty MacDowell in the thirteenth chapter of *Ulysses*.

[100] Evidence for the popularity of *Pericles* may be found in the anonymous contemporary pamphlet, *Pimlyco or Runne Red-Cap* (1609), written largely in Skeltonics and containing one of the earliest references to the play: "Amazde I stood, to see a Crowd / of Ciuill Throats stretched out so lowd; . . . So that I truly thought all These / Came to see *Shore* [i.e., Thomas Heywood's *Edward IV*] or *Pericles*" (E.K. Chambers, *William Shakespeare*, Oxford, 1930, II, 217). It is uncertain why Olson attributes the poem to "Sheppard"; perhaps he is thinking of playwright Samuel Sheppard, whose *Epigrams* (1651) included one to Shakespeare.

[101] *Webster's Collegiate Dictionary*, 5th ed., p. 285.

[102] Basaldella Mirko (b. 1910), Italian sculptor; Corrado Cagli's brother-in-law.

[103] (b. 1902), Italian painter and writer; author of *Christ Stopped at Eboli* (note IV. 13).

[104] William W. Joseph, who had studied painting with Josef Albers at Black Mountain.

[105] See note VI. 168. For a portrait, see George Martin, *Madam Secretary: Frances Perkins* (Boston, 1976), pp. 469–72.

[106] Cf. Olson's 23 June 1950 letter (I. 147): " 'Wot Olson don't know IZ, / I hate Swedes as much as I do Jewz.' "

[107] Greek "to flow"; root of "rhythm" (*Webster's Collegiate Dictionary*, 5th ed., p. 857). See also "The Cause, The Cause" (*Archaeologist of Morning*, p. [132]) and "Against Wisdom As Such" (*Human Universe*, p. 70).

[108] John Boman Adams, teaching at Black Mountain.

[109] The river forming the boundary between North Dakota and Minnesota, terminating in Lake Winnipeg.

[110] A local paramilitary organization — more a social club and marching band — started in 1876 at the time of the nation's centennial, with a uniform that was a facsimile of the one worn by officers of the Continental Army during the Revolution. A photograph of Olson's father in uniform survives.

Louisburg Square, with a central park, brick walks, cobblestone streets, gaslight lampposts and homes with Bulfinch doorways, is on Beacon Hill in Boston. It was where such notables as William Dean Howells and Louisa May Alcott lived during the nineteenth century.

[111] Rimbaud writes: "I dreamed of . . . the migration of races and continents," in "Délires II: Alchimie du Verbe" (*A Season in Hell*, trans. Delmore Schwartz, Norfolk, Conn., 1939, p. 63), and see also, e.g., "Promontoire" and "Soir Historique" in *Les Illuminations* (*Prose Poems from the Illuminations*, trans. Louise Varèse, New York, 1946, pp. 86–93). See also Olson's "Knowing All Ways, Including the Transposition of Continents" (*Archaeologist of Morning*, p. [108]).

[112] Ignatius Donnelly, *Atlantis: The Antediluvian World* (New York, 1882), and James Churchward's fantasy classic, *The Lost Continent of Mu* (New York, 1931). Evidence in Olson's notebook "#3" from December 1939–January 1940 indicates he consulted these works while reading Thomas Mann's *Joseph and His Brothers* and considering myth in relation to Melville. Both Donnelly and Churchward are also cited in the *Mayan Letters* bibliography from 1953 (*Selected Writings*, p. 129).

113 *The Autobiography of William Carlos Williams*, p. 241:
". . . Shakespeare's, 'To hold the mirror up to nature' — as vicious a piece
of bad advice as the budding artist ever gazed upon. It is tricky,
thoughtless, wrong. It is NOT to hold the mirror up to nature that the
artist performs his work. It is to make, out of the imagination,
something not at all a copy of nature, but something quite different,
a new thing, unlike any thing else in nature, a thing advanced and apart
from it."

114 Henry Forbush Howe, *Salt Rivers of the Massachusetts Shore* (New
York, 1951).

115 The unpublished "Purgatory Blind" from 1940 and its later revision,
"Marry the Marrow," with these lines:

> The Annisquam and the Atlantic
> At high fulfilled the land,
> Brimmed and eased it.
> Stretched fabric across the hips of the earth,
> French cut,
> Discovering the global curve beneath.

See also *The Maximus Poems*, p. 86: "As I had it in my first poem,
the Annisquam / fills itself, at its tides, as she did / the French dress,
cut / on the bias."

For the "tidal rivers rushing" dream from 1950, see "ABCs (2)": "the
yelping rocks / where the tidal river rushes" (*Archaeologist of Morning*,
p. [51], and see notes in Butterick, *Guide to The Maximus Poems*, pp.
129–30 and 535).

116 See note I. 100.

117 A 400-word statement for a catalogue of Twombly's exhibition held
at the Seven Stairs Gallery, Stuart Brent's, in Chicago, 2-30 November
1951.

118 Entitled simply "Cy Twombly" (see *OLSON*, no. 8, Fall 1977, pp.
12–15), although the Washington and Lee University exhibition never
took place.

119 "The elegancy, facility, and golden cadence of poesy," says
Holofernes in *Love's Labour's Lost*, V. ii. 126.

[120] Richard Grant White (1821–1885), in his Riverside edition of *Mr. William Shakespeare's Comedies, Histories & Poems, Tragedies . . .* (Boston, 1901), III, 699 (annotating *Lear* V.iii.318ff.): "Were it not that S. always falls into feebleness with rhyme, I should believe that these words and the seven following lines were a tag added to please the players and the vulgar among the audience. Without them Albany's speech would close the tragedy with a note like that of the last lines of *Hamlet.* Indeed, I am at every reading of them nearer being sure that they are not from the hand that wrote the rest of the tragedy."

[121] See Bérard, *Did Homer Live?*, especially chapter V, "The Phoenicians and the Odyssey." Berard writes, e.g., on p. 122 concerning the Cyclopes: "Their country, known in ancient times as the Phlegraean Fields, is riddled with great eyes, some of them single, or blind, or empty sockets, others full of gleaming water or green growth; each one is an old crater or volcanic subsidence, and their fires, smokings, outpourings of stone, belchings and vomitings . . . have terrified or still terrify the country round." See also Olson's 1 April 1951 letter (V. 118) and note V. 116.

Jim Bridger (1804–1881) was the first white man, as far as is known, to visit the Great Salt Lake in Utah (fall of 1824). He also visited the site of Yellowstone National Park before 1840, although actually John Colter, a member of the Lewis and Clark expedition, had been there earlier, in 1807. See also *The Maximus Poems*, p. 158.

[122] Latin "against nature," "against the order of nature"; one of Pound's most emphatic denunciations (see especially Canto 45).

[123] See Olson's 25 July 1951 letter (VI. 204–05) and note VI. 203.

[124] Possibly Black Mountain student Victor Kalos (see Olson's 18 July 1951 letter). Olson would write Ben Shahn the following spring about his efforts to secure conscientious objector status (letter 19 May 1952 at Archives of American Art).

[125] See Creeley's 18 May 1950 letter (I. 31) and note I. 19.

[126] "Nothing is without efficient cause" stands as a headline or epigraph to Pound's letter that prefaces his *Jefferson and/or Mussolini* (p. v), and see also *Guide to Kulchur,* p. 45. Olson refers to the phrase in *Call*

Me Ishmael, p. 81, and again in "A Bibliography on America" (*Additional Prose*, p. 13).

For Pound's complaint of a "30-year lag," see also Olson's 27 May 1950 letter (I. 52) and note I. 51.

[127] Victor Sprague (b. 1908), who had been teaching previously at Louisiana State University.

[128] Ellinor Helene Behre, a zoologist at Louisiana State University.

[129] Selections from Louis Agassiz' works by Kasper were eventually published as *Gists from Agassiz, or Passages on the Intelligence Working in Nature* (New York, 1953).

[130] Williams' 3 March 1950 letter to Creeley in *Origin*, no. 1, p. 34, beginning: "My own (moral) program can be briefly stated. I send it for what it may be worth to you: To write badly is an offence to the state since the government can never be more than the government of words."

[131] See Olson's 7 April 1951 letter (V. 128) and note V. 124.

[132] Franklin D. Roosevelt's relationship with his wife's former social secretary, Lucy Rutherfurd, is alluded to (she had gone to visit Roosevelt, e.g., at Warm Springs in April 1945 at the time of his death, accompanied by an artist friend, Elizabeth Shoumatoff, who was to paint a portrait of the President).

[133] Callisto was the daughter of Lycaon (see note VII. 49), changed by Hera into a she-bear. She was also the mother of Arcas, eponymous hero of Arcadia, where Odysseus' father was born, himself son of a she-bear, according to Pausanias (VIII. 3 — a passage marked in Olson's copy, with his note next to mention of Arcas' son: "investigate him, as ancestor of Odysseus"). See also Olson's 8 August 1951 letter to Louis Martz (VII. 00) and note VII. 46; also his hymn "The She-Bear" (*Alcheringa*, no. 5, Spring-Summer 1973, pp. 8–11).

[134] I.e. *ciruelas*, Spanish "plums."

[135] A variation of the account in Herodotus (II. 73), who says nothing of the father's body being dropped into the Nile.

[136] Animal-headed god of the ancient Egyptians. See especially Plutarch, "Of Isis and Osiris," section 18 (in *Plutarch's Morals: Theosophical Essays*, trans. C. W. King, London, 1908, pp. 14-15).

[137] Richard Chase writes in "The Real Melville?," *Nation*, 173, 1 December 1951, p. 479: "Within Melville criticism we seem to be in a period during which Mr. [Newton] Arvin's book will be thought fundamentally to be just as indefensibly wild, 'Freudian,' and intellectual as Charles Olson's 'Call Me Ishmael' is usually said to be."

[138] Richard Burbage (ca. 1567-1619), English actor, associate of Shakespeare (probably the original Hamlet, Lear, and Othello), and builder of the Globe Theatre.

[139] Pound, in his "Translator's Postscript" to Remy de Gourmont, *The Natural Philosophy of Love* (New York, 1942), writes that "the brain itself, is, in origin and development, only a sort of great clot of genital fluid held in suspense or reserve" (p. 295), and of "driving any new idea into the great passive vulva of London, a sensation analogous to the male feeling in copulation" (p. 297).

[140] J. Dover Wilson (1881-1969), editor of Cambridge University Press's The New Shakespeare through the 1930s, and the great English textual critics, W. W. Greg (1875-1959) and W. W. Pollard (1859-1944).

[141] Olson first wrote Robert Giroux with his suggestion for "The Objectist's Shakespeare," 6 December 1951 — apparently without success — and then, from his sister-in-law's home in Weymouth, Mass. on 21 December 1951, to Edward A. Weeks of Little, Brown in Boston, with similar lack of success (carbon copies of letters among his papers).

[142] Albert Erskine, editor at Random House, formerly with Reynal & Hitchcock.

[143] Sir Laurence Olivier, in Shakespeare's *Antony and Cleopatra* and Shaw's *Caesar and Cleopatra* (with Vivien Leigh as Cleopatra in both), opened at the Ziegfeld Theatre in New York on December 19th for a sixteen-week run, following a successful London engagement.

[144] *Literary Essays*, p. 42: "The arts give us a great percentage of the lasting and unassailable data regarding the nature of man, of immaterial

man, of man considered as a thinking and sentient creature. They begin where the science of medicine leaves off or rather they overlap that science. The borders of the two arts overcross."

[145] *Call Me Ishmael*, p. 12: "Some men ride on such space, others have to fasten themselves like a tent stake to survive. As I see it Poe dug in and Melville mounted. These are the alternatives."

[146] See "In Cold Hell, In Thicket" (*Archaeologist of Morning*, p. [69]).

[147] See Klee on "objective images" and "constructions" in *On Modern Art*, e.g. p. 43: "each formation, each combination will have its own particular constructive expression, each figure its face — its features."

[148] Olson's "An Ode on Nativity" (*Archaeologist of Morning*, pp. [81]-[84]), written December 1951.

[149] Not an exact quotation, but accurate in spirit. Jonson is reported to have reproached Shakespeare with "the want of learning, and ignorance of the Ancients" (*The Shakspere Allusion-Book: A Collection of Allusions to Shakspere from 1591 to 1700*, ed. John Munro, London, 1932, I, 373) — "wanting art" in that sense, as Olson would appear to know from a 1954 fragment concerning the Elizabethans, whom he observes said "in so many words that, by comparison with the classics, they wrote 'without art,' and so were always borrowing, stealing or imitating those models."

[150] *The Portable Coleridge*, ed. I. A. Richards (New York, 1950). Creeley's copy, with flyleaf dated 1951, later found its way into Olson's library.

[151] *The Oxford Book of Modern Verse, 1892-1935*, ed. W B. Yeats (New York, 1936), in which Yeats writes concerning Pound's *Cantos* (p. xxiv), "There is no transmission through time, we pass without comment from ancient Greece to modern England, from modern England to medieval China; the symphony, the pattern, is timeless, flux eternal and therefore without movement."

[152] From Robert Frost's famous poem, "Stopping by Woods on a Snowy Evening."

[153] From Coleridge's "Dejection: An Ode."

[154] Olson's "Ode on Nativity."

[155] Douglas D. Paige, editor of *The Letters of Ezra Pound 1907–1941* (New York, 1950).

[156] Olson's *This*, published at the Black Mountain College Graphics Workshop as Black Mountain Broadside no. 1.

[157] Writer Robert Hellman (1919–1984), who would later teach at Black Mountain and publish stories in the *Black Mountain Review*.

I. Index of Persons Named in the Letters

II. Index of Works by Charles Olson and Robert Creeley Cited in the Text

Printed January 1987 in Santa Barbara & Ann Arbor
for the Black Sparrow Press by Graham Mackintosh
& Edwards Brothers Inc. Design by Barbara Martin.
This edition is published in paper wrappers; there
are 500 hardcover trade copies; 200 hardcover copies
have been numbered & signed by Robert Creeley; &
26 lettered copies have been handbound in boards
by Earle Gray & signed by George Butterick &
Robert Creeley.

GEORGE F. BUTTERICK studied with both Charles Olson and Robert Creeley at the State University of New York at Buffalo, where he received his Ph.D. in 1970. He is Curator of Literary Archives at the University of Connecticut, and lives with his family in the nearby city of Willimantic. He recently completed his edition of Charles Olson's *Collected Poems* (outside of the *Maximus* series) and is presently at work on Olson's *Collected Prose*. His essays and reviews have appeared widely in journals, including, most recently, *American Poetry*, *Conjunctions, Credences, Exquisite Corpse, Sagetrieb*, and *Sulfur*. He is also the author of four books of poetry.